LEGACY IN THE LANDSCAPE

With its focus on the city rather than the disaster event, this book situates natural disasters in the context of urban growth and change. It offers an original, interdisciplinary perspective by connecting the technical and socioeconomic dimensions of disaster risk and highlighting the commonalities of hazards such as riverine flooding, coastal flooding, and earthquakes. The book begins by proposing a novel Urban Risk Dynamics framework that emphasizes the roles of economy, landscape, and technology in influencing hazard, exposure, and vulnerability. This framework is then used to support the examination of six contrasting cities from around the world, offering generalized insights that apply to a wide range of urban risk contexts. The book will be of significant interest to students and researchers working in urban planning, civil engineering, earth sciences, and environmental science and to policy-makers and practitioners concerned with reducing future disaster risk in cities.

STEPHANIE E. CHANG is a professor at the University of British Columbia with a joint appointment in the School of Community and Regional Planning and the Institute for Resources, Environment and Sustainability. Her recognitions include: a Shah Family Innovation Prize from the Earthquake Engineering Research Institute (EERI) in 2001; a Distinguished Lectureship from EERI in 2011; and a Distinguished Research Award from the Integrated Disaster Risk Management Society in 2018. She coedited *Modeling Spatial and Economic Impacts of Disasters* (Springer, 2004) and held a Canada Research Chair in Disaster Management and Urban Sustainability from 2004 to 2013.

LEGACY IN THE LANDSCAPE

How Urbanization Shapes Disaster Risk

STEPHANIE E. CHANG
University of British Columbia

CAMBRIDGE
UNIVERSITY PRESS

CAMBRIDGE
UNIVERSITY PRESS

Shaftesbury Road, Cambridge CB2 8EA, United Kingdom

One Liberty Plaza, 20th Floor, New York, NY 10006, USA

477 Williamstown Road, Port Melbourne, VIC 3207, Australia

314–321, 3rd Floor, Plot 3, Splendor Forum, Jasola District Centre, New Delhi – 110025, India

103 Penang Road, #05–06/07, Visioncrest Commercial, Singapore 238467

Cambridge University Press is part of Cambridge University Press & Assessment, a department of the University of Cambridge.

We share the University's mission to contribute to society through the pursuit of education, learning and research at the highest international levels of excellence.

www.cambridge.org
Information on this title: www.cambridge.org/9781009633543

DOI: 10.1017/9781009633574

When citing this work, please include a reference to the DOI 10.1017/9781009633574

First published 2025

A catalogue record for this publication is available from the British Library

Library of Congress Cataloging-in-Publication Data
Names: Chang, S. E. (Stephanie Ei-Ling) author
Title: Legacy in the landscape : how urbanization shapes disaster risk / Stephanie E. Chang, University of British Columbia.
Description: Cambridge, United Kingdom ; New York, NY : Cambridge University Press, 2025. | Includes bibliographical references and index.
Identifiers: LCCN 2025006317 | ISBN 9781009633550 hardback | ISBN 9781009633543 paperback | ISBN 9781009633574 ebook
Subjects: LCSH: Risk management – Law and legislation | Disaster relief – Law and legislation | Urbanization | Hazard mitigation
Classification: LCC HC79.D45 C43 2025 | DDC 363.34/2091732–dc23/eng/20250306
LC record available at https://lccn.loc.gov/2025006317

ISBN 978-1-009-63355-0 Hardback
ISBN 978-1-009-63354-3 Paperback

For
my father and mother,
my brother,
my husband,
and my son

Contents

Preface

When the Loma Prieta earthquake struck San Francisco in 1989, some of the most severe and dramatic destruction occurred in the Marina District: Large fires broke out, the water system was severely damaged, the ground buckled and fractured. Several multistory apartment buildings collapsed. Hundreds of neighborhood residents were displaced from their homes. Now pause and turn back the clock to 1906, to the infamous San Francisco earthquake. At that time, the Marina District was just a sparsely settled lagoon. In subsequent decades, the lagoon was filled in to make space for urban development. The fill materials included debris from the 1906 earthquake.

In 1992, when Hurricane Andrew left a trail of devastation in the Miami region, observers noticed a surprising pattern of housing damage. In general, one would expect newer buildings to perform better in a natural hazard event than older ones; in Hurricane Andrew, however, newer housing was damaged at higher rates than older residences – even in areas that experienced similar windspeeds. Houses built in the 1970s and 1980s fared more poorly than those from the 1960s.

Along Japan's northeastern Tohoku coast, hundreds of inscribed old stone markers warn of the danger from tsunamis. In the aftermath of one such disaster in 1933, many villages and towns were relocated uphill. Over time, however, the population returned to the low-lying coastal areas and built them up again. When the devastating 2011 Great East Japan Earthquake occurred, many such settlements were once again destroyed by the ensuing inundation. One village called Aneyoshi survived, however, even in the face of a nearly 39 m (128 feet) high tsunami. It had remained at the higher elevation, heeding the carved injunction to avoid building below its tsunami stone. Aneyoshi is tiny: At the time of the 2011 catastrophe, it had a population of just 34 people.

In my research and teaching about natural hazards and disasters, I have often come across examples like these that have given me pause. How could it be that in San Francisco one of the worst concentrations of the 1989 earthquake damage was located literally atop debris from the 1906 earthquake? Why didn't the data in Miami cohere to the standard narrative of science and technology steadily improving safety over time? Why was Aneyoshi, the village that stayed safe on high ground, so tiny – or more to the point, have there been any examples of actual cities that have moved, wholesale, away from hazard zones? Over the course of nearly 30 years of studying hazards and disasters, whenever I came across such curious anecdotes that did not fit neatly within standard ways of thinking about disaster risk, I mainly filed them away. But the more such examples I collected, the more I became convinced that something critical was missing in the standard ways of thinking – something fundamental about the relationship between urban development and disaster risk.

* * *

I wrote this book to delve into what I see as a critical gap in the hazards field – the need to understand urbanization as a systemic driver of disaster risk. Much has been written about disasters *in* cities, but insights are scarce on how city-building itself influences disaster risk. To address this need, I have adopted an approach that is distinctive in several ways. First and foremost, this book centers the narrative around the city, rather than the disaster event. It takes a historical approach to explain current-day disaster risk, and it seeks to develop insights on urbanization processes as an underappreciated driver of risk. The book examines a series of cities in order to develop generalized, rather than case-specific, insights. And it draws commonalities across different hazards instead of focusing on just one type.

The story in this book starts with the city. We already know much about urban disaster events. What has been largely missing for cities is the longer-term view – an understanding of what came before the disaster, how this shaped the event's impacts, what happened afterward in the recovery process, and how this conditions what will happen in a future natural hazard event. In other words, the disasters research field has been largely ahistorical.

This book presents cities as continually evolving entities. It examines the dynamics of cities' past and present to draw insights into future trends and possibilities. What is it about urbanization that gives rise to disaster risk? Answering this question is foundational to addressing more proximate ones: Why did a specific flood (or storm or earthquake) turn into a disaster? What is likely to happen in the next event? Why are disaster losses increasing? And ultimately, how can urban disaster risk be reduced?

It is worth emphasizing that this book focuses on cities as the unit of analysis. The social science literature on hazards and disasters is rich in studies that have examined key concepts – vulnerability, risk, recovery, and resilience, for example – at other scales. Much has been written about these issues at the level of the individual person, household, or business; social, demographic, or economic groups such as low-income populations or small businesses; and spatial units such as neighborhoods or countries. Here, the city is taken as the unit of analysis in order to shine a light on risk factors that operate at that scale, for example, urban encroachment onto hazardous lands or economic competition between cities. This also enables insights into how risk dynamics change as small towns grow and evolve into large, dense, heavily built-up population centers.

This book is not about one particular city but rather seeks insights into cities in general. Every city is of course unique, so it is not a given, by any stretch, that one urban area's experience with disaster risk will resemble another's. The literature on urban disasters is dominated by in-depth, informative case studies. But is every city so unique that every disaster is context-specific, or are there some basic commonalities in the evolution of disaster risk? The core of this book comprises six case studies, six very distinct cities. It turns out that common themes do indeed resonate across them. Understanding what generalized insights might be possible is important for sharing and transferring lessons about risk reduction between cities.

In this book, I do not treat disasters as random, external, exogenous events. Rather, I am interested in how a disaster's impacts arose out of the intersection of a hazard event with urban conditions at that particular point in the city's development history. Importantly, the hazards themselves are viewed as characteristic of the city's physical environment, so that the changing relationship between the city and its landscape is of central interest. Such a perspective allows insights to be gained into how even in periods when no hazard event occurs, the city's potential for disasters continues to evolve.

This book offers an integrated, interdisciplinary synthesis – a "big picture" view of urban disaster risk. For each of the six cities, it provides a concise narrative of urban development from origins to the present, relying on secondary sources and emphasizing aspects of urbanization that relate most closely to disaster risk. Looking across the six cases, it develops a cohesive view of how urban disaster risk tends to change over the long term.

Core material for the case studies comes from research in urban history, environmental history, urban geography, and urban planning. The framing of the study also relies on insights from urban economics and regional science, as well as interdisciplinary disaster social sciences. And foundational knowledge from the natural sciences and engineering – geomorphology, geotechnical engineering, and structural engineering, for example – provides crucial pieces of the overall picture. As a consequence, this study may be difficult to classify and is inherently interdisciplinary.

* * *

This book emphasizes the physical city. In terms of natural hazard impacts, it focuses on damage to the built environment. Cities are certainly much more than the buildings, highways, flood protection levees, and other constructed elements within their boundaries. The built environment provides but the physical context for urban lives and livelihoods; production, trade, and economic activities; politics and institutions; social interactions and culture; and many other important dimensions of urbanization. Similarly, disasters cause much more loss, suffering, and transformation beyond the physical damage to structures and infrastructure. But what happens to the built environment is at the core of what turns a natural hazard event into a disaster, and global long-term trends show that even as human casualties have been on an overall decline, direct physical damage has been on a substantial rise. This book emphasizes the physical city in order to shed light on what – and especially what about urbanization processes – may be driving these trends.

Such a focus necessarily entails many limitations. The social dimensions of disasters and risk are not emphasized, and readers are referred to the rich literature on social vulnerability and disaster resilience for these perspectives. Valuable starting points include Blaikie et al. (2014) and Tierney (2019).

Since the case studies here are drawn from Europe, the USA, Canada, Japan, and New Zealand, conclusions and insights are likely to have lesser applicability to cities of the Global South where somewhat different factors and forces may drive the pace and patterns of urbanization.

Moreover, because this book focuses on long-term trends in the built environment, the case study narratives do not mention individual people. Urban history is full of influential, often colorful personalities who have made consequential decisions – mayors, business leaders, even visionary urban planners. Real estate developers, speculators, citizen protest groups, and other often anonymous actors also exert influence on urban development. By stepping back from the actions of specific individuals, I have sought to develop a broader, cumulative perspective on urban change over a timespan of decades and centuries.

At the same time, however, this book does pay more attention to the physical landscape than is typical in social science research. For disaster risk, geography matters. A central thesis of this study is that as a city develops, its relationship with the land also changes. As far as the evolution of disaster risk is concerned, the city cannot be understood without reference to the land that it occupies.

This book is intended to be accessible to readers from a range of backgrounds. Hence while I draw on many disciplines, I have sought to avoid technical terms, to provide lay explanations, and to elaborate on some concepts that would be elementary to specialists. Experts may wish to skip over the discussions of basics in their particular domains, whether that be geomorphology, earthquake engineering, or urban economics. In order to portray the big picture, I have endeavored to keep the presentation simple, without verging into the simplistic.

This book is intended for researchers, students, and practitioners in the many fields that relate to urban disaster risk: the earth sciences, civil engineering, environmental studies, geography, sociology, and urban planning, among others. While interest in natural hazards and disaster risk reduction is growing in these fields, training remains specialized, and few books deliberately bridge technical issues with socioeconomic insights. By providing such a bridge, I hope this book can help those from varying disciplinary backgrounds to connect their specialized knowledge to the larger problem of disaster risk in cities.

* * *

I am grateful to the many researchers whose published work I have drawn on in order to assemble an overall picture from what often seemed like numerous puzzle pieces. The content of each case study draws extensively from other studies regarding the city's development history or a specific disaster event. As much as possible, I have looked to sources by scholars with deep local knowledge, especially those who live and work in the specific case study city. These sources are cited in the notes, and I refer interested readers to them for more in-depth, detailed discussion than was possible within the scope of this book.

In addition to published sources, I have also drawn on field visits, interviews, and informal conversations for background understanding of the case study cities. These include numerous visits to Japan, several of which were hosted by the Disaster Prevention Research Institute at Kyoto University, as well as by Kobe University; a sabbatical year in Vienna at the International Institute for Applied Systems Analysis; and a visit hosted by Resilient Organisations in New Zealand that gave me a glimpse into Christchurch before the Canterbury earthquake sequence.

I am grateful to the many mentors, collaborators, colleagues, and students who have helped shape my thinking over the years. My undergraduate advisor, Masanobu Shinozuka, encouraged me to bridge the gap between engineering and the social sciences. My graduate advisor, Barclay Jones, taught me to appreciate cities empirically, historically, and holistically. I have learned much from my other mentors, many collaborators, and graduate students and postdocs, including how to think about hazards and disasters from the perspectives of different disciplines. I especially thank Kathleen Tierney, Ron Eguchi, Tom O'Rourke, Adam Rose, Tim McDaniels, Phil Berke, David Edgington, Ken Elwood, and Charlotte Brown. I gratefully acknowledge Charlotte Milne's assistance in producing the case study maps. Most of all, I thank my husband, Leo Shin, for being with me throughout this project and for helping me get over the hurdles near the finish.

1

Reconsidering Disaster Risk

1.1 Natural Hazards and Cities over Time

Most people would agree that cities need to plan for disaster risk not just today but into the future. In practice, however, anticipating what disaster risk will look like in the future is not an easy task. Most studies that forecast future risk anticipate changes in the natural hazard events, such as an increased likelihood of powerful storms due to climate change. Very few attempt to forecast how the cities at risk may themselves transform over the period. For example, it is standard for an analysis of future coastal flooding to take into account sea-level rise projections and, somewhat less commonly, changes in storm likelihood and other characteristics. Only rarely will the analysis consider future urban population growth, densification, or land-use changes. Yet we all know that cities change, and sometimes do so very rapidly.

This book addresses the challenge of understanding how urban disaster risk changes over time. At its core is a simple argument – to understand how urban risk changes, we need to understand how cities change. Here, cities are viewed as continually evolving entities whose past and present dynamics provide insights into future trends and possibilities. I ask this central question: What is it about urbanization that gives rise to disaster risk?

In this chapter, I propose a conceptual framework for thinking about the dynamics of urban disaster risk. I first argue that we know less than we think we do about how disaster risk in cities is changing. Established tools and frameworks for thinking about risk have some significant shortcomings when it comes to understanding how it changes. I then propose a simple conceptual framework to serve as a lens through which to examine evolving disaster risk in any city. To operationalize this framework, I suggest several questions that can help guide the empirical study of evolving disaster risk in actual cities. The framework provides the basis for delving into a series of empirical case studies in subsequent chapters.[1]

* * *

The statistics tell us that disaster trends are worsening. According to the most commonly used global database on disasters, the EM-DAT database maintained by the Centre for Research on the Epidemiology of Disasters, the number of disaster events has shown an increasing trend over the last several decades. Extrapolating from this, the United Nations Office for Disaster Risk Reduction (UNDRR) anticipates around 550 disasters per year by the year 2030 – over five times more than the annual count back in 1970. It further notes that annual economic losses from disasters in the last three decades have on average more than doubled, from $70 billion in the 1990s to some $170 billion in the 2010s. Similar databases are maintained for individual countries and by the private sector, such as the insurance and reinsurance industry, and they show similar trends.[2]

Such trend data and analyses provide valuable information, but they should not be taken at face value. First, what counts as a "disaster"? To be included in the EM-DAT database, an event has to meet at least one of several criteria: 10 or more deaths; 100 or more people affected/injured/homeless; declaration by the country of a state of emergency; and/or an appeal for international assistance. When data are insufficient, supplementary criteria may also be used, such as "worst disasters in the decade." Compiling a global database with reasonable consistency in the face of widely varying data quality, reporting reliability, and contextual significance is a difficult task. Yet if these data are to be used to consider how risk is changing, questions should be raised about whether systematic biases may exist in the data. Researchers have noted, for example, that smaller events tend to be underrepresented in the database. Completeness may also have shifted over time. Multidecadal trends in disaster data can thus be unreliable for many reasons.[3]

But let us suppose that data quality issues notwithstanding, in actuality, the total numbers of disaster events and amount of losses really are increasing over the long term. Do these indicators meaningfully measure how risk is changing? Some have argued that other metrics are more suitable. For example, if annual deaths from disasters doubled over a period when total population has quadrupled, deaths per capita would have been halved – a significant improvement in risk to any

[1] This chapter expands on some unpublished ideas that I presented in my 2011 Distinguished Lecture for the Earthquake Engineering Research Institute (EERI).

[2] EM-DAT database: www.emdat.be. For UNDRR estimates, see (United Nations Office for Disaster Risk Reduction, 2022). For insurance/reinsurance data, see, for example, Munich Re, www.munichre.com/en/risks/natural-disasters.html.

[3] For data inclusion criteria, see www.emdat.be/guidelines. For underrepresentation of smaller events, see (Vereinte Nationen, 2015).

individual person. Similarly, economic losses can also be expressed in relation to the size of the economy at the time (e.g., as a share of a country's gross domestic product (GDP) or the global total). Moreover, if economic losses are adjusted for price inflation over time, their increase looks less ominous.

But let us further suppose that data quality issues aside, and suitable metrics considered, we find that indeed disasters are becoming more common and losses are growing. There is still another reason why such trends do not really tell us much about how risk is changing. This is because global disaster trends cannot be extrapolated down to the local level.

A simple thought exercise illustrates why. Imagine a hypothetical world in which there are only two cities and both are at risk from earthquakes. Let us assume that between Year 0 and Year 20, nothing changes – the probability of earthquakes in both cities remains the same, as do their populations. However, it so happens that in Year 0, an earthquake strikes City A (population 20,000) and causes a 1% loss, or 200 deaths. Then in Year 20, an earthquake strikes City B (population 100,000) and causes a 1% loss, or 1,000 deaths. Connecting these two datapoints over time, the global trend would show a fivefold increase in annual earthquake deaths. Yet this increasing loss trendline tells us nothing about how risk in cities A and B has been changing. Indeed, for city A as well as city B, the actual *risk* of earthquake loss has remained constant between Years 0 and 20 because neither the seismicity nor the population changed. Global metrics do not tell us about local conditions.

Understanding how urban disaster risk is changing requires investigation at the local level. City-scale studies have adopted different approaches to answering this question. One is to look for "repeat" events to see whether a given hazard event striking a city caused more (or different patterns of) losses than a similar hazard event in a previous period. Such repeat events are not very common, but they do happen.

Los Angeles experienced two similarly sized earthquakes about 23 years apart, the 1971 San Fernando earthquake (M_w 6.6) and the 1994 Northridge earthquake (M_w 6.7). Both events had epicenters in the San Fernando Valley; ground motion patterns and intensities were, overall, quite similar. In the years between these two events, however, Los Angeles County's population had grown by some 2 million people. Since there were many more people in harm's way, was the 1994 Northridge earthquake much more devastating than the 1971 San Fernando earthquake? In some ways, no: The San Fernando earthquake caused 58 deaths, while Northridge caused 57. While injuries were higher in Northridge (over 9,000, compared with 2,000 for San Fernando), data on injuries are harder to compare reliably because of definitional differences, reporting sources, and the like. But it seems clear that economic losses were much higher in Northridge – at least $24 billion, or 13 times higher than San Fernando's $1.8 billion (in inflation-adjusted 1994 dollars). At the time, the 1994 Northridge earthquake was the costliest disaster in US history. Comparing these two disasters, analysts have noted that the 1971 earthquake spurred seismic safety legislation and initiatives such as improved building codes and retrofit programs, and these significantly reduced damage in the 1994 earthquake compared to what would have otherwise occurred. The empirical evidence from Los Angeles, at least, does not support a simple story of increasing urban disaster risk due to growing population.[4]

Another approach is to examine how factors influencing risk have been changing over time and to quantitatively estimate the overall effect on future risk. Studies have focused for instance on modeling how the risk-reducing improvements in building codes for earthquakes or hurricanes balance out against population growth and the accompanying increase in buildings at risk. Similarly to the "repeat events" approach, models can be used to estimate losses (such as casualties, property damage, and business interruption) if the same hazard event were to occur, hypothetically, at different points in time. More generally, such modeling approaches can be used to examine "what if" scenarios – how would losses in a disaster be different under different conditions or policies? As with the example comparing the actual 1971 and 1994 earthquakes in Los Angeles, the findings of modeling studies point to a complicated story in which risk trends depend upon the hazard, the impact metric, the scope of the analysis, and the underlying assumptions. But what such scenario approaches can tell us is still limited by how they consider risk.[5]

1.2 Frameworks about Risk

What, then, is risk? Perhaps the most common framework for thinking about natural hazards-related risk, particularly from a science and engineering perspective, is that risk is an adverse outcome that has some likelihood of occurrence. The basic idea is:

$$\text{Risk} = \text{Probability} \times \text{Consequences}$$

where Probability refers to the likelihood of an event (such as an earthquake) and Consequences are the losses that would be experienced if that event were to occur.

[4] The Census population of Los Angeles County was 7.0 million in 1970 and 8.9 million in 1990. For data on Northridge earthquake costs, see (Eguchi et al., 1998). The $24 billion figure is a tabulation of documented costs, but actual direct economic losses were probably closer to $44 billion. These numbers exclude indirect, or business interruption, losses. For a comparison of the two events and discussion of policy changes after San Fernando, see (Olshansky, 2001).

[5] For risk dynamics modeling studies, see, for example, (Chang et al., 2012) and (Chang, Yip, & Tse, 2019) on earthquakes and coastal flooding in Vancouver, Canada, as well as (Jain & Davidson, 2007) on hurricanes in North Carolina. Hallegatte et al. (2011) modeled economic losses under different levels of sea-level rise in Copenhagen.

This basic idea can be specified more precisely in mathematical terms, taking into account aspects such as the risk of what (e.g., human casualties), the probability of many possible adverse events (e.g., earthquakes of different magnitudes and epicentral locations), and the conditionality of consequences (e.g., deaths conditional on building damage, which are in turn conditional on earthquake ground shaking). This idea of risk as "probability times consequences" is foundational to many sophisticated quantitative analyses of urban disaster risk.

It is not, however, very amenable to thinking about how risk changes over time. There are at least a couple of ways in which to introduce time into the basic formulation. One is comparative statics: Risk can be evaluated separately for two points in time, say today (T_1) and 50 years from now (T_2). This requires quantifying what each factor that influences risk – say, a city's population or the probability of a hurricane – would be at T_1 and T_2. In T_2, it may be expected that the probability of a hurricane would be higher due to climate change, that the accompanying coastal flood extent would be greater due to sea-level rise, that the urban population would have grown a certain percentage with especially high increase in certain neighborhoods, that improved building codes would reduce the likelihood of building damage to some degree, and so on. Models can be used to estimate flood risk with conditions in T_1 and T_2; the difference quantifies how much risk would be expected to change over this period. A variation would be to decouple the analysis from a specific timeline and to examine questions such as: If (or when) sea level rises by X amount, by how much would hurricane losses be expected to change? Alternatively, a more challenging approach would be to integrate rates of change directly into the analysis, for example, using equations that are temporally specified.

Either way, the conceptual framing of risk as "probability times consequences" has some important limitations when it comes to considering urban risk dynamics. First, while it enables assessing *how much* risk changes, *how* it changes – the underlying mechanisms, such as building code improvements – are assumptions that are built into the analysis. Second, the approach does not elucidate *why* risk changes, that is, what is driving the underlying dynamics. Third, factors influencing risk are considered independently of one another; for example, it is assumed that changes in building codes occur independently of changes in hurricane hazard. Further, specific actions that influence risk – for instance, government disaster relief policies or construction of protective infrastructure – are difficult to include in the risk analysis except by assumption, through "what-if" scenario analyses. And finally, the framing focuses on direct factors influencing risk, for the most part ignoring indirect drivers. The "probability times consequences" framing enables detailed analysis into risk today, but not into how we got to where we are today or where we are headed.

In the social science literature on hazards and disasters, risk is often framed a little differently than "probability times consequences." The basic idea is commonly conceptualized as:

$$\text{Risk} = \text{Hazard} \times \text{Vulnerability}$$

At some level, "hazard" is akin to "probability," and "vulnerability" to "consequences." But there are some key differences. The framing is not intended literally, in a mathematically multiplicative sense, but rather to indicate the intersection between hazard and vulnerability – for example, in terms of low-income populations occupying steep slopes that are prone to landslides. The hazard is generally not treated probabilistically but more commonly taken as a given, while the weight of attention is afforded to understanding the vulnerability side, especially social vulnerability. A key difference is that this framing more integrally conceptualizes issues of how and why risk changes, especially in terms of how social vulnerability to disasters is created and perpetuated.

One influential version of this framing, the disaster pressure-and-release (PAR) model, underscores the importance of the underlying drivers that give rise to risk conditions. In the PAR model, "a disaster is the intersection of two opposing forces: Those processes generating vulnerability on one side, and the natural hazard event … on the other." In order "to relieve the pressure, vulnerability has to be reduced." Vulnerability itself is thought of as comprising three layers: *Unsafe Conditions*, which are influenced by underlying *Dynamic Pressures*, which are in turn influenced by *Root Causes*. Unsafe conditions can be physical (e.g., populations living on steep slopes) as well as socioeconomic (e.g., low income levels, lack of disaster preparedness). Of particular interest here are the dynamic pressures that give rise to these unsafe conditions – forces such as rapid urbanization and deforestation, as well as lack of local investments or corrupt governments. Root causes such as capitalist economic systems "reflect the exercise and distribution of power in a society" and provide the context within which these dynamic pressures arise. A substantial body of knowledge has been developed that examines vulnerability from this perspective, especially differential vulnerability across social groups and the heightened vulnerability of marginalized populations.[6]

From the perspective of understanding how urban risk changes over time, however, there are a few key aspects that are missing or obscured. First is specific reference to the processes by which change happens in cities. What are the dynamic pressures *within* cities that give rise to unsafe conditions? Does urban disaster risk invariably increase over time? Do particular processes of urban development

[6] (Wisner et al., 2004); quotes are from pp. 50, 53. For an overview of the vulnerability literature, see, for example, (Wisner, 2016).

exacerbate social vulnerability and thereby worsen disaster risk? Second, also missing are the processes of change on the hazard side. And third, how do actions, investments, and policies – including but not limited to those intended to address disaster risk – figure into the picture? Ultimately, where are the most promising opportunities and what are the most promising approaches for mitigating the propagation of risk in cities over the long term?

Another foundational framework about risk consists of the interdisciplinary approach developed by the Intergovernmental Panel on Climate Change (IPCC). Within this framework, risk is defined as "the potential for adverse consequences for human or ecological systems, recognising the diversity of values and objectives associated with such systems." Hazard is "the potential occurrence of a natural or human-induced physical event or trend that may cause loss of life, injury, or other health impacts, as well as damage and loss to property, infrastructure, livelihoods, service provision, ecosystems and environmental resources." Exposure refers to "the presence of people; livelihoods; species or ecosystems; environmental functions, services and resources; infrastructure; or economic, social or cultural assets in places and settings that could be adversely affected." Vulnerability is defined in terms of "the propensity or disposition to be adversely affected and encompasses a variety of concepts and elements, including sensitivity or susceptibility to harm and lack of capacity to cope and adapt."[7]

Risk emerges from the intersection of hazard, exposure, and vulnerability, which can be viewed as three blades of a "risk propeller." Driving this propeller are the underlying forces of interconnected climate, ecosystems, and human society, which can be summarized briefly:

> Human society causes climate change. Climate change, through hazards, exposure and vulnerability generates impacts and risks that can surpass limits to adaptation and result in losses and damages. Human society can adapt to, maladapt and mitigate climate change, ecosystems can adapt and mitigate within limits. Ecosystems and their biodiversity provision livelihoods and ecosystem services. Human society impacts ecosystems and can restore and conserve them.[8]

In many ways, this framework provides a valuable basis for thinking about risk dynamics. It focuses on how risk changes, rather than on how much risk exists; in particular, it highlights the underlying systems interactions that may drive change. It integrates consideration of change in both natural systems (climate, ecosystems) and human systems, recognizing their fundamental interconnections. Changes in hazard are considered, especially as arising from human society's actions, alongside changes in exposure and vulnerability. Furthermore, this framing of risk

[7] (Intergovernmental Panel on Climate Change [IPCC], 2023); quotes are from p. 5.
[8] (IPCC, 2023, Figure SPM.1).

allows the identification of opportunities to reduce risk by modifying the underlying systems processes and interactions that give rise to it.

But from the perspective of understanding risk dynamics in cities, there are still many gaps. How does the "risk propeller" play out – how do hazard, exposure, vulnerability, and ultimately risk evolve – in cities? Where does urbanization fit into the picture? And to what extent does the framework also apply to hazards such as earthquakes that are not climate-related?

1.3 A Framework about Urban Risk Dynamics

In order to examine why, how, and how much disaster risk is changing in a city – and ultimately, how risk-producing processes can be effectively addressed – we need a modified framework, one that centers the urban development process and relates it to the central concepts of disaster risk. The framework should be sufficiently structured to support systematically understanding how and why disaster risk changes over a city's history, yet open to a broad range of factors and diversity of urban contexts.

A simple framework for Urban Risk Dynamics is proposed here (Figure 1.1). Consistently with the IPCC risk framework and much of the disasters literature, risk is viewed as arising from the interaction between hazard, exposure, and vulnerability. These interactions are set in the context of urban development processes, particularly as they relate to the focus of this book – changes in the built environment, or the physical city at risk of damage from natural hazards.

The Urban Risk Dynamics framework emphasizes three interrelated dimensions of urbanization: landscape, economy, and technology. Landscape comprises the physical terrain and environment, including water bodies. A key premise of this study is that local geography is vital to understanding urban disaster risk. Economy pertains to activities such as the production of goods and services, as well as trade. A second premise here is that cities must be understood as economic entities. (Chapter 2 elaborates on how cities' location, functioning, internal structure, growth, and decline are all influenced by economic forces.) Technology refers broadly to the application of human ingenuity to urban needs such as for water supply or transportation mobility. A third premise of this study is that technological change is a key driver of urban change. Many other factors also influence urban development processes (e.g., the role of governments) but are omitted from the diagram for simplicity of presentation.[9]

The Urban Risk Dynamics framework provides a lens through which we can approach any city to understand how its risk from natural hazards has been

[9] For the role of technology in global change, see (Grübler, 2003).

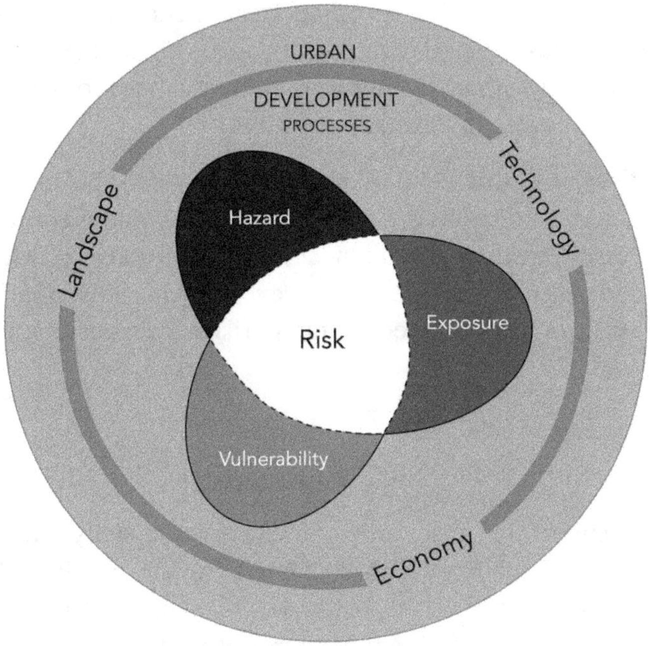

Figure 1.1 Urban risk dynamics framework

changing over time. Specifically, the framework can be implemented through asking a series of broad questions:

- **How has urban development influenced the local hazard?** This question does not pertain specifically to the effects of climate change which, while part of the evolving hazard context, derive from processes that are global in scope. Rather, it refers to local processes such as flood control technologies and land-use changes that affect the probability and severity of hazards that are faced by the city.
- **How has urban development influenced exposure?** This question relates to the particulars of settlement in areas that are especially susceptible to hazard, such as floodplains. It is perhaps the most straightforward to examine but raises complex issues of not only how much but when, how, why, and by and for whom. It raises, for example, questions of the role of land-use planning in generating disaster risk.
- **How has urban development influenced vulnerability?** This question relates to the propensity for loss in a hazard event that affects people, property, and economic activity exposed to the hazard. It includes, for example, changes to building codes and construction practices. But it also includes societal preparedness for hazard events (e.g., risk perceptions, warning systems), capacity to respond to and recover from disasters, and differential vulnerability across socioeconomic groups within society.

In answering these questions, it is also important to consider how the interactions between hazard, exposure, and vulnerability may have changed. Furthermore, beyond examining how urban development processes lead to risk, it is also valuable to consider influences in the other direction:

- **How have disasters influenced urban development?** This question considers hazard events as part of a city's development history and draws attention to the specific processes of urban development in disaster recovery, when the pace of change is often accelerated. Does urban development in the aftermath of disasters tend to occur in ways that reduce future risk or, conversely, that exacerbate it? How, and why?

1.4 Six Case Studies

In subsequent chapters, the risk stories of several case study cities are explored through the lens of this Urban Risk Dynamics framework. In order to provide some bounds and coherence to the study, several scoping decisions were made. First, the analysis emphasizes only three types of natural hazards: riverine flooding, coastal flooding, and earthquakes. These in some ways represent "classic" natural hazards affecting urban areas – hazards that have threatened cities across the ages, that directly damage the built environment, and for which the scientific knowledge base is well established. These hazards are well understood as physical phenomena and in terms of societal impacts, yet the connection to long-term urbanization processes remains understudied.

But why earthquakes alongside floods? In part, this juxtaposition serves to expose any similarities in urban risk dynamics across hazards that at first glance might seem to have nothing in common. In other words, is there anything about urbanization that shapes flood risk in ways that parallel earthquake risk? Another rationale, too, is to address the reality that while flooding and seismicity may be compartmentalized in academic inquiry, the reality for many cities that face earthquakes is that they are also prone to flooding.

A second key scoping decision pertains to the selection of the case study cities. For each hazard, I explore two cases: for riverine flooding, Vienna (Austria) and Calgary (Canada); for coastal flooding, New Orleans (USA) and New York City (USA); and for earthquakes, Kobe (Japan) and Christchurch (New Zealand). Some of these may seem obvious choices to natural hazards researchers, while others may be surprising. Table 1.1 lists some key characteristics of the six cases.

These six cases were selected to meet several key criteria individually, in pairs, and as a set. First and foremost, each city must of course be facing a significant risk from the particular hazard. Equally importantly, there must exist a sufficient body

Table 1.1 *Case study cities*

Chapter	City	Country	Population[(1)]	Major disaster[(2)]
Chapter 3: Riverine flooding	Vienna	Austria	2,006,000	–
	Calgary	Canada	1,307,000	*2013 flood*
Chapter 4: Coastal flooding	New Orleans	USA	364,000	2005 hurricane
	New York	USA	8,258,000	*2012 hurricane*
Chapter 5: Earthquakes	Kobe	Japan	1,494,000	1995 earthquake
	Christchurch	New Zealand	396,000	*2010–2011 earthquakes*

Notes:
(1) Population for 2023 except Calgary (2021) and Kobe (2024). Data from city government websites except New Orleans (US Census).
(2) Disasters since 1995 only. *Italics* = since 2010.

of English-language scholarly literature on the city's hazard risk, urban development history, and major disasters. Indeed, the source material for each of the case studies is especially rich in some way that is important for this study, such as environmental history, urban geography, or multifaceted postdisaster investigation.

Each pair of cities was selected to provide an insightful but not overwhelming degree of contrast. Vienna and Calgary are both medium-sized river cities but differ importantly in other ways – notably, region of the world, political centrality to the nation, and temporal span of urban history. Their physical setting also differs, as the Danube is a major navigational waterway and a much larger river than the Bow. These contrasts, as will become apparent in Chapter 3, do matter when it comes to riverine flood hazard and the cities' efforts at risk management.

New Orleans and New York are both US cities that have experienced major hurricane disasters with coastal flooding. Hurricanes Katrina and Sandy are not only two of the most expensive disasters in the nation's history but also among the best documented. As will be shown in Chapter 4, the predisaster background of urban development strongly conditioned the similarities and differences between these two infamous disasters. While the two cities share a national context (e.g., with regard to flood insurance policy), they differ in important ways – in terms of population size but also with regard to predisaster growth or decline trajectory, hazard event frequency, and physical setting (New Orleans sits on a massive coastal delta, while New York is located on a deepwater estuary).

Kobe and Christchurch take the story beyond Europe and North America to Asia and Oceania. Both cities experienced major earthquake disasters that are among the most thoroughly studied in the literature, and both face not only seismic but also flood hazards. They differ in terms of country as well as economic history, urban setting, and physical geography. In contrast to Christchurch, Kobe has one of the largest ports in the world, is part of a much larger metropolitan region (Osaka-Kobe), and is sandwiched between mountains and sea. Chapter 5 reveals how such similarities and differences matter for earthquake impact and recovery.

A further selection criterion was that for each pair one of the cities had to have experienced a major disaster about a decade before this writing. This timing strikes a balance between recency and data availability. In 2013, Calgary (along with much of southern Alberta province) was flooded in Canada's costliest disaster up until that time. In 2012, Hurricane Sandy caused extensive destruction in New York City and the broader region. In 2010–2011, Christchurch experienced a devastating sequence of earthquakes. Each of these disasters represented a milestone event that spurred public reactions, policy responses, changes in professional practice, and considerable academic research. After a decade of postdisaster recovery and a profusion of investigative studies, these cases provide valuable opportunities for reflection as well as synthesis.

As a set, the six cases together represent a diversity of urban types. These contrasts allow some insight into how urbanization occurs across different landscapes and what implications that might hold for disaster risk. While most are medium-sized cities, New York has over 8 million residents and is one of the largest urban economies in the world. In contrast to the other cases, Vienna is an old city – a long-time imperial capital and for centuries a major European urban center. Kobe's development reflects patterns of rapid industrialization in East Asia. Only two US cities are included here, even though the literature is rich in US case studies, in order to capture sufficient global variation in urban experiences. Yet for all their diversity, the six cities are similar in that they are all set within industrialized economies in what is referred to as the Global North.

Before delving into these six cases, however, it is important to establish the concepts of "urbanization" and "urban development processes" and to demonstrate what it means to view cities as economic entities. These topics, which are central to this study but rarely encountered in textbooks and studies of hazards and disasters, are the subject of Chapter 2.

2
How Cities Evolve

Cities are, fundamentally, economic entities. Their location, functioning, internal structure, growth, and decline are all heavily influenced by economic forces. Indeed, many of the reasons why cities exist at all are economic. Archeologists, urban historians, economic historians, and others have long examined where and why cities began. The particulars may have changed over millennia, but through to the present day, cities exist because the dense clustering of people in a landscape provides economic advantages to the people and organizations that locate there.[1]

These economic forces and their logic – the way they operate and manifest in the urban environment – are the subject of this chapter, which draws from the fields of urban economics, economic geography, and regional science in order to present fundamental concepts about long-term urban dynamics. It focuses on three questions: Why are cities where they are? What drives urban growth and change? And how does urban form change as cities grow across a landscape? While the chapter does not examine disaster risk per se, the broad contours of urban dynamics that it outlines are central to the six case studies of disaster risk that follow in Chapters 3–5.

2.1 Why Are Cities Where They Are?

Imagine that you had the power to found a new city. You face a landscape of possible locations – let's say in a coastal region with a broad plain, a mountain range, hills, valleys, and a river flowing down through the valleys to the sea. You have free choice as to where to place the beginnings of your new city. Where would you locate it?

[1] For a classic work on urban origins, see (Bairoch, 1991). For a comprehensive recent synthesis, see (Bosker, 2022).

You might begin by considering that you would like your new city to have easy access to the river and the ocean, for ships to bring in goods like food, clothing, and machinery for your city's population. It wouldn't make sense to place your new city on a mountain peak (how many real cities can you name that are located on mountain peaks?). Perhaps the flat areas near the river are prime agricultural land, which would be advantageous for growing food to feed the city's residents. With a series of considerations like these, which are essentially economic considerations, you might end up locating your city at the mouth of the river, where it meets the ocean. Or perhaps in a wide valley along the river, where it would still have plenty of space for expansion and easy access to a water source and river transport.

Many cities were established in locations such as a natural harbor at the mouth of a navigable river, or the confluence of two rivers. Sites that afford ready access to water transportation are economically advantageous, as shipping typically provides a cheaper means of moving goods (and people) over long distances than land-based transportation. But goods, such as grain, must first be transported over land to harbors and again over land after being unloaded from ships to reach their final destination. Locations that facilitate the movement of goods from one transport mode to another, particularly between water and rail or road, are thus economically advantageous. Moreover, since cities function as trade centers, such locations help with controlling trade routes. The advantages of access to water transport were arguably especially important in earlier centuries, when many of today's cities were being established.[2]

Other geographic features besides transportation access can also provide important locational benefits. Soil quality in the surrounding region and agriculturally favorable climatic conditions are important geographical advantages. Early cities also needed access to fresh water supply, building materials, and wood as an energy source. A river can provide not only water for drinking and agriculture but also fish for food and an outlet for waste disposal. All of these advantages support economic activity. Even when town sites were chosen for different reasons – for example, for military defense or strategic political control of lands and resources or to mine an ore deposit – it can be argued that these reasons promoted and protected economic activity.[3]

[2] The term "first nature" is sometimes used in the academic literature to refer to the influence of physical geography, such as rivers, mountains, fertile plains, and climate. See, for example, (Lin & Rauch, 2022). The role of "break of bulk" in transportation economics was identified by Cooley (1894). See also (Harris & Ullman, 1945). Other types of locations away from water routes could also be advantageous for controlling trade routes, for example, at a mountain pass or desert oasis. See (Bosker, 2022) for a useful overview of economic factors influencing city origins. Jedwab et al. (2022) provide an interesting discussion of cities in the Middle Ages (c. 800–1500 CE) in regions around the world, from an urban economic perspective.

[3] See (Jedwab et al., 2022) and (Bosker, 2022). Bosker and Buringh (2017), in a study of city origins in Europe, examined the statistical likelihood of a city forming across hundreds of thousands of potential sites. They found that locational advantage for water- or land-based transportation was a key factor. Other variables such as favorable agricultural conditions were also significant but with statistically smaller and less robust effects.

This does not mean that physical geography alone predetermines urbanization. Highly favorable natural advantages do not guarantee urban fortunes. Notably, technology can augment a location's economic advantages or make up for its disadvantages. For example, in an influential study of the city of Chicago, environmental historian William Cronon argued that "if waterway geography were the determinant of urban growth, the major inland city would surely be St. Louis … Located at the confluence of two of the continent's greatest rivers, the Mississippi and the Missouri, St. Louis could reasonably expect to draw resources from the entire country to its north and west." Yet Chicago predominated, its fortunes strongly bolstered by the routing of the railroad network when it was constructed in the 1850s.[4]

Human modifications to the landscape can take many forms, but they have one aspect in common: They require investment. Construction of railways, road networks, canals, bridges, tunnels, and the like is expensive. Generally, such investments are made – whether by autocratic rulers, elected governments, or speculatory capitalists – because they are expected to bring economic advantages and payoffs. In a similar vein, construction of water control structures such as irrigation channels, aqueducts, dams, and reservoirs can also make arid locations more economically viable. The costs of draining swamplands are offset by the benefits of being able to settle the newly drained lands.[5]

For a city, location matters also in relation to other places; that is, the economic logic of urban location has a lot to do with spatial interactions. Early cities served as "central places" for their agricultural hinterland, or what can be considered their agricultural catchment area. Farmers could bring their products to a town market to sell and trade. Access to a fertile agricultural hinterland was thus an important locational advantage for early, preindustrial, cities, when transport costs were high. It became less and less important over time, however, as technological advances were made in agriculture, transport, and storage. Instead, a city site's advantages in terms of transport connections with other cities for long-distance trade – whether by land or by water – became more prominent, and cities could be founded in locations without an agriculturally rich hinterland.[6]

So why are cities located where they are? The discussion so far has emphasized an urban economic perspective. Cities are economic entities, and their locational fundamentals such as access to water transportation are important because they confer economic advantages. Technology, such as railroads, can augment a location's economic advantages. Such human modifications to the landscape

[4] (Cronon, 1991); quote is from p. 37.

[5] The term "second nature" is sometimes used in the academic literature to refer to durable, constructed, locationally fixed investments such as canals and railroads. See, for example, (Lin & Rauch, 2022).

[6] See (Bairoch, 1991; Bosker, 2022; Duranton, 1999).

require investment, and they are undertaken for their expected economic benefits. Transportation connection to other cities is a further important locational advantage. This simple characterization recognizes the fundamental economic logic underlying the location of cities, but it is just the starting point for a more complex perspective on how urban development leads to disaster risk.[7]

2.2 What Drives Urban Growth and Change?

How many of today's major cities were already predominant 300 years ago? If you were to take a guess at answering this question, you might approach it in many ways. You might consider today's large cities, say those with over 1 million residents, and consider whether they could plausibly have existed three centuries ago. Alternatively, you might look up the 10 largest cities in the world today and consider whether they would likely have been the 10 largest cities back then. You might try to imagine the world of the early 1700s – before the Industrial Revolution – and how it differed from today, and what that might mean for cities. You might think about major cities that you have visited and recall whether they had archeological sites such as temples and castles that dated from before the eighteenth century. In some regions of the world, such as the west coast of the USA, you might figure that there were no cities at all three centuries ago. The world map of cities today is a snapshot in time.

The reasons why cities grow – and why once-flourishing cities decline – are myriad, complex, and particular to each one's historic circumstances. But amid all the rich and idiosyncratic narratives of individual cities, three observations about the long-term dynamics of urban fortunes are particularly important for this book, because they have subtle yet profound implications for cities and disaster risk. The first is that a city's economic competitiveness changes over time, due to both internal and external forces. The second is that technological change alters the ways in which cities gain economic advantage from their physical location. And third, many forces resist change; indeed, persistence is a defining feature of urbanization.

A few brief examples are selected here to illustrate these urban dynamics across the centuries in different parts of the globe. These examples are neither exhaustive nor deliberately representative, but they are diverse, interesting, and insightful in complementary ways. We begin in the centuries after the fall of the Western Roman Empire with the "resetting" of the urban network in Europe. Following this, we

[7] This simple characterization is distilled from a considerable body of literature in urban economics that is based on abstract mathematical models. These models are unable to account for many of the particularities of actual cities, their distinct physical settings, and their social histories. But they are very powerful in their capacity to generate fundamental insights about urban location, growth, and change.

consider the medieval port city of Bruges, review Chicago's emergence in the early railroad era, move forward to post-World War II urbanization in Japan, and finally examine the impact of containerization on port cities in the latter decades of the twentieth century.

* * *

The ancient Romans built cities across their domain, and the collapse of the Western Roman Empire in 476 CE devastated urbanization in Europe. In what had been Roman Britain, by around 450–600 CE, cities had essentially disappeared. By contrast, in France, many formerly Roman towns were occupied by the Franks and survived, even if the settlements declined. Thus when urban networks began to reemerge centuries later in the Middle Ages, Britain's cities effectively developed from a blank slate – that is to say, the urban network was "reset" – while France's retained the imprint of Roman city-building. Analysts have found that this "resetting of Britain's urban network gave it better access to natural navigable waterways, which mattered for town growth from 1200 to 1800," whereas "history trapped many French towns in suboptimal locations." In the Middle Ages, coastal access became more important for two reasons: The long-distance road network was deficient compared with Roman times, and technical improvements had been made in waterborne transport (in particular, new shallow-draft ship designs that enabled ocean-going vessels to access inland waterways, thereby reducing transport costs). Between 1200 and 1800, overall, towns that had coastal access grew faster than those that did not. The legacy of this era of reurbanization remains today: While 16 out of France's 20 largest cities are near Roman town sites, in Britain, only 2 out of 20 are.[8]

This example illustrates that while locational advantages matter across the ages, the value of particular attributes (in this case, access to water for transportation) is related to the economic systems and technologies of the day. Moreover, locations with advantage in one era could become disadvantageous in another time. In the absence of wholesale "resetting," however – which rarely occurs – cities will generally persist where they were established.

The historic city of Bruges in current-day Belgium offers a second insightful example of changing urban fortunes. Bruges is perhaps best known today as a tourist destination with well-preserved medieval architecture, but around 1400, it was one of the largest cities in Europe. As the preeminent commercial hub of northwestern Europe, it was a key trading center for textiles and other goods. Over the next century, however, its fortunes declined precipitously – a decline that is often ascribed simply to the silting up of Bruges' harbor.

[8] This example is drawn from (Michaels & Rauch, 2018); quote is from p. 378.

But such a simplistic interpretation has been challenged by historians. The navigability problems of Bruges' waterways long predated the period of economic decline and were actually an inherent condition of the site. The city's government made numerous costly attempts to engineer a solution, including deepening and straightening the channel, constructing canals and locks, and funneling in water to increase scouring – all of which ultimately failed. Just as significant as the long-standing challenges of waterway navigability, moreover, was the changing structure of Europe's economy, especially the decline of the Flemish cloth industry that was central to Bruges' prosperity. Other towns became more competitive, and by 1560, Antwerp had become preeminent in the region. In other words, "the decline of Bruges in the late Middle Ages as a major trading center has been attributed to silting in the channel leading to the sea, but it is far more reasonable to say that regional shifts in trade, which reduced the city's role, discouraged the burghers from regular dredging of the waterway."[9]

The story of Bruges thus illustrates some key points about the dynamic processes behind rising and falling urban fortunes: that urban change is closely tied to the underlying economic context; that locational advantages are not simply natural but reinforced and maintained by capital investments in the built environment; and that the physical environment is subject to continual natural processes of landscape change.

The city of Chicago provides a third example, illustrating how technological change in the Industrial Revolution impacted urbanization processes. City-building is a much more recent phenomenon in North America than in Europe, and the formative period of rapid urbanization was intricately connected with the development of railroads and steamships in the mid-1800s.[10]

Chicago emerged as a major city in the nineteenth century. In 1840, it was just a small lakeshore settlement with fewer than 5,000 residents. It did not have a particularly advantageous natural site: The mouth of the Chicago River was actually prone to siltation, and expensive engineering works and dredging were needed to first create and then maintain a harbor for shipping. Rather, it was the construction of canals and especially railroads that endowed the city with more important competitive advantages. After the railroads reached Chicago, the city's population

[9] See (Dewilde et al., 2018; Van Houtte, 1966). Centuries later, the city of Bruges and the national government invested in a new seaport, Zeebrugge (Brugge on the Sea). Opened in 1907, today it serves as an important port for Belgium. In the context of this larger picture, Hein and Schubert (2021) argue that Bruges can be seen as exemplifying the adaptation capacity of port cities. Quote is from (Hohenberg & Lees, 1985, p. 31).

[10] The impact of the Industrial Revolution on cities is considered to have begun from the late 1700s in Britain and after 1800 in continental Europe. For an accessible overview of urbanization around the world since 1700 and implications for environmental change, see (Berry, 2008) (originally published in 1990). In 1820, only 6% of the US population lived in towns with 5,000 or more people, compared with 13%–14% in Europe. Between 1820 and 1870, US urban population increased by 14 times. Dozens of new cities emerged in the nineteenth century, many linked to the expansion of railroads (Bairoch, 1991).

ballooned to 109,000 by 1860 and then to over 1 million by 1890. Chicago's paramount geographic advantage was actually its critical location at the junction of two major railroad networks, one on its eastern side and the other on its western. This location enabled Chicago to become a gateway city – the principal wholesale market for the midcontinent USA, connecting that region's towns and natural resources with the commercial and industrial networks of New York City and the northeast.[11]

In other words, Chicago's physical location (connecting the Great Lakes and Mississippi River watersheds) conferred an economic advantage (connecting the east and west of the country into a single trading system) that was made compelling by the technological development, routing decisions, and substantial capital investments that created the railroad network. And as the city grew, its advantages compounded, attracting more people and enabling businesses to operate more economically with better access to information, wholesalers, credit, retail demand, and the like, compared with other cities. Chicago remains the largest city in the central USA, its history illustrating the confluence of the three fundamental observations made earlier: that economic competitiveness is dynamic, that technological change alters how cities gain economic advantage from their location, and ultimately, that self-reinforcing forces lead to persistence.

But to what extent do these broad and fundamental observations also apply outside of the Western world, in regions with very distinct histories of urbanization? One study of Japan over many centuries of urban history found strong evidence for stability in terms of where populations concentrated: "There is tremendous persistence in which regions are most densely settled, even as the economy passes through multiple economic revolutions – the rise of agriculture, the rise and decline of feudalism, the move to autarky and the reversal to free trade, and finally the rise of the industrial revolution."[12]

Over the four centuries between 1600 and 1998, Japan's population grew by roughly 10 times, yet the spatial pattern of population concentration across the country changed little. Remarkably, even the extensive destruction of many cities in World War II did little to shift the long-run relative sizes of cities. Some cities lost as much as half their populations due to casualties and displacement from bombing, while other cities were not bombed. Despite these disparities, most cities recovered their prewar relative city rank within about 15 years. Indeed, "cities that suffered the largest population declines due to bombing tended to have the fastest postwar growth rates, while cities whose populations boomed conversely had much lower growth rates thereafter."[13]

[11] This example is drawn from (Cronon, 1991), the classic work on Chicago's urban economic and environmental history.

[12] This example is drawn from (Davis & Weinstein, 2002); quote is from p. 1285.

[13] (Davis & Weinstein, 2002, p. 1280). Comparing rankings of regional population densities between 1600 and 1998, the study found an 83% correlation.

The overall picture of urban persistence, then, suggests that some strong locational fundamentals may be at work – that is, geographic characteristics of locations that provide a comparative advantage for growth. But there was one notable exception in this broad pattern: After the Industrial Revolution began in Japan in the 1870s, differentials in regional population densities increased – an observation that would be hard to explain on the basis of location fundamentals alone. In other words, location fundamentals appear important in establishing basic patterns of human settlement, but the self-reinforcing dynamics of density – particularly after the technological disruption of the Industrial Revolution – become more influential thereafter.

One final example, the impact of containerization in global shipping, provides a striking illustration of how technological change can impact the relationship between cities and location fundamentals. Invented in the USA in the mid-1950s and diffusing worldwide from the mid-1960s, containerization represented a transportation revolution with major consequences for port cities, no less than for global trade flows. Before containerization, the "loading and unloading of individual items in barrels, sacks and wooden crates from land transport to ship and back again on arrival was slow and labor-intensive … almost as labor intensive after World War II as it was during the beginning of the Victorian age." With containerization, two critical innovations – mechanization (of container handling) and standardization (especially of container dimensions) – allowed all manner of cargoes to be moved swiftly and efficiently. Transport costs were drastically reduced as ships spent much less time in port, as mechanization reduced delays and uncertainties from labor strikes, as regular freighters were replaced with faster containerships, and as ever-larger vessels reduced shipping costs per container.[14]

Containerization spread rapidly around the world from the mid-1960s to the mid-1980s, transforming port cities in the process. The economic logic of containerization incentivized shipping companies to consolidate traffic in a hub-and-spoke system and maximize the use of the largest vessels. Ports competed to capture this shifting traffic but to do so required substantial capital investments and physical changes. In this environment, the competitive edge lay not in a port's hinterland but rather in its capacity to rapidly adapt to the new technology. The traditional waterfront consisted of numerous finger piers and associated warehouses, located

[14] For a comprehensive narrative of the containerization story, see (Levinson, 2006b). Quote is from (Bernhofen et al., 2016, p. 38). See also (Brooks et al., 2021). Standardization also allows the container to be readily transferred across sea, rail, and truck modes. Containerization reduced port turnaround times for vessels from 3 weeks to about 24 hours. Overall, it reduced transport costs by about 30%. For manufactured products, maritime transport costs used to account for 5%–10% of the final retail price; after containerization, this dropped to 1.5%. A 5,000 TEU (twenty-foot equivalent unit) capacity containership transports a container for 50% less cost than a 2,500 TEU vessel (Rodrigue et al., 2007). Regarding strikes, see (Bernhofen et al., 2016). The first generation of containerships had a capacity of around 1,000 TEU; today's largest vessels can carry over 20,000 TEU (Rodrigue, 2020).

centrally in the city. In contrast, container shipping required deeper harbors that could accommodate much larger ships, new infrastructure such as gantry cranes, convenient connections to roads and railway, and substantially more land for moving and storing containers.[15]

Some port cities invested heavily while others did not, could not, or were late to the game. In the UK, for example, London and Liverpool had dominated maritime trade for centuries but lost out in the era of containerization to places like Felixstowe, "whose traffic at the dawn of the container age had been too small even to merit statistical mention," and Rotterdam, which after the war had been investing heavily in modern port infrastructure. On the US East Coast, a new container port at Newark diverted business from New York; indeed, the Port of Manhattan never containerized and no longer exists as a freight port. On the West Coast, there was a flurry of port construction from the 1950s and 1960s. A new container port at Oakland took business away from previously dominant San Francisco. In Southeast Asia, the newly independent country of Singapore pursued containerization aggressively, capturing the trade as it was just emerging in the region and growing rapidly for decades to become in 2005 the largest port in the world for general cargo.[16]

One study of US port counties from 1950 to 2010 found that population and employment in port counties that did containerize – generally those with deeper harbors – grew twice as fast as those that did not. Moreover, consistent with containerization's large requirements for land, the gains were concentrated in areas with initially low land values. These findings illustrate how economic advantages of specific location attributes (such as a deep harbor) depend on how they relate to the technological regime of the times.[17]

Cities are not only economic entities but *dynamic* economic entities that are continually under multiple pressures, some of which push for change and others that resist. The aforementioned examples span many centuries, disparate regions of the globe, and spatial scales from individual city to entire continent. Nonetheless, across this diversity of contexts, a few themes emerge. One is persistence. Once basic patterns of human settlement are established, the economic advantages of urban centers accumulate. This leads to a self-reinforcing dynamic that overshadows the underlying location fundamentals, which may become economically less important or even obsolete. A second theme is the importance of capital investment in modifying the physical environment in ways that confer economic benefits to the city. The advantages of locating, say, on the shores of a water body require

[15] The average draft for a 1,000 TEU containership is 8.3 m, compared to 16 m for a 14,000+ TEU vessel (Rodrigue, 2020).

[16] (Levinson, 2006b); quote is from p. 207. See also (Brooks et al., 2021). [17] (Brooks et al., 2021).

the construction, maintenance, and upgrading of water transport infrastructure. Third, the economic value of locational attributes relates to the technologies of the era; consequently, it shifts as technologies change. It follows, then, that the location fundamentals of new cities may differ in some ways from those of old ones (as in the case of Chicago, established in the railroad era). Encompassing all of these is the observation that urban dynamics are shaped by the complex and evolving relationships between economic activity, landscape, and technology.[18]

2.3 How Does a City Grow across a Landscape?

Suppose you are flying on an airplane, approaching a city that you are visiting for the first time. Looking out the window, you can see the urban area spread out below you. Which part of the cityscape is the oldest? To take an educated guess, you might make a few observations: The city is located on a river; there is a cluster of high-rise buildings that look like office towers; further away from the river and the high-rises, there is a clear grid pattern of streets with lower-density development that seems to be housing. Looking a little closer, you might notice that between the river and the high-rises, there appears to be a jumble of mid-rise buildings that look like they may be made of brick or stone, or at any rate are not clad in walls of glass. Perhaps that jumble is the oldest part of the city?

How a city grows across a landscape has profound implications for its disaster risk. And cities being dynamic economic entities, there is an economic logic that drives the internal structuring of the urban environment, at the land parcel level as much as at the metropolitan region scale. There is a considerable body of literature that considers "cities as systems within systems of cities."[19] The economic forces seen to be operating in relation to cities' existence and fortunes over time also influence development within the city – among them, location fundamentals, capital investments, spatial competition, spatial interaction, and technological change. Within the city, there is also considerable persistence, punctuated by episodic change.

Perhaps the most fundamental logic, however, relates to why cities exist in the first place. From an urban economic perspective, cities exist because both people and businesses find it advantageous to locate in dense clusters. ("Businesses" here refer broadly to entities producing goods and services, from the medieval craftsman to the current-day corporation.) Businesses reap many types of benefits from urban density. In a city, they have ready access to a large pool of labor, to services such as those rendered by accountants and lawyers, to a range of real estate properties,

[18] See (Hanlon & Heblich, 2022) for a review of how historical perspectives are being used in contemporary scholarship in urban economics.

[19] This is the title of (Berry, 1964).

to public amenities such as universities and transportation infrastructure such as airports, and so on. They also benefit from a concentration of businesses in their own or related sectors, for example, by gaining access to specialized workers, suppliers, customers, and the like. A dense concentration of related businesses can also facilitate the exchange of ideas and information and promote innovation. In various ways, then, density promotes interactions that benefit businesses by lowering their costs or increasing their productivity. In the terminology of urban economics, these effects are referred to collectively as "agglomeration economies." Similarly, households benefit from greater access to jobs, urban amenities, and more goods and services than would be available in non-urban locations.[20]

The benefits of urban density are balanced by associated costs, and this tension is fundamental to understanding urban economic development. Housing costs are higher in cities than elsewhere. As urban density increases, so too does congestion, which elevates transport costs. (Broadly construed, transport costs include not only direct monetary payouts, such as for gasoline, but also other factors such as travel time.) Greater urban density also entails greater exposure to disease and pollution, particularly in cities with low levels of public infrastructure and regulatory controls. While the benefits of density encourage spatial concentration, the associated costs push in the opposite direction, for dispersion.

Most cities have a downtown or central business district where building density and rents are higher than elsewhere in the city. At a basic level, density is highest downtown because many people and businesses find it advantageous to be located near the center, and since land is limited, there is a demand for high-rise buildings that can accommodate more people and businesses than can low-rise structures. This economic logic plays out over time:

> Anything that makes a city relatively more attractive (such as a productivity increase or improved amenities) draws population from other places, which puts upward pressure on house prices, which in turn translates into higher land prices. Faced with a higher price per unit of land, developers opt to build with a greater capital-to-land ratio (essentially, taller buildings). Faced with a higher price per unit area of floorspace, residents opt for smaller residences … [and] density increases. In this sense, density is a consequence of urban evolutions.[21]

But at the same time, density itself is part of the locational attraction for businesses and people. As noted previously, businesses benefit from "agglomeration

[20] Collectively, the benefits of clustering are referred to as "agglomeration economies." Those related to production inputs in cities that are available to many businesses, such as airports, are termed "urbanization economies." Benefits related to locating near other related businesses, such as access to specialized labor, are referred to as "localization economies." For a textbook discussion, see (Jones, 2022). For a more in-depth treatment, see (Duranton & Puga, 2020).

[21] (Duranton & Puga, 2020, p. 1).

economies" of dense locations that reduce their costs and increase their productivity – for example, greater access to workers, information, specialized services, nearby suppliers, infrastructure services, and customers. Households benefit from greater access to jobs, goods and services, and amenities. In a word, density's pull is accessibility.[22]

Since there is a high demand for the accessibility of the central area, households and businesses must compete for more central locations. Some are able to pay more than others, that is, to outbid others by paying higher rents. In principle, the kinds of businesses for whom a central location is most advantageous and profitable are able to make the highest bids to locate centrally. From a business's point of view, there is a basic trade-off between the benefits and costs of any potential location within the city. Similarly, for households, a more central location with good accessibility means that transport costs (to jobs, services, etc.) would be low but housing costs would be high. Conversely, a more peripheral location reduces housing costs but increases transportation costs, including not only out-of-pocket expenses but also travel time for commuting and other purposes. At the same time, developers are making profit-maximizing decisions about the amount and type of housing and nonresidential buildings to construct, for example, in terms of how many stories to build at a given location. These decisions involve some degree of speculation about future demand and profitability.

In the simplest conceptualization of urban economics, the outcome of all these individual decisions is that, at each location, land is used by the highest bidder: "The market mechanism ensures that, at each location, land goes to its highest and best use, and that resources are allocated efficiently over space." It is important to recognize that "best" in this perspective refers to economic efficiency and that an economically efficient land-use outcome can nonetheless be less than desirable in relation to other criteria – social equity, for example, or environmental quality.[23]

Moving outward from the city center, urban development typically becomes progressively less dense, with lower building heights, more dispersed structures, and more open space. The outskirts or suburbs are where one typically finds the single-family houses on larger plots of land. Overall, density can be described as declining along a gradient that is highest at the city center and lowest at the outskirts. This essentialized characterization of a typical city is referred to as the "monocentric city" model.[24]

[22] See (Duranton & Puga, 2020).

[23] Quote is from (Arnott, 2011, p. 67); this outcome is conditional on assumptions including the absence of market failures.

[24] Clark (1951) was the first to mathematically define and empirically estimate density gradients for a diversity of cities. That work, as well as many subsequent studies on urban density gradients, focused on population density (i.e., number of people per unit of land area). Here, I emphasize density in relation to the built environment because of the book's focus on property damage in disasters.

As an essentialized characterization of a typical city, the "monocentric city" model provides a useful starting point for clarifying the underlying economic logic that shapes urban development. Nonetheless, this general narrative of a single urban center from which density declines outward – so commonplace that it could apply anywhere – is at the same time so abstract that it fits awkwardly with the grounded description of any real city. It is clearly important to complicate the story by introducing additional critical influences.[25]

* * *

The monocentric city model essentially assumes that market mechanisms operate freely in the urban environment; consequently, it pays scant attention to nonmarket influences on land use, housing, and urban development. Yet in reality there are many nonmarket factors that influence how cities are structured and change over time. Four are emphasized here because of their significance for the evolution of disaster risk in the built environment: the physical landscape; changing transportation technologies; urban planning; and the durability of the built environment.[26]

The physical landscape contains many features that influence how a city develops across it. The original city site, as noted previously, was often chosen in relation to some geographic feature such as proximity to a navigable river, mountain pass, or coastline. By implication, this feature also poses a constraint to city-building. Eventually, however, development pressures, technological developments, and capital investments may be sufficient to overcome this barrier, for example, by constructing a bridge or tunnel. Economically advantageous locations typically include some areas that are easier to settle and other sites, such as swamps or steep slopes, that are less amenable. It would be reasonable to hypothesize that the more favorable areas would have been settled first, while more troublesome sites would be developed later, again with the requisite combination of development pressures,

[25] The monocentric model of cities is a core formulation in urban economics, dating from pioneering work in the 1960s by W. Alonso, R. Muth, and E. Mills. For basic concepts and principles of this approach, see (Arnott, 2011). For a synthesis of the classical contributions in this area, see (Capello, 2014). For a more formal overview of the model and how it has been refined, applied, and tested in recent studies, see (Duranton & Puga, 2015). For a detailed economic perspective on urban density, see (Duranton & Puga, 2020). Duranton (1999) argues that the monocentric model is applicable to the industrial city, or in a general sense to contexts where land markets serve as the institutional mechanism regulating urban population growth and land allocation; in contrast, in medieval European cities, these functions were often performed by guilds. One of the assumptions of the basic monocentric model is that there is a single central business district where all the jobs, services, and so on are located; critiques and refinements are discussed in (Duranton & Puga, 2015).

[26] Regarding critiques, Duranton and Puga (2015) acknowledge: "When we do comparative statics in the monocentric model, we are implicitly letting the city be completely rebuilt from scratch to fit the new conditions. This is often seen as a reasonable simplification … However, some important details of the standard monocentric model conflict with reality" (p. 497). They note that some recent research has extended the monocentric model to consider, to a limited degree, aspects such as natural geography, durable housing, investors' expectations and decision-making over time, leapfrog development, construction delays, and land-use regulations.

technology, and capital. At a general level, urban morphology – the shape and structure of the physical city – is related to landscape geomorphology. This relationship is likely to be strongest in early historic eras and to diminish over time as increasingly sophisticated technologies enable overcoming landscape barriers or constraints to urban development.

A second critical factor that influences the evolution of urban form consists of changes in transportation technology. In principle, when transport costs are high, more people want to locate near the city center; when new technologies reduce transport costs, people are able to locate further out. Historically, this effect has played out vividly in cities around the world. Urban settlements before the Industrial Revolution were walking cities and did not extend more than a few miles from the center. People lived close to where they worked. In European cities from the mid nineteenth century onward, mobility was transformed by a series of new transportation technologies, beginning with horse-drawn omnibuses and leading to electrified streetcar networks. Subsequently, automobiles became popularly accessible in the 1960s and led to further decentralization.[27]

In American cities, most of which were newer than those in Europe, innovations in transportation technology had an even greater effect on urban expansion. Urban geographers have identified four broad eras of US cities: the walking-horsecar era (1800–1890), the electric streetcar era (1890–1920), the recreational automobile era (1920–1945), and the freeway era (1945–present). Remarkably, even as the built-up areas of American cities expanded greatly over time, the radius of urban areas as measured in terms of travel time from the center has remained fairly constant, at around 45 minutes.[28]

A third critical force consists of the influence of governments – especially through regulations, policies, and planning – that impose constraints on free markets in urban development. The strength and specifics of government interventions vary considerably around the world and over the centuries. Studies have found that cities where market mechanisms are particularly constrained, such as Moscow and South African cities under apartheid, stand out as exceptions to the otherwise robust empirical observation of an urban density gradient that declines from the city center toward the outskirts. Similarly, studies have found that urban development shows different spatial patterns in areas with stronger government restrictions compared to those with fewer constraints on market mechanisms.[29]

[27] See, for example, (Bairoch, 1991).

[28] Other factors also influenced contrasts between European and American cities in terms of flattening of the density gradient over time, including differences in land scarcity, land ownership systems, and the role of government. See (Muller, 2017).

[29] For the finding on Moscow and South African cities under apartheid, see (Duranton & Puga, 2015). Angel et al. (2012) used satellite imagery for 120 cities around the world to examine fragmentation, or the extent of developed versus undeveloped land in urban areas. They found distinctive patterns in Portland, Oregon,

Urban planning can influence the physical urban form through many mechanisms. Land-use zoning, for instance, typically specifies restrictions that relate to how land can be used (e.g., for residential or industrial purposes) as well as its intensity (e.g., number of stories, developable share of a land parcel, minimum lot size). Such planning interventions set the parameters by which the private sector can undertake development but do not guarantee that such development will actually occur. Depending on the specific context, zoning can be used by local governments to maintain low residential density in some areas, encourage high-density development in others, or require mixed commercial–residential land uses in places like public transit hubs. Historic preservation planning is another mechanism that can prevent market forces from tearing down older structures in order to replace them with higher-rent newer ones. It is worth noting that urban planning institutions such as land-use zoning are comparatively new in urban history. Yet once instituted they tend to change slowly. In some cities, visionary master plans have had a profound effect on the direction and pattern of urban development for decades or more into the future.

Governments also invest directly in the urban built environment, especially in terms of infrastructure systems such as streets, parks, and networks for potable water, sewer, and energy, not to mention infrastructure for safety, including flood protection. Infrastructure systems are often taken for granted, but they underpin development processes: Extending urban development onto new tracts of land requires extending streets and utility service connections as well.

Finally, the durability of the built environment is crucial to how cities evolve over time, and often overlooked in urban economics. Buildings and civil infrastructure such as bridges are constructed to last many decades. Indeed, high-rise buildings and large infrastructure assets are rarely demolished once constructed, and when they are torn down, they are often replaced by a more intensive use (e.g., a taller building or larger bridge) at the same location. Even so, there are other elements of the cityscape that are even more durable, namely, streets and land plots. Streets distinguish public space from privately held property, so once laid out, they tend to resist transformation. Similarly, the land plots or land parcels system of a city pertains to ownership and is very stable; although processes for subdividing or amalgamating plots of land exist, they are exercised much less frequently than changes to development on the existing plots. Since decisions about street networks and land parcels are generally made early in a city's history, these represent one mechanism resisting urban spatial change in subsequent periods.[30]

which has an urban growth boundary, and cities in China, where government policies constrained conversion of agricultural land to urban uses. Similarly, Burchfield et al. (2006) examined urban sprawl patterns in US cities using remote sensing data. They found more dispersed development in unincorporated areas just beyond city boundaries, where there are fewer land-use regulations than in incorporated municipalities.

30 Regarding durability of streets and land plots, see (Oliveira, 2016).

The imprint of older urban systems is often detectable in the cityscape even after those systems have become obsolete. This is evident in the many historic cores of older cities, such as in Europe, that retain the street structure of a walking city. In China, one study compared cities that once had city walls during the later imperial period with those that never did; it found that even today, long after the walls had been torn down, the previously walled cities had higher population densities than the other urban areas. In many formerly industrial cities in Europe, suburbs on the eastern side of town are poorer than those on the western side. Analysts have argued that this is a historic legacy of the industrial era: "While wind direction no longer constitutes an important issue in these cities, it certainly did at the peak of the industrial era, when a windward location helped the affluent avoid factory emissions and smells." Prevailing winds for these cities come from the west. In Los Angeles, the streetcars-based urban transit system that was removed over 60 years ago continues to influence present-day spatial patterns of density, through both mechanisms of land-use regulation and the cumulative effects of agglomeration.[31]

* * *

Cities are dynamic economic entities in terms of how they develop over time across the local landscape. Fundamental observations made previously for cities as a whole also apply to the city's internal dynamics. The original sites often relate to landscape features such as water access. Once basic patterns of settlement are established, economic advantages accumulate and lead to a self-reinforcing dynamic that persists, even if the original reasons become obsolete. Capital investments and technological advances overcome barriers posed by physical geography and problems associated with density, such as congestion and pollution, thereby enabling the city to accommodate growing populations. Eras of rapid population and economic growth are accommodated through new construction that embodies the technological regimes of the day. Economic competition underlies the city's physical form, reflected in gradients of density and rent that decline from the central city outward to the outskirts. At the same time, powerful forces also constrain change and lead to considerable persistence in the urban landscape – forces including street networks, land ownership systems, urban planning institutions, and the durable construction of buildings and civil engineering works. Internally, the physical forms of cities are shaped by complex and evolving relationships between economic activity, landscape, and technology.

[31] For Chinese walled cities, see (Du & Zhang, 2019). For eastern and western suburbs and wind direction, see (Duranton & Puga, 2015); quote is from p. 535. See (Heblich et al., 2021) for an in-depth analysis of this effect in English cities. They note that this east-side effect did not exist prior to the Industrial Revolution. For Los Angeles, see (Brooks & Lutz, 2019).

And what does all this have to do with disasters? At one level, it is important to acknowledge that the urban built environment at risk from hazards is a tangible accumulation of the city's economic history. At another level, we can think of earthquakes, floods, and other disasters as disruptive events along a spectrum that could also encompass – from the perspective of a city's history – other types of disruptions such as pandemics, wars, and even major technological changes such as containerization or the Industrial Revolution. More fundamentally, by viewing cities as dynamic economic entities, we can begin to examine the forces underlying urban development over time that the disaster temporarily disrupts. The dynamic forces that created the city before a disaster will continue to do so afterward, during the recovery and into the future.

3

Cities and Riverine Flooding

3.1 Riverine Flooding

Why do rivers flood? From the vantage point of any location such as a city, the answer might initially seem straightforward: A river floods when an excessive amount of rain falls in a short period of time across the city and upstream of it, leading to more water than the river channel can hold. The water level therefore rises, overtops the river's banks, and spills out over low-lying areas, thereby flooding streets, homes, and businesses. In a few days or weeks, the floodwaters recede and the city has to deal with the cleanup and recovery. In this simple picture, the city is merely an unfortunate, passive recipient of floodwaters.

But upon closer investigation, this simple picture turns out to be rather misleading. Behind this simple picture lies a much more complex long-term dynamic of geomorphological processes playing out over eons, entangled with urbanization processes transpiring over centuries and decades, leading to the conditions in which a particular flood event unfolds over weeks and days. Climate conditions that give rise to extreme weather events are also part of the picture, but riverine flooding would impact cities even without anthropogenic climate change. The focus of this chapter is on how urban development processes relate to riverine flood risk.

Rivers drain watersheds. Rain or snow falling over a river's catchment area will generally make its way first into a small stream, then down into a larger waterway, from there into the main channel of the river, and eventually to the river's outlet at the sea. The amount of water flowing through the river system depends on precipitation that weather systems have brought over the watershed, cumulatively and with some lag time. River flows thus vary with fluctuations in precipitation levels, and there is often a seasonality associated with these variations. For example, some rivers are characterized by high water levels in the springtime when winter snowpack in the watershed melts. In some years, extreme flows may occur, such as when there is a combination of an especially high snowpack, sudden temperature warming, and simultaneously a substantial rainfall event. In other years, different conditions may lead to very low water levels. In the context of this variability, then, "out-of-channel flows are simply part of the continuum of river dynamics." That is, floods are part of the naturally variable processes of river systems.[1]

Flooding is influenced by many other factors besides temperature, precipitation, and other atmospheric conditions. Conditions of the landscape in the watershed are just as important, as the landscape regulates how quickly and how much water is delivered to the river: "Streamflow involves more than a simple response to rainwater trickling off the land. It is as much, or more, a response to landscape and its capacity to intercept precipitation, route it underground, reduce its volume, and slow its delivery rate." Characteristics such as hillsides and steep slopes, tree cover and other vegetation, and soil type all influence how quickly rainwater enters the river. Conditions such as how saturated the ground may already be from prior rainfall are also important. Attributes of the river itself such as its channel shape and depth also influence the volume and speed of water flowing through it; for example, water flows more quickly through steeper, straighter, smoother, deeper channels. It follows that changes in any of these myriad contributing factors – whether relating to atmospheric, watershed, or river conditions – may alter the likelihood of flooding at different locations along the river. The net effect turns out to be complex and region-specific; for example, flooding appears to be increasing in some parts of Europe at the same time as it has been decreasing in others.[2]

Flood events demonstrate in palpable and often dramatic terms that rivers are dynamic entities, but what may be less self-evident is that rivers are changing continually. On a map, the blue line indicating the path of a river as it makes its way from mountains to sea is a snapshot in time. In flat valleys, rivers tend to form meanders, sweeping bends that snake through the landscape. Without human intervention, the meanders will shift over time:

> At channel bends, the faster-moving water responds more to centrifugal force than slower water does and slides toward the outside of the bend … Where channels swing back and forth in meanders, the belt of fast-moving water is thrown from one side of the channel to the other in successive bends much as a bobsled team does in negotiating its run.

In the process, the water erodes the riverbank on the outside of the meander and deposits the sediment in zones of lower velocity on the inside of the bend, so that over time the river channel migrates sideways through the landscape. Since this process tends to take place more on the lower side, the overall effect is one of meanders migrating both laterally and down a valley over time. Sometimes, a river

[1] Quote is from (Davies et al., 2021, p. 285).

[2] Quote is from (Marsh & Kaufman, 2013, section 15.2). See (Hall et al., 2014) for a comprehensive review of changing flood regimes in Europe, including potential drivers and evidence of change. See (Merz, 2017) for a discussion of flood risk factors, analysis, and modeling.

will make a sudden change in its route, such as by breaching one of its meanders. With this cut providing a shorter, steeper, and more efficient route to convey water, the river abandons the old loop, which becomes an oxbow lake that eventually transforms into a wetland.[3]

We often view a river as running *through* a landscape, without appreciating its role in the formation of that very landscape. Rivers transport sediment. When a river transitions from the steeper gradients of a mountainous area to flatter terrain, it slows down, and as a result drops some of the sediment it has been carrying. Over long periods of time, especially during episodes of high flow and flooding, the accumulation and movement of sediment forms an alluvial plain – the floodplain. In other words, the floodplain is not simply land that is at risk of getting inundated in a flood event but land that was formed by the river in the first place. Floodplains, moreover, typically contain many types of features that are also bound up with riverine processes. For example, natural levees often form on the banks of rivers; these slightly elevated areas are mounds created in past flood events when floodwaters overflowed the channel, slowed down, and dropped some of their sediment load. Behind the levees, backswamps can form when floodwaters are trapped for long periods of time in these low-lying areas. From a fluvial geomorphological perspective,

> River channels are the conduits that drain runoff from the surface of the land. Water flowing over the land surface is capable of eroding soil and even rock material, so that rivers carry and redistribute sedimentary material as well. In the short term, the sediment transporting activity of rivers creates the channels in which streams and rivers flow and it affects the quality of water in the channels; in the very long term, it creates the landscape.[4]

Along with the benefits that alluvial plains provide for urban settlement come the hazards of flooding. Cities around the world have dealt with riverine floods from their earliest days. Urban adaptations to the hazard have taken many forms, transforming over the ages in tandem with population expansion, scientific and technological advances, and socioeconomic change. But cities have nonetheless continued to be devastated by floods. Scholars have cautioned against "maladaptation" – actions undertaken to deal with hazards such as flooding that end up being counterproductive. How have cities tried to deal with the risk of floods over the ages, to what extent have they been successful or maladaptive, and what do the patterns portend for future risk?

This chapter considers these questions by delving into two case studies. Vienna, capital of the modern-day Austrian nation and formerly of the Austro-Hungarian empire, is an old European city situated on the banks of the Danube River. It is not especially well known in the disasters literature, not having experienced a

[3] (Marsh & Kaufman, 2013, sections 21.2 and 21.4); quote on page 31 "At channel bends…" is from section 21.2.
[4] (Church et al., 2009, p. 103).

devastating flood in recent times, yet flood risk has been a part of its environmental context throughout the centuries. Vienna provides an instructive case because it has been especially well documented and analyzed by local urban environmental historians. The second case, Calgary in western Canada, is a very different city – young even by North American standards, it is a regional commercial center situated at the confluence of two comparatively small rivers, the Bow and Elbow. In 2013, Calgary experienced a severe flood; at the time, the event was considered the costliest disaster in Canadian history. Ten years later, postflood analyses and the unfolding of disaster recovery patterns provide insights into urban adaptation to flood risk today. From these two contrasting cases, common themes nonetheless emerge regarding urbanization and riverine flood risk, suggesting some key insights into the core questions of how urban development influences hazard, exposure, and vulnerability and, in turn, how disasters influence urban development.

Riverine flooding is not the only type of flooding that affects cities. Coastal and pluvial flooding are also increasingly important urban hazards. But rivers overflowing their banks perhaps represent flooding in its "classical" form and provide a useful entry point for investigation.

3.2 Vienna

The Danube River flows over some 2,860 km from the Alps to the Black Sea. In the Austrian section, which is part of the Upper Danube, it runs through a series of narrow valleys and broad floodplains. Here, it exhibits high degrees of energy, variability in flows, and movement of sediments from the mountains. The city of Vienna is situated on an alluvial flat stretch of the river where the floodplain is over 6 km wide. In this flat stretch, historically, the river exhibited continual sedimentation and erosion, as well as sudden changes in its numerous channels, as it traversed the landscape (Figure 3.1). Prior to large-scale engineering interventions, the Danube was a shifting, braided river in this section, shaping "an amphibious landscape in which land was replaced by water and vice versa incessantly." Floods of varying magnitudes occurred regularly and the river was prone to ice jam flooding in winter. In the 21-year period from 1768 to 1789, for example, the river flooded 36 times, of which 7 were considered severe events. Smaller tributary rivers that joined the Danube in this area were also dynamic, so that the overall regime was characterized by periods of low as well as high flows, both of which caused problems for human settlements.[5]

[5] For the Danube River, see (Schober et al., 2015). Quote is from (Winiwarter et al., 2013, p. 106). For visualizations of the changing riverscape over the centuries, see www.environmentandsociety.org/arcadia/struggle-river-vienna-and-danube-1500-present. For flood history, see (Hohensinner et al., 2013) and (Winiwarter et al., 2016).

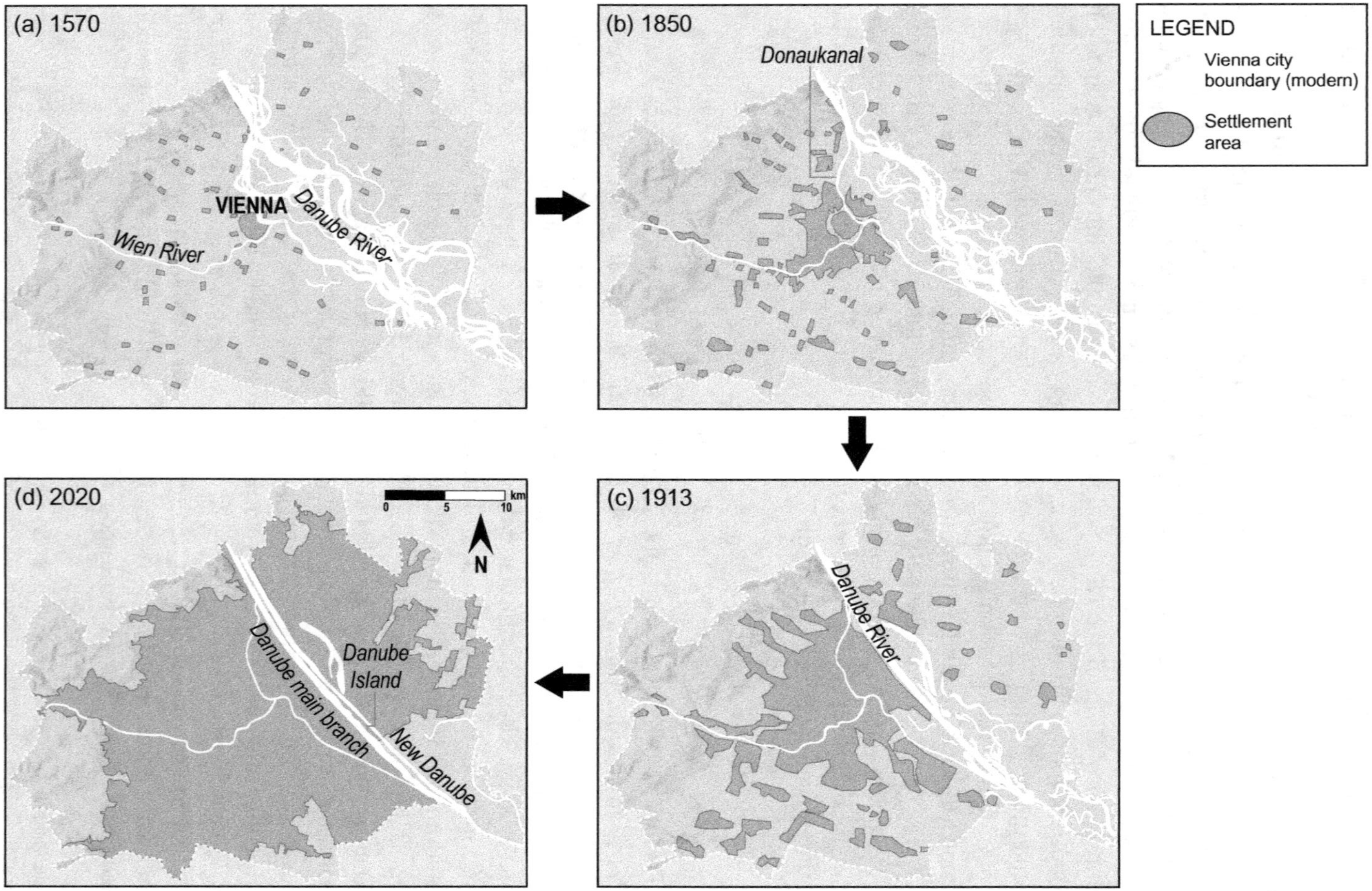

Figure 3.1 Vienna, urban expansion 1570–2020. (Data based on: Eigner & Schneider, 2005; Encyclopædia Britannica, Inc., 2024a; Haidvogl et al., 2013; Hohensinner et al., 2013. Maps by Charlotte Milne.)

The city of Vienna's historic core dates back to its establishment as Vindobona, a minor garrison town on the border of the Roman Empire. The original settlement was located relatively securely in relation to floods, on a terrace some 15 m above the river on its right bank. As the population grew in later centuries, the town expanded outward from this core into more flood-prone areas. Until well into the nineteenth century, this growth mainly took place on the right bank of the Danube toward the surrounding hillsides. The alluvial floodplain itself, with its marshlands and shifting watercourses and islands, was too unstable for settlement. Land in the floodplain outside the city gates was sometimes used for vegetable farms. In the medieval era, Vienna's site was on the main arm of the Danube, which played a key role in urban trade and transportation; however, the ever-changing river gradually shifted away from the city from the fourteenth century onward. Numerous schemes and investments were made to try to stop this movement of the river but to no avail. Roads and bridges had to be relocated whenever the river changed course. By the early seventeenth century, the authorities gave up trying to halt the northward migration of the main arm of the Danube and sought instead to maintain minimum water levels in the shipping channel (the Donaukanal) that served the city.[6]

Well into the nineteenth century, the urban population developed numerous practices for dealing with and adapting to frequent flooding. For example:

> One important measure involved removing ships and rafts from the *Donaukanal* each autumn when the shipping season came to an end because they would have increased the risk of ice jam floods by blocking the flow … In less risky areas, wood had to be prepared to install boardwalks in case of floods and construction wood to brace houses had to be made available. In case of floods, the Water Engineering Agency … was responsible for closing the bridges to heavy vehicles and pedestrians. Ships to cut the ice on the Danube arms had to be ready as well as ships for crossing the *Donaukanal* to compensate for destroyed bridges. Bakers, butchers and other commercial food traders on the island were obliged to stock enough food for at least 14 days. The municipal council had to store flour … The monastery was also responsible for stocking drinking water in barrels. When floods were believed to be imminent, house owners were ordered to ensure older and ill people were moved to upper floors. Likewise, animals had to be brought to safe locations.[7]

When the single bridge over the Danube was destroyed by flooding, which happened frequently, ferries were used. Even hydropower facilities were flexible enough to accommodate flooding. Numerous ship mills that ground flour were

[6] For original settlement, see (Barendrecht et al., 2017; Kryžanowski et al., 2014). For Vienna's urban development history, albeit with little reference to flood risk, see (Hall, 1997; Lichtenberger, 1993). For a historical, spatial reconstruction of how the riverine landscape changed over the centuries, see (Hohensinner et al., 2013). For efforts by authorities, see (Haidvogl et al., 2018; Hohensinner et al., 2013; Sonnlechner et al., 2013; Winiwarter et al., 2013).

[7] (Haidvogl et al., 2013, p. 201).

operated on the Danube. These ship mills were adaptable to variations in water levels on the river and could be moved or removed as needed, for example, in response to ice jams.[8]

* * *

The relationship between the city and the river changed dramatically in the 1870s with what is referred to as the Great Danube Regulation. This massive engineering project was undertaken to "provide a secure passage for ships, to protect Vienna from floods and create large tracts of land that could be developed for new railways stations … and railway tracks, docks, new roads along the river and building sites for residential use." The Great Danube Regulation involved excavating a new main channel for the river in the vicinity of the city, cutting through the meanders to unify and straighten the riverbed. It yielded a channel 280 m wide with a 450 m floodplain on the left bank and a flood protection dike. Excavation utilized machinery that had recently been employed (by the French) in digging the Suez Canal, and the unearthed material was used to fill in remaining river arms in the landscape. Thereafter, shipping on the river largely used the new main channel, although the preexisting Donaukanal remained in service for local traffic.[9]

Channelization of the Danube River was not the only major urban infrastructure transformation of the nineteenth century. Urban water systems were radically altered – modernized – in this period. The Wien River, which meets the Danube in the Vienna urban area, was also channelized, buried in some sections, and disconnected from its floodplain to allow for railroad construction. Numerous other tributaries and small streams had previously flowed into the rivers; these, too, were altered and brought by means of tunnels, channels, and pipes into an integrated underground sewer system. Two pipelines, the first and second Alpine Water Pipelines, were constructed to access new sources of clean drinking water from springs 100 km away, allowing urban water consumption to increase greatly. These new and abundant water sources also helped to flush the integrated sewer system. By 1879, over 70% of homes in the city were served by water pipeline.[10]

From an urbanization perspective, the latter part of the nineteenth century was clearly a critical period in Vienna's history, the infrastructural imprint of which remains to this day. What drove these massive, costly investments in new urban infrastructure? It is no coincidence that during this period Vienna's urban

[8] (Haidvogl, 2012) and (Haidvogl et al., 2018).

[9] Quote is from (Lichtenberger, 1993, p. 123). The width of the channel is reported variously in different sources; for example, (Kryžanowski et al., 2014) notes a 280 m riverbed and 450 m floodplain, (Haidvogl et al., 2018) reports a 470 m wide inundation area, and (Lichtenberger, 1993) indicates a 670 m wide channel with 400 m wide flood control strip. For excavation machinery and navigational use, see (Haidvogl et al., 2018; Winiwarter et al., 2013).

[10] (Gierlinger et al., 2013; Haidvogl et al., 2018; Winiwarter et al., 2016).

population also expanded rapidly, increasing nearly fivefold from some 500,000 to over 2 million between 1850 and 1918. Such large-scale population growth entailed a concomitant increase in requirements for food, water, energy, and sanitation, not to mention housing, developable land, and protection from floods.[11]

Industrialization was transforming the economy. Early industrial cities were notoriously crowded, polluted, disease-ridden, and unhealthy environments. According to one estimate of pollution in that era, nitrogen concentration in the Wien River exceeded levels allowable today by over six times. A cholera epidemic in the 1830s spurred efforts to improve urban hygiene. At the same time, engineering capabilities and medical knowledge, including ideas regarding disease, were also developing. Moreover, new transportation technologies that emerged in the Industrial Revolution required different forms of supporting infrastructure; for example, the use of steamships "necessitated a technically shaped, homogeneous riverbed."[12]

Vienna's urban environmental historians have highlighted two additional drivers of the city's transformation in relation to the river: the need for a stable landscape and the separation of river functions. With urban expansion in the nineteenth century, "the growing and industrialising metropolis needed a stable riverscape for new settlements … and to protect infrastructure in the floodplain, such as bridges, roads and railways." Historically, the continually shifting riverine landscape with its eroding and emerging islands posed problems for land rights; in one documented case, litigation between two large landowners over timber harvesting "began in 1547 and lasted for 112 years," during which period "the Danube … changed its course several times, islands grew and diminished, appeared and disappeared." Such legal disputes were ultimately resolved with the Great Danube Regulation of the 1870s. Land stability was – and of course remains – a requirement for land ownership and land-use rights.[13]

The channelization of the Danube and the burying of smaller urban waterways also reflected – and enabled – a transformation in the city's relationship with the riverine landscape, one in which the investment in modernizing infrastructure technologies served to separate, and make more efficient, the many ways in which people used the waterways. In terms of drinking water, the new water mains allowed large volumes of clean water to be brought into the city from distant alpine springs, rather than sourced locally. With the development of railroads, fish began to be imported from faraway sources, supplanting the demand for local

[11] This discussion draws on (Haidvogl et al., 2018; Winiwarter et al., 2016).

[12] (Douglas, 2013; Gierlinger et al., 2013). Quote is from (Haidvogl et al., 2018, p. 728).

[13] Quote "the growing and industrialising metropolis …" is from (Winiwarter et al., 2013, p. 112). The authors also mention other more indirect objectives, such as the demonstration and maintenance of political power and social structure. Quote "began in 1547 …" is from (Sonnlechner et al., 2013, p. 190).

catch. Channelization improved the navigability of the Danube for the steamships that came to dominate river transport in the latter part of the century. The large-scale shift to coal as an energy source, which led to a substantial rise in energy use, reduced the demand for local hydropower from mills on the rivers.[14] While the Danube retained its role as a transportation artery, the upshot for local tributaries and small streams was that "only their role as waste and wastewater recipients remained, leading to their integration into the underground sewage system. By the end of the nineteenth century, they had been vaulted, their waters were now solely needed to flush sewage downhill."[15]

Reducing flood risk was an important objective in this transformation, bound up with changes enabling rapid population growth, sanitation improvements, industrialization and economic change, and technological development in the city. A damaging flood in 1862 had served as an immediate trigger for the 1870–1875 Great Danube Regulation.[16]

* * *

The nineteenth century seems remote and archaic, perhaps even quaint. The era of steamships has passed and the Industrial Revolution has long been succeeded by other technological revolutions leading into the current digital era. Why does the nineteenth-century transformation of the city's relationship with its riverine landscape matter? Specifically, why does it matter for the city's flood risk today, and in future decades? Indeed, Vienna has not experienced a severe flood in many decades – is flooding even still a problem? The legacy of the nineteenth-century urban transformation is profound, but it is hard to see. With regard to flood risk, two impacts are particularly consequential: the long-term effects on urban development patterns and on flood management strategies.

The Great Danube Regulation of 1870–1875 enabled and encouraged the city to expand into the floodplain. Floodplain development was not a coincidence but part and parcel of the authorities' considerations in making the massive capital investment. Developable land was needed to accommodate the burgeoning population and urban industrial activity. Annexation of former suburbs, including lands in the floodplain, brought a greater area within the purview of the local authorities. Vienna's city government, which had to cover one-third of the costs of channelization, "hoped to recover these expenses by selling the newly gained land." Zoning plans that were issued following the channelization designated different areas of the floodplain for residential, commercial, industrial, and recreational uses.[17]

[14] (Gierlinger et al., 2013; Haidvogl et al., 2018; Winiwarter et al., 2016).
[15] (Winiwarter et al., 2016, p. 223). [16] (Barendrecht et al., 2017).
[17] (Haidvogl, 2012); quote is from p. 125.

Population and construction on the floodplain grew apace. The city of Vienna is divided into districts, of which four are located on the floodplain. Of these, by 1888, the 2nd district (Leopoldstadt) had grown to become the most populated in the city, with some 115,000 residents. Between 1888 and 1918, population in the other floodplain areas (Vienna's 20th, 21st, and 22nd districts) exhibited some of the highest growth rates in the city, expanding by over 100%. By 1910, some 420,000 people, or 20% of Vienna's inhabitants, lived on the Danube floodplain, protected by dikes. Today, some 24% of Vienna is situated on the floodplain, reliant on the large-scale engineering works for flood protection:[18] "From the mid-19th century onward, urban development was a main driver for major changes in the riverine landscape. Today, immense economic value is inextricably linked to the former floodplains and continuous investment to maintain all the technical facilities required to prevent inundation is therefore indispensable."[19]

Development in the former floodplain meant that ever-greater populations, buildings, and infrastructure had to be protected from flooding – and that these same expanses of land were no longer available to help hold floodwaters during times of high flow in the river.

The large-scale engineering projects of the nineteenth century set the direction for flood management in subsequent eras. The Great Danube Regulation did not solve Vienna's flood problem, but thereafter, efforts to reduce flood risk had to be designed in the context of the river channelization. Major floods occurred in 1897 and 1899 (maximum discharge 10,500 m^3/s) and led to the enhancement of the dikes, which were deemed too low. In 1954, the largest flood of the twentieth century (maximum discharge 9,600 m^3/s) caused considerable damage and prompted further massive flood protection works, which were begun in 1972 and eventually completed in 1988. A new river channel, the "New Danube," was dug.[20]

Parallel to the main channel from the first Danube Regulation, the New Danube is some 210 m wide and designed as a flood bypass to retain excess water in times of high river flow. The excavated earth was deposited between the two channels to form a 21 km long artificial island, the Danube Island (Donauinsel), which is mainly used for recreational purposes. Water levels in the New Danube are

[18] The period of rapid urban growth ended with World War I and the collapse of the Austro-Hungarian Empire: "Vienna found herself no longer the capital city of an imperial empire of 52 million people, but simply the capital of a small republic of 6.4 million. Consequently rapid urban growth gave way to a steady population decline. This is one of the main reasons why there is no ring of inter-war residential areas round Vienna, or any encircling suburbs from the post-war period" (Hall, 1997, pp. 208–209). For population on the floodplain, see (Haidvogl, 2012; Haidvogl et al., 2013, 2018). Haidvogl (2012) specifically identifies certain areas of the city that experienced major development in the floodplain: Leopoldstadt, Brigittenau, Floridsdorf, and Kaisermühlen.

[19] (Haidvogl et al., 2013, p. 196).

[20] (Haidvogl et al., 2018). Discharge levels are from (Blöschl et al., 2013). For 1954 flood and subsequent flood protection, see (Barendrecht et al., 2017). A hydropower plant was added to the project and completed in 1988.

regulated using sluice gates and weirs at the canal's upstream and downstream ends. The discharge capacity of the flood bypass (5,200 m^3/s) significantly augments the main channel's capacity of 8,800 m^3/s. The safety level from this structural system is one of the highest in Europe, providing protection for a 10,000-year return period flood. This is comparable to the largest flood ever recorded along this reach of the Danube (14,000 m^3/s peak discharge, in 1501).[21]

Once again, following the construction of the New Danube, the city expanded into the newly flood-protected areas. Urban development included housing as well as construction of a commercial area, centered around the site of one of the United Nations' global headquarters.

> After the completion of the project, the urban development on the left banks of the Danube took place more rapidly. Of course, other factors, such as the introduction of a new subway line, also increased the attractiveness of the area, but proper flood protection made sure that investments in property were more secure. The once neglected districts on the left side of the Danube became the major development areas for services and industry as well as for new housing projects. Since the implementation of the project, the population in these two districts approximately doubled.[22]

The enhanced flood protection system performed well in subsequent major events in 2002 and 2013. The latter event was one of the largest in the last two centuries, with peak flood discharge of 11,000 m^3/s at Vienna.[23]

The Danube River today is "tamed." From the perspective of flood protection for people and assets in the city, this conversion has undoubtedly been beneficial. Indeed, it has been a requirement for urban growth and development. Vienna's flood protection system is considered a success story, a "visionary example of dealing with urban floods." Not only does the system provide some of the highest flood protection levels in Europe but co-benefits of the system, especially the recreational amenities of the Danube Island, are enjoyed during nonflood times. River regulation is also bound up with hydroelectric power generation, an important source of renewable energy in Austria. It is worth noting that it was due to public engagement, protest, and environmental advocacy that government authorities were persuaded to incorporate some more natural (i.e., less constructed) elements of the river management arrangements, such as more naturally sloping channel banks, designating the Danube Island as a recreational area, and creating the Donau-Auen National Park downstream of the city. It is also worth recognizing that flood protection, by operating to reduce impacts of the river's extreme flows on the landscape, simultaneously reduces the benefits of those same extreme flows for the landscape. In terms of local ecology, for example, species composition in

[21] (Kryžanowski et al., 2014). [22] (Kryžanowski et al., 2014, p. 138).
[23] (Barendrecht et al., 2017; Blöschl et al., 2013).

the national park “differs fundamentally from that of earlier days due to anthropogenically influenced flood dynamic.”[24]

The Vienna case illustrates how industrialization transformed the city’s relationship with its riverine landscape, at once enabling and requiring a much greater degree of control over its form and processes. In this sense, it is far from unique. Similar stories underpin transformations in other cities in the industrial era. One comparative study of four European cases (Vienna, Munich, Lyon, and Brussels) found that despite rather distinct settings, histories, and drivers of change, all of the cities emerged from the era of industrialization with modernized urban infrastructural transformations that led to remarkably similar urban forms:[25]

> While each river-city story is different, the ensuing set of drivers led to similar outcomes. The fossil-based networked cities’ waters run either belowground or between concrete walls and dams, their flow regulated by weirs and locks, their energy used for large-scale hydropower in some cases, or for flushing wastes towards treatment plants. Their ecology has been thoroughly transformed; their uses are mono-functional … While aboveground aquatic remains are greatly simplified in their appearance, the sophistication of the underground networks has been greatly increased.[26]

In all four cities, over the course of the nineteenth century, technological development and capital investments in flood-protection systems allowed previously avoided floodplains to become densely populated.

The Vienna case is especially instructive because it has been painstakingly reconstructed and analyzed in recent years by urban environmental historians. What does the evolution of urban flood risk look like in other types of cities? Do similar dynamics play out in newer cities, elsewhere in the world, in other types of riverine settings, and even for other types of hazards? Which aspects of this story are unique to Vienna or to old European cities, and which are common across the globe?

3.3 Calgary

The Bow River in Canada flows down from the Rocky Mountains in the area of the iconic Banff National Park, emerging in a forested foothills region to drain eastward through a vast expanse of dry prairie lands. Over 600 km long, it is a major tributary of the Saskatchewan River system whose waters eventually flow into

[24] (Kryžanowski et al., 2014). Quote “a visionary example …” is from (Hruby, 2021). For an overview of hydropower in Austria, including the role of public resistance leading to the establishment of the Donau-Auen National Park, see (Wagner et al., 2015). Quote “differs fundamentally …” is from (Winiwarter et al., 2013, p. 104).

[25] See (Castonguay & Evenden, 2012) for a range of European and North American urban case studies. For the comparison of Vienna, Munich, Lyon, and Berlin, see (Winiwarter et al., 2016).

[26] (Winiwarter et al., 2016, pp. 229–230).

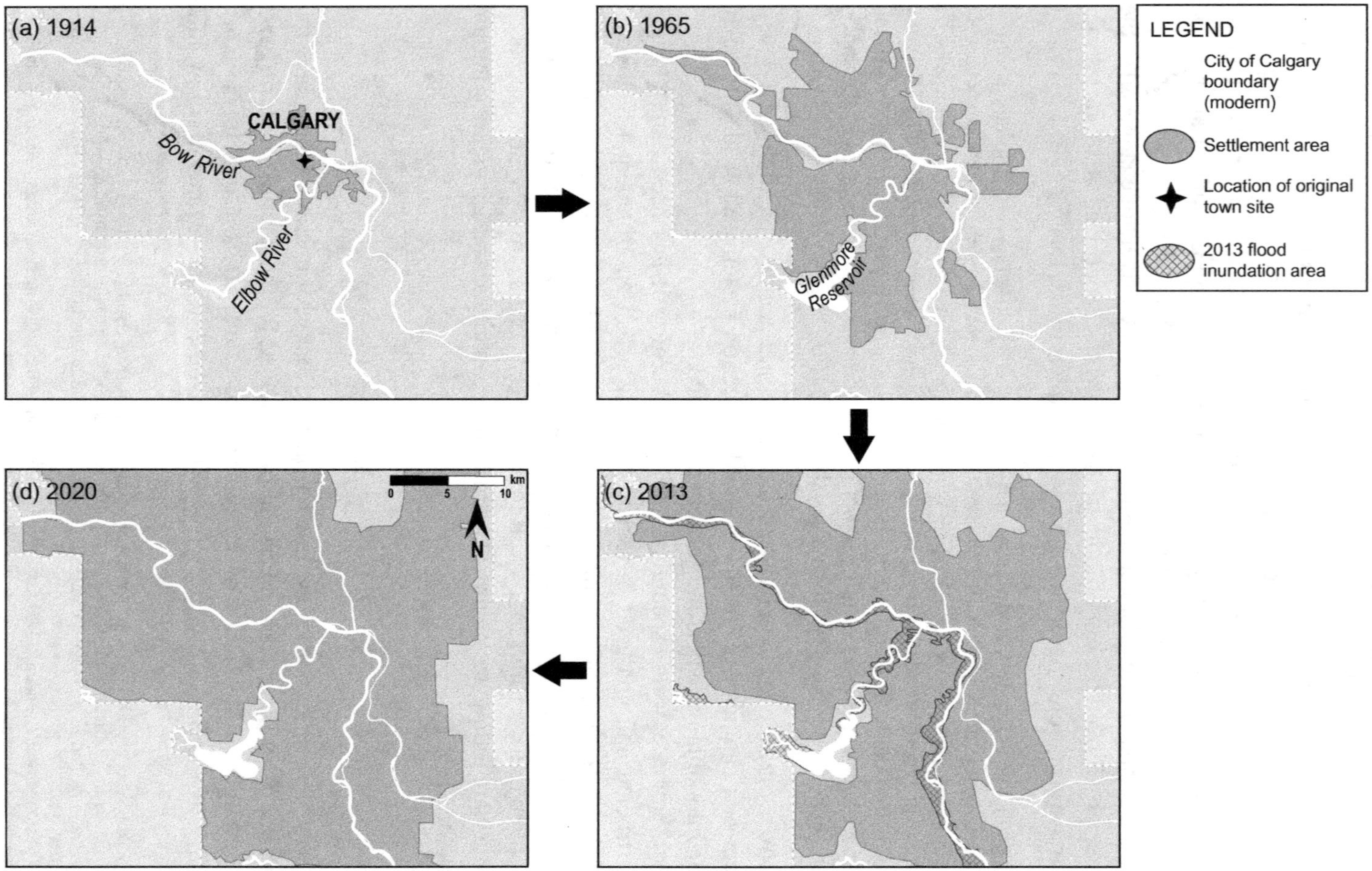

Figure 3.2 Calgary, urban expansion 1914–2020. (Data based on: Ejiagha et al., 2022; Gray-Scholz et al. 2019; Sandalack & Nicolai, 2006; The Globe and Mail, 2013. Maps by Charlotte Milne.)

Hudson Bay, thousands of kilometers away. Most of the Bow River's water comes from precipitation in the mountainous area of the watershed, so that variability in the river's flow is largely governed by the annual melting of the mountain snowpack and spring rainfall in the foothills. And flow variability is high:[27]

> Snow does not fall evenly upon the mountains. Nor does the same quantity of snow or rain fall each year. And on the dry southern Alberta prairie the rain is famously unreliable. The flow of the Bow – and all other mountain rivers, for that matter – fluctuates with these climatic variations. In retrospect we can observe long-term cycles in the patterns of precipitation and flow: long wet periods, long dry periods, intervals of stability, and periods of erratic weather and corresponding flow behaviour. As a result, the flow of the Bow as measured at Calgary, for instance, varies enormously … People who lived near the river learned to expect change from year to year, rather than sameness and constancy.[28]

Within the course of a year, flooding on the Bow tends to occur in the early summer, when peak flows from snowmelt coincide with major rainfall events.[29]

Prior to the founding of the city of Calgary, for thousands of years, a succession of different Indigenous peoples inhabited the area. On the riverbanks, they set up seasonal encampments rather than permanent settlements. They located trail systems on higher ground, used the valleys for seeking shelter and food, and could move their camps to avoid floods. The arrival of Euro-Canadian settlers in the late eighteenth and nineteenth centuries brought profound changes, among them the displacement and marginalization of the Indigenous inhabitants and the beginning of town settlements. From one perspective, "the history of settlement in the Bow valley begins with an environmental catastrophe," the collapse of bison populations upon which Indigenous hunter-gatherer livelihoods had long depended.[30]

The city of Calgary is located on the Bow River where the foothills meet the prairies (Figure 3.2). More precisely, its original town site sits at the confluence of the Bow and one of its tributaries, the Elbow River. Initially, a frontier police fort had been set up at a traditional location for fording the river. In 1883, the Canadian Pacific Railway (CPR), extending westward to the Pacific, chose to route its transcontinental railroad through Calgary; in so doing, it secured the future of the frontier town. The location was economically promising: "Calgary's fortuitous setting at the intersection of the early north-south and east-west routes gave it a strategic nodal location and great growth potential." The specific tract of land chosen by the railroad company, which formed the nucleus of the town as it expanded, was "a level, gravelly expanse by the river, ideal for railroading and real estate

[27] See (Armstrong et al., 2009) for an in-depth and multifaceted environmental history of the Bow River.
[28] (Armstrong et al., 2009, p. 121). [29] (Armstrong et al., 2009; Pomeroy et al., 2016).
[30] See (Armstrong et al., 2009, ch. 1 and 2) and (Calgary Public Library, 2014). Quote is from (Armstrong et al., 2009, p. 45).

speculation … in fact a flood plain." Eventually, development in this area would form the central business district of today's metropolitan area.[31]

Calgary is a new city even by North American standards. As it grew, its early form was strongly influenced by factors related to the dominant transport technology of the era, the railroad, which left a lasting imprint on the city:[32]

> By 1914, then, the essence of the modern land use pattern had emerged … At the heart of this pattern is Calgary's railway system with its controlling influence on industrial siting, but even more basic than this is the pattern of entrenched river valleys and abandoned stream channels followed so closely by the railways. Surface form, then, through its influence on railway location, has played a very significant role in establishing Calgary's urban pattern.[33]

In this early era, the local terrain also contributed in other ways to shaping development in the floodplain: "Local relief, degree and direction of slope, and natural drainage patterns … directly influenced the provision of city utilities. In Calgary's early decades, development occurred only where services could be easily extended. The city therefore expanded on the relatively flat river valley bottoms, and the escarpments and ravines presented barriers to growth." The steep slopes of the escarpments also deterred development when in-town transport technology consisted of horses and horse-drawn vehicles. Even up to 1945, Calgary's urban form still broadly followed the contours of the river valleys and escarpments. Technical and economic constraints thus effectively concentrated the original settlement in the floodplain.[34]

The early town experienced floods frequently from the Bow, Elbow, and other waterways. In the 50-odd years between 1879 and 1932, for example, the Bow River was reported to have flooded somewhere on the order of 8–17 times. As the population and settlement grew, so did the magnitude of flood damages reported. In 1883, a flood carried away the town's only bridge; it was replaced. In 1884, another flood destroyed "all" of Calgary's bridges along with railroad infrastructure, but no buildings. The flood of 1897 (with a maximum flow of 2,265 m^3/s at Calgary above the Bow–Elbow confluence) was especially large:[35]

[31] See (Armstrong et al., 2009). Quote "Calgary's fortuitous setting …" is from (Sandalack & Nicolai, 2006, p. 6). Quote "a level, gravelly expanse …" is from (Armstrong et al., 2009, p. 244).

[32] (Sandalack & Nicolai, 2006; Smith, 1962). Calgary formally incorporated as a town in 1884 with a population of just over 400 people.

[33] (Smith, 1962, p. 319).

[34] Quote "Local relief …" is from (Sandalack & Nicolai, 2006, p. 7); see also p. 52. For mid twentieth-century urban form, see (Sandalack & Nicolai, 2006; Smith, 1962).

[35] (Armstrong et al., 2009; Calgary Public Library, 2014; Pomeroy et al., 2016; The City of Calgary, n.d.). Pomeroy et al. (2016) mention eight Bow River flood events reported in contemporaneous sources. The list of twentieth-century floods at Calgary (beginning in 1897) in (Armstrong et al., 2009, p. 248) is based on city engineering archives and includes 17 events in the period 1897–1932. Peak discharge data are from the City of Calgary's River Flood Story: https://maps.calgary.ca/RiverFlooding/.

> The Bow raged up over its banks, tearing out bridges, uprooting trees, dislodging buildings, and turning large parts of northwest Calgary into a swirling, silt-laden sea. Three inches of rain had fallen in the previous day and a half. The swollen river drove more than sixty families from their homes on the flats southwest of town … [T]he water reached a maximum height of 14.9 feet … No subsequent flood in the twentieth century would come even close to this level and volume.[36]

Yet even in the smaller subsequent floods, the growing town reported more and new types of losses. For example, the 1915 flood (1,130 m^3/s) caused rail damage that temporarily isolated the city, destroyed bridges, flooded several residential neighborhoods, and damaged waterworks, gas, and electric power infrastructure, the latter shutting down the city's streetcar system. After each flood, the city rebuilt, improved its infrastructure, and expanded. The potential impact of a large flood in 1932 (1,520 m^3/s) was mitigated by the newly constructed Glenmore Dam upstream, whose reservoir at the time had fortuitously not yet been filled.[37]

In the first few decades of Calgary's growth, then, it was perhaps unsurprising that lands along the rivers were not highly valued and were relegated to industrial and lower-value uses. "Floods regularly coursed through the district, sweeping away the more fragile structures, depositing muck and debris, doing little to enhance property values or encourage extensive investment. The south bank of the Bow thus became a gritty working-class, commercial part of the town … In the process, Calgary's backyard, as sometimes happens, became something of a junkyard."[38]

Riverside land was mainly used for sawmills and lumber yards, power plants, storage yards, warehouses, garbage dumps, and similar purposes. Calgary's Chinatown was established in 1910 at its present location near the Centre Street Bridge, which crosses over the Bow River; at the time, the land was considered undesirable, being close to a low-income neighborhood. (The bridge was subsequently destroyed in the 1915 flood and replaced by a grander one, which remains in use.) The south bank of the Bow River at Calgary was considered a "decaying and derelict" district through the 1950s.[39]

* * *

Calgary's urban expansion did not truly take off until after World War II. The city's economy, which had originally been tied to agriculture and the cattle industry, was transformed with the discovery of oil in the region: "Within twenty

[36] (Armstrong et al., 2009, p. 244). [37] (Calgary Public Library, 2014; The City of Calgary, 2022b).

[38] (Nelles, 2005, p. 29).

[39] For Chinatown, see (Lai, 1988). In this era of discriminatory policies, Chinese immigrants in Canadian cities settled into enclaves. For Centre Street Bridge, see (Calgary Public Library, 2014). For south bank district, see (Armstrong et al., 2009; Nelles, 2005; Sandalack & Nicolai, 2006). Quote is from (Nelles, 2005, p. 31).

years (1945–1965) Calgary grew from a small provincial city to an urban metropolis of national importance, serving as the Canadian headquarters of an international oil industry." Population swelled – from 100,000 to nearly 600,000 in the 35 years from 1946 to 1981 and then to 1.39 million in the next 35 years from 1981 to 2016.[40]

The city accommodated this rapid population growth through suburbanization, a series of land annexations, and extensive sprawl. Over the course of the twentieth century, the distance from the city's center to its edge grew from 1.6 km to 24.1 km, and the area of development spread to over 500 km^2. Urban form in these new areas related to the dominant transportation technology of this era, the automobile. Low-density suburban tracts proliferated and spread to areas that had previously been avoided, such as the adjoining plateaus. Underground utilities, although less visible than transportation, played a highly influential role in where, when, and how the city expanded. In some areas, the high capital cost of providing utility services delayed development until expensive infrastructure investments were made.[41] "For example, the height of land and accompanying water pressure problems necessitated reservoir construction, and compromised development in the north above the 3,700-foot contour. Extensive expansion beyond this altitude had to wait until the 1970s when a gravity water supply from the Bearspaw Dam to the west became available."[42]

Market forces largely drove this rapid development, but urban planning emerged as an increasingly important influence on how Calgary was to grow. The City established its Planning Department in 1950, issued its first municipal plan in 1963, and institutionalized planning processes such as land-use zoning. For many decades, however, the city government did not actively seek to contain the sprawling pattern of development; rather, land-use planning mainly served to accommodate market-driven development. Indeed, in the postwar period, land-use planning could "best be described as the rationalization of land market forces to accommodate growth … [and in] the already developed portions of the city … to protect property values." From the 1990s onward, though, the local government did seek to slow down suburban sprawl; for example, in 2007, the City adopted a series of sustainability principles that sought to create higher densities in parts of the city that had already been developed. The City instituted growth management

[40] (Foran, 2009; Sandalack & Nicolai, 2006; Smith, 1962; Townshend et al., 2020). Quote "Within twenty years …" is from (Sandalack & Nicolai, 2006, p. 77). Population data are from (Townshend et al., 2020, p. 193). Figures refer to the Calgary census metropolitan area (CMA).

[41] See (Sandalack & Nicolai, 2006). Distance to city edge figures are for 1900 and 2005, respectively. Foran (2009) argues that utility servicing was crucial since it was a requirement for home mortgages and that when the City decided to transfer its responsibility for installing utilities to developers in the early 1950s it effectively "lost the real power to direct growth" (p. 22).

[42] (Foran, 2009, p. 21).

policies such as transit-oriented development, infill development, large-scale redevelopment of underused sites, and higher density developments in suburban areas that had been built in the 1950s and 1960s.[43]

What happened to Calgary's flood risk during the postwar period of rapid urbanization? At one level, the percentage of the city exposed to riverine flooding declined as the city expanded outward from the floodplain. But a closer examination reveals a rather more complex shift in Calgary's flood risk – for in the face of economic development pressures, the older settlements in the floodplain did not remain static, either.

To accommodate the rapid population growth, the city not only expanded massively outward but also intensified and renewed development in the urban core. By the early 1960s, in the older neighborhoods, pre-1914 housing in the floodplain was being torn down and "replaced by modern apartment blocks of a generally high standard of construction." From the 1960s to the early 1980s, much of downtown Calgary was thoroughly rebuilt:[44]

> The city's skyline was transformed by office towers that sprang up to form a dense and concentrated business core, and much of the historic urban fabric of commercial and residential buildings was removed in a vast urban renewal program … replaced by institutional blocks including a new municipal centre and some major cultural facilities. The construction crane was referred to as Calgary's official bird during this time.[45]

High-rise condominium towers were erected in parts of the inner city surrounding the central business district.

The social and economic geography of the city's residents shifted along with these transformations in the built environment. After 1980, although incomes rose overall, income inequality worsened and income differentials across the city became more spatially pronounced. The broad pattern of relative income change showed a sharp contrast between the fortunes of the central city and the outer areas. According to census data, the inner-city census tracts that had experienced high-rise condominium construction and extensive redevelopment also showed high gains in income relative to the city as a whole. At the same time, relative income losses occurred elsewhere, predominantly in neighborhoods that had been established from the 1960s to early 1980s. Moreover, the areas falling furthest behind were clustered in suburban northeast Calgary, where there was a high concentration of low-income and visible minority populations. Strikingly, in 1980, the

[43] See (Foran, 2009) for an in-depth look at Calgary's urban development in the period 1945–1978, with focus on the relationship between developers and the municipal government. See also (Nelles, 2005; Sandalack & Nicolai, 2006; Smith, 1962). Quote "best be described …" is from (Gordon & Hulchaski, 1985, p. 23). The description pertains to land-use planning in the province of Alberta and its municipalities, including Calgary. For growth management policies, see (Han, 2019; The City of Calgary, Planning, Development & Assessment, 2015; Townshend et al., 2020).

[44] Quote "replaced by modern …" is from (Smith, 1962, p. 320).

[45] (Sandalack & Nicolai, 2006, p. 105).

city's lowest-income census tract was located in the oldest part of the town, but by 2015, this same area had become middle income. In a word, much of Calgary's older urban core had gentrified.[46]

Arguably, a key reason why development intensified in the flood-prone areas of the city was that, over time, flooding became perceived as less and less of a threat. After 1932, no major summer flood occurred for many decades. Without destructive floods, collective memory of the threat faded and gave way to the public perception that the river had been "tamed." Local residents commonly credited the disappearance of summer floods to the dams and reservoirs that had been constructed in the mountains; although designed for hydroelectric power generation, they were thought to also incidentally benefit flood control. The city did experience ice jam floods in the winter, but this problem also seemed to have been resolved through the construction of dikes and an upstream dam in the late 1950s. Surveys found low levels of flood awareness.[47]

As the threat of flooding receded in the collective memory, new proposals were made for repurposing land along the riverbanks. In the 1960s, the CPR rail company sought to turn its valuable central city land holdings from railway uses into developable real estate. It proposed moving the rail tracks out to the underutilized riverbanks, which would be transformed by both new highway and railway infrastructure running atop a dike system. This major redevelopment proposal floundered, but though it was never implemented, it came close to being implemented – and would have transformed the city's flood risk, at a minimum by situating critical transportation infrastructure on the banks of the river, and perhaps committing the city to a flood protection strategy based on diking.[48]

Instead, in several areas along Calgary's rivers and streams, land was converted into something quite different – a system of river parks. Several influences led to the creation of these parks, among them urban planning, citizen campaigns, and private philanthropy, but notably, changing attitudes toward the environment were also instrumental:

> Sometime during the mid-twentieth century the Bow River passed in the public mind from being a working river, privately and publicly appropriated, altered and used for economic purposes, to something completely different, a park appreciated more for the public amenities and pleasure it provided. It came to be valued more for its aesthetic, recreational, and cultural attributes than its narrowly defined economic applications.[49]

[46] See (Townshend et al., 2020). This study compared 1980 and 2015 but did not report on conditions in the interim. Note that the 2015 situation postdates the 2013 flood; however, as will be discussed later in this chapter, the 2013 flood does not appear to have caused major changes to urban development trends.

[47] See (Armstrong et al., 2009). Surveys were conducted in 1976, 2006, and 2014 in high-risk neighborhoods; in all cases, only about one-third of residents were aware of the flood risk before moving to their locations (Abboud et al., 2018).

[48] See (Nelles, 2005). [49] (Nelles, 2005, p. 28).

The concept of a system of river valley parks was incorporated into city planning efforts, as reflected for example in Calgary's 1973 general plan, its 1984 River Valleys Plan, its 1994 Urban Park Master Plan, and its 2009 Municipal Development Plan (and its 2020 update). In addition, in the 1970s, the provincial government bought out land in a more outlying part of the city that was under pressure to be developed and created Fish Creek Provincial Park. Over time, the river parks became important to Calgary's urban identity. From a flood risk perspective, establishing the river parks prevented urban development in some of the most flood-prone lands in the city – yet this seems to have been an incidental benefit, rather than a driving force.[50]

Indeed, early public advocacy for the river parks revealed that flood risk reduction was not, in fact, a high priority for many citizens. In the 1970s, engineering studies of the flood risk debunked public perceptions that the problem of flood risk had disappeared:

> The main cause of the decline, [the engineering studies] concluded, was the relative absence of the conditions that created floods: concentrated periods of rainfall on previously saturated foothills watersheds, not the dams. These conditions could return … A flood of the magnitude of 1879 or 1897 might recur perhaps once a century, and for floods of this magnitude, the city was ill-prepared and the dams would provide little aid or comfort.[51]

In response, the municipal government made efforts to manage the risk, acquiring properties in flood-prone locations, widening and deepening the river channel, and stabilizing the riverbanks – but it encountered popular resistance. In public meetings, residents "unanimously condemned a program that involved indiscriminate clearing of the floodway and rezoning of threatened districts": "When confronted with the technical data about flood threats, many ratepayers' groups became alarmed at the maps of huge swaths of urban real estate declared to be in the putative flood plain and began worrying, not about remote floods, but rather about sinking property values." A public commission reported that "residents were prepared to take the risk of any flood damage," and moreover, they "rejected intrusive excavations of the river or wholesale rezoning of property for flood control protection in favour of better flood forecasting, upstream flood control projects, and a flood insurance program." As a result, in the 1970s, "something like a social contract was entered into by the interested and organized citizenry and the city over assessment of flood risk. The population preferred to accept the risk of floods rather than undergo the tree removal, diking, and zoning changes necessary to minimize that danger."[52]

[50] (Nelles, 2005; The City of Calgary, 2013, 2021; The City of Calgary, City & Community Planning Division, 1984). Fish Creek Provincial Park was developed using ecological design principles and a watershed framework (Foran, 2009; Taylor et al., 1995).

[51] (Armstrong et al., 2009, p. 255).

[52] See (Armstrong et al., 2009; Nelles, 2005). Quotes are from (Armstrong et al., 2009, pp. 268–269 and 392).

Yet the city did institute land-use planning tools specifically to address flood risk. The 1980 Land Use Bylaw 2P80 and the 2007 Land Use Bylaw 1P2007 that later replaced it included special regulations regarding development on lands at risk of flooding. For example, land in the *floodway* – "the river channel and adjoining lands indicated on the Floodway/Flood Fringe Maps that would provide the pathway for flood waters in the event of a flood of a magnitude likely to occur once in one hundred years" – could only be used for purposes such as parks, recreational facilities, and agriculture. Buildings already existing in the floodway as of 1985, however, were grandfathered in. No new buildings would be allowed to be constructed in the floodway "except for the replacement of existing single family, semi-detached, duplex dwellings and accessory buildings on the same locations." In practice, however, a municipal report noted that "at times these limitations are relaxed for development." On the *floodplain*, or the designated areas adjacent to the floodway, risk was managed through less restrictive regulations such as minimum setbacks from waterways and building design requirements. In broad terms, then, land-use planning tools were used to prevent new development from exacerbating flood risk but were not aimed at reducing the risk that already existed as of 1985.[53]

* * *

For over eight decades, Calgary grew rapidly without experiencing any severe flood. By 2013, its population exceeded 1.1 million people. In June of that year, heavy rainfall and rapid snowmelt caused flooding of a magnitude not experienced since 1932. Precipitation in the watershed areas upstream of Calgary was "torrential," with rainfall rates "more typical of a tropical storm in quantity and intensity" and similar to what had occurred in the 1929 and 1932 floods. The disaster impacted a broad area across southern Alberta province. All of the Bow River's tributaries essentially flooded simultaneously, compounding the peak flow in the river. At Calgary, river levels reached 5–6 m higher than typical summer levels. From a hydrometeorological standpoint, this event was indeed large – but not exceptional for the region. Hydrologists determined that on the Bow River at Calgary, a flood of that size had a return period of about 1 in 40 years and that it was "likely neither the flood of a century, nor the flood of a lifetime for those in the region." At downtown Calgary, flow on the Bow River peaked at 1,840 m^3/s,

[53] Doberstein et al. (2019) characterize Calgary's flood risk management approach as an "avoid" strategy. Section 19.1 in (The City of Calgary, Land Use Section, Development and Land Use Division, 1980) refers to the "floodway," "floodplain," and "overland flow area." Part 3, Division 3 in (The City of Calgary, Land Use ByLaw Sustainment Team, Development & Building Approvals, Planning Implementation, 2007) refers to the "floodway," "flood fringe," and "overland flow area." Quote "the river channel …" is from Part 3, Division 3 in (The City of Calgary, Land Use ByLaw Sustainment Team, Development & Building Approvals, Planning Implementation, 2007). Quote "except for the replacement …" is from (The City of Calgary, Land Use Section, Development and Land Use Division, 1980), Section 19.1. Quote "at times …" is from (The Globe and Mail, 2021).

greater than the flood in 1932 but less than the one in 1897. On the Elbow River, it was estimated to be a 1 in 100 year (i.e., 1:100-year) flood.[54]

At the time, the 2013 Southern Alberta flood was considered the costliest disaster in Canadian history. It caused some Can$5–6 billion (in Canadian dollars) in damage, including a record Can$1.7 billion in insured losses, across the region. Within the city of Calgary, substantial damage was caused by riverine flooding as both the Elbow and Bow Rivers overtopped their banks in several locations; damage also occurred from rising groundwater, stormwater backup, and sewer backup. Major roadways and over 20 bridges were closed, some 34,000 homes and businesses lost electric power, and the main wastewater treatment plant was flooded. At the Saddledome sports arena, floodwaters reached up to the tenth row of seats. The downtown core was inundated and inaccessible for a week. One person died and some 110,000 were evacuated. Around 4,000 businesses were affected and 3,000 buildings damaged. Thirty parks were flooded. The disaster cost the City over Can$400 million in infrastructure damage and Can$55 million in emergency response costs. Consistent with the city's urban development history, flooding mainly affected the older neighborhoods in the floodplain.[55]

Damage and disruption could have been worse. In anticipation of the flood, the City had preemptively lowered water levels in the upstream Glenmore Dam reservoir, allowing it to contain more floodwater and reducing peak flow on the Elbow River by 44%. This action is estimated to have reduced damage, economic loss, and population affected by 20%–30%. The electric utility also made operational adjustments at its reservoirs, which reduced flood levels in the Bow. A preflood investment in an advanced water filtration system enabled the City to maintain potable water supply throughout the flood disaster.[56]

One might expect the costliest disaster in the city's history, not to mention in the nation's history, to have triggered transformational changes. After all, the flood risk was visible, immense, and undeniable – no longer just an abstract hazard map or stories from the distant past. It is instructive to consider what did change in the decade following the 2013 flood, and what did not.

[54] See (Pomeroy et al., 2016; The City of Calgary, 2022b). Quote "more typical ..." is from (Pomeroy et al., 2016, pp. 107–108). Quote "likely neither the flood of a century ..." is from p. 116. The authors note that return period calculation is subject to considerable uncertainty due to the short history of scientific data on streamflow in the region. Bryant et al. (2022) also cite a 2014 engineering study by Golder Associates that estimated the return period at 80 years. For the 1 in 100 year flood estimate, (Abboud et al., 2018) cites a 2015 Government of Alberta Environment and Parks report.

[55] As in many disasters, the preliminary rough estimate (Can$6 billion in 2013 dollars) has been frequently quoted but was never publicly detailed or officially revised. See (Bryant et al., 2022). City cost is from (Environment and Climate Change Canada, 2013; The City of Calgary, 2022b). See maps and images at Calgary's River Flood Story (https://maps.calgary.ca/riverflooding/). See also (Abboud et al., 2018) regarding groundwater flooding in the older neighborhoods along the Elbow River.

[56] For reservoir water lowering and water supply, see (The City of Calgary, 2022b). For estimated loss reduction, see (Reynolds et al., 2014).

In many ways, the 2013 flood catalyzed action on the part of institutions whose mandate involved dealing with the risk of flooding to society. For one, the disaster was a turning point for the insurance industry. Prior to the disaster, insurance for overland or riverine flooding had not been available to homeowners in Canada. Insurance companies considered the risk an "uninsurable peril," one for which the business case did not warrant selling the product. After the 2013 flood, with public expectations high, it became clear that such a position was untenable. The insurance industry became concerned about reputational risk to its brand, as well as regulatory risk – the possibility that provincial and federal governments might decide to institute flood insurance regulations without industry input. Major companies began offering flood insurance in 2015.[57]

Scientific understanding of the regional flood hazard also improved. For example, "previous floods of this magnitude on the Bow River were not gauged … similarly, the area and duration of inundation in urban areas were previously estimated using hydraulic models, but now the extent of inundation is well documented." Moreover, the flood demonstrated that damage could be caused not only by overland flooding but also by groundwater flooding, "when the water table rises due to … propagation of the rising river stages into permeable, river-connected alluvial aquifers." New flood models were developed that included this additional dimension of the flood hazard. Flood maps had last been updated in 1983; the provincial government, which has responsibility for flood hazard studies and mapping, engaged in a substantial update of the flood maps and incorporated methodological enhancements.[58]

Capital investments were made to redress vulnerabilities that the flood had revealed to buildings and infrastructure. For example, the main wastewater treatment plant had suffered Can$13.5 million in damages, and untreated effluent had been discharged into the Bow River for days during the flood. The utility subsequently invested Can$22 million in flood protection measures at the plant so that it could withstand a repeat event.[59]

Perhaps most significantly, the City established a Flood Resilience Program in 2014 with a charge to continuously assess progress in and opportunities for flood risk reduction. The goal was protection for a 1 in 200 year flood. The city updated its flood damage model, estimated the cost of doing nothing, and undertook a Flood Mitigation Measures Assessment to examine a range of possible flood mitigation alternatives. In 2017, it adopted a formal Flood Resilience Plan. The plan did not rely on a single approach but instead combined many strategies. Upstream of the city, dams and reservoirs (including a new "dry reservoir" to

[57] (Thistlethwaite, 2017).

[58] Quote "previous floods …" is from (Pomeroy et al., 2016, p. 114). Quote "when the water table rises …" is from (Abboud et al., 2018, p. 1). For new flood models, see (Bryant et al., 2022). For flood map updating, see www.alberta.ca/final-flood-maps.aspx and (The City of Calgary, 2022b).

[59] (Nadeau-Bonilla & MacDonald, 2015).

which floodwaters could be diverted temporarily) would be used to slow down flood flows. Within the city, flood barriers would be built in a few especially at-risk neighborhoods. Floodplain land-use policies would also help guide development. At the level of individual properties, building regulations and public education would be improved. Enhancements would also be made to flood forecasting, monitoring, and emergency response planning. In the decade after the 2013 flood, the city invested over Can$150 million in new infrastructure that was expected to reduce Calgary's flood risk by 55%; with completion of the new dry reservoir, risk would be reduced by 70%. The City began updating its Disaster Risk Assessment annually and releasing a detailed Disaster Risk Report "every four years in alignment with the municipal budget cycle."[60]

The City's communication about flood risk is straightforward and clear. Its websites include spatially detailed interactive maps and aerial photos of the 2013 flood extent, as well as information on historic floods and other hazard information. The resources are attuned to popular misconceptions about risk, clarifying for example that

> a 1:100 (100-year or 1% flood) flood has a one per cent chance of happening in any given year or a 22 per cent chance of happening during the lifetime of a 25-year mortgage. This doesn't mean that after a 1:100 flood occurs it won't happen again for another 100 years. It's possible for major floods to happen in back-to-back years.

Its Flood Resilience Plan acknowledges that with climate change, "our high river flow season may shift earlier in the year and we could see bigger floods happening more often. Our city and the region are also growing. Density and land use is increasing in some river communities and spaces. This can leave more people and businesses vulnerable to the impacts of flooding." It notes that approximately 75,000 Calgarians live in the floodplain, that a 1:100-year flood is expected to cause direct and indirect damages of Can$2.2 billion, and that a 1:1,000-year flood would inflict Can$12.3 billion in losses.[61]

[60] (The City of Calgary, 2022a). Without flood mitigation, it was estimated that the city could expect Can$168 million per year on average in flood damages (The City of Calgary, 2022b). As of 10 years after the flood, the city was in the process of updating its Calgary River Valleys plan, which "directs how we develop and regulate in the floodplain" and "will respond to new Government of Alberta Flood Hazard Maps and consolidate floodplain policy to direct updates to the Land Use Bylaw, Municipal Development Plan, and other plans and regulations" (p. 24). Quote "every four years …" is from (Calgary Emergency Management Agency, 2022, p. 8).

[61] See Calgary's Disaster Risk Explorer (https://maps.calgary.ca/DisasterRiskExplorer/) and Calgary's River Flood Story (https://maps.calgary.ca/RiverFlooding/). Quotes are from (The City of Calgary, 2022b, pp. 4, 3). The dollar figures include "direct damage to buildings and infrastructure during river floods (including groundwater flooding), as well as indirect damages due to impacts to traffic, waste disposal, emergency operations costs, and habitat restoration" (The City of Calgary, 2022b, p. 4). Note that while the Flood Resilience Plan (The City of Calgary, 2022b) mentions 75,000 people in the floodplain, the city's Disaster Risk Explorer website mentions 27,000 in the 1:100-year flood hazard area in 2015 and 42,000 in the 1:200-year flood hazard area in the same year (https://maps.calgary.ca/DisasterRiskExplorer/). It is unclear whether the discrepancy is due to differences in the areas assessed or to population growth in the interim.

What did not change were the fundamental pattern and trends in Calgary's urban development. In contrast to the numerous engineering initiatives to reduce flooding, there were few efforts to reduce human occupancy of the floodplain. In the aftermath of the 2013 flood, the Alberta government did implement a limited and ultimately unsuccessful Floodway Relocation Program to buy out homes located in floodways. Crucially, it was voluntary. In Calgary, it hardly made a dent; only 50 homes were eligible, and only one-third of the homeowners accepted the offer, even knowing that if they refused, they would be ineligible for government disaster assistance in future floods. A full-scale effort was not a viable option. According to the Flood Resilience Plan, "buyout of all properties in the floodplain would cost billions and was considered financially and socially infeasible." The media put it more bluntly:[62]

> Moving people out of harm's way after decades of poor planning decisions, on the other hand, is expensive and politically fraught. In Calgary, it was a complete non-starter: A 2014 municipal report discouraged that option except in the most vulnerable areas, while barely bothering to provide a justification. It came down to money: The city has estimated that it would cost more than $2-billion to buy out all properties at risk of flooding. Alberta Transportation documents estimated that removing homes, businesses, roads and other vulnerable infrastructure "could cost total in the tens of billions of dollars."[63]

Nor was there much consensus or collective voice on the part of residents advocating for restricting development in flood-prone areas. Land-use planning with regard to flood-prone areas was clarified but not fundamentally changed.[64]

Urban development trends do not register any noticeable impact from the 2013 flood. Calgary's population continued to grow, exceeding 1.25 million five years after the flood. The oldest part of the city, the Inner City sector, showed significant increase in population and dwelling units between 2010 and 2015 and continued to be stable or growing in subsequent years. Development continued in flood-prone areas "owing largely to developers' political and economic clout."[65]

> Since the 2013 flood … [d]evelopment of new residential communities … continues along the river on the southern side of the city … But recent efforts to half urban sprawl also have pushed redevelopment inward to the city's older river-adjacent communities, allowing builders to raze existing homes and build two (or more) in their place. Known locally as "infills," those homes mean that the population is also growing in existing neighborhoods near the rivers, not solely on the outskirts … [I]n Calgary the wealthiest people buy property *near* hazards because of amenities like scenery and recreation.[66]

[62] See (Abboud et al., 2018). Quote "buyout of all properties …" is from (The City of Calgary, 2022b, p. 15).

[63] (McClearn & Keller, 2021). For the Can$2 billion estimate, see (IBI Group and Golder Associates, 2017).

[64] For lack of consensus, see (Haney, 2022). For lack of fundamental change, see section 4.4 Flood Hazard Areas of the 2020 Municipal Development Plan (The City of Calgary, 2021).

[65] Data are from Calgary's annual Civic Census. For Inner City sector, see (The City of Calgary, 2016; 2018). Quote is from (Haney, 2022, p. 22).

[66] (Haney, 2022, p. 27).

Even after the 2013 flood, the City's development planning analysis categorized numerous land parcels near the rivers as "underutilized," with "potential for additional units."[67]

Detailed postflood analysis of one flooded neighborhood, on the north bank of the Bow, is especially revealing. Researchers found that between 2013 and 2018, structural mitigation projects reduced flood risk by an estimated 47% – but at the same time, urban development trends like densification increased flood risk by 4%. They concluded: "These results demonstrate that the flood management revival in Southern Alberta has largely been successful at reducing flood risk; however, the gains are under threat from continued development and densification absent additional floodproofing regulations." Even in a city recovering from a catastrophic flood, then, "development pressure can continue to increase vulnerability absent robust regulation."[68]

3.4 Urbanization and Riverine Flood Risk

Every river city is unique in the specifics of how flooding has intersected with its urban history. At the same time, at some level, cities also exhibit broad patterns that are characteristic of their type of urbanization. By considering cities as different as Vienna and Calgary – an old European imperial capital and a young North American commercial center – it is possible to gain insight into how and why riverine flood risk changes over time as a result of city-building processes and legacies.

The Urban Risk Dynamics framework from Chapter 1 provides a structure for considering the forces at play in Vienna and Calgary, as well as any other city at risk from riverine flooding. With an emphasis on evolving interactions between economics, landscape, and technology in urbanization, the framework asks how urban development influences changes in the local flood hazard, exposure, and vulnerability – and how flood disasters in turn affect urban development.

How has urbanization influenced flood *hazard*? In both Vienna and Calgary, the relationship between the city and the river has been one of technological control of the river, intensifying over time – sometimes overtly for flood control and sometimes incidentally so. In one case, this involved straightening and channelizing the river, and eventually increasing the channel capacity and providing areas to accommodate excess flow during floods. In the other case, upstream dams and reservoirs initially built for other purposes became increasingly central to flood management strategies. Why each city adopted its particular engineering solution undoubtedly revolves around many factors, technical as well as economic and

[67] (The City of Calgary, 2016, p. 22). [68] (Bryant et al., 2022); quotes are from pp. 1, 12.

political. It is worth keeping in mind that engineering approaches themselves also evolve, and the potential solutions on offer will invariably reflect the technical know-how, practices, and preferences of the times.

Regardless of the specific technology, engineering works served to reduce the local flood hazard by modifying riverine processes to mitigate the natural uncertainty, variability, and extremes in flows. While riverine flood events are still possible, they have become much less frequent. Moreover, since smaller events are well controlled, if a flood does occur, it would likely be a very large one that exceeds the capacity of the protective mechanisms. Controlling the river reduces the flood hazard but entails other kinds of costs – most notably, environmental impacts such as loss of riparian habitat, ecosystem health, and biodiversity. In both Vienna and Calgary, following an initial period of traditional engineering works, environmental considerations were later incorporated into more multilayered enhancements of the basic strategy, which nonetheless remained one of reducing the flood hazard by stabilizing and controlling the river.

This trend is far from unique to the two case studies. Although the engineering particulars differ from city to city, analysts have observed that "the United States, like most developed countries, shows a marked disposition to control nature rather than work with it" in addressing riverine flooding.[69]

How has urban development influenced flood *exposure*? The original town site of a river city is, almost by definition, close to the river channel. The particulars of the siting rationale may differ. In the case of Vienna, the Romans built a fortified town on a terrace to the side of the Danube. In contrast, Calgary's reason for being was the railroad, which required corridors of flat lands; this led the original town site to be located on the floodplain at a little distance from the Bow River. Regardless, the locational logic of the founding era is reflected in how the original town site relates to the river. As the cities grew, they expanded out from this original core, densifying over time. Even as the original rationale for the town site became obsolete, the urban center remained where it had been planted, near the river. Inevitably, then, flood exposure increased as more people and property came to be located in the floodplain with urban growth.

Nonetheless, as Vienna and Calgary both showed, flood exposure over the course of a city's history changes in nonlinear ways. The general trend is one of increasing urban exposure, in the sense that development in the floodplain tends to increase in quantity and density. But this may entail long periods of little change followed by years of rapid and intense change. There may be periods where most of the new urban expansion is away from the floodplain and other eras where growth extends into more hazardous lands.

[69] (Birkland et al., 2003, p. 46).

In terms of how a city expands, there may be constraints arising from the physical landscape that over time may be overcome by technology and economic investments; these dynamics have implications for flood risk. In Calgary, early urban development was largely limited to the river valleys. Only in the latter half of the twentieth century, when population boomed, when the automobile transformed transportation, and when expensive investments were made in utility infrastructure, did new urban development expand onto the plateaus. For Calgary, then, flood exposure mainly increased during its early history, rather than in the post-war period of major urban expansion. Vienna's story is strikingly different. The Danube is a much larger and very dynamic river. For many centuries, urban settlement stayed on the edge of the floodplain. The Great Danube Regulation of the 1870s stabilized the riverine landscape, enabling and encouraging substantial urban expansion onto the historic floodplain. For Vienna, controlling the river meant that land in the floodplain became stable and viable for urban settlement.

A key point here is that capital investments in engineering works for flood protection are expensive. They are generally undertaken only when there is sufficient financial justification for the outlays. This implies that from an urban economic standpoint, major investments in critical infrastructure for flood control tend to be made in eras when a city is on the cusp of, or in the midst of, a period of rapid growth at a substantial urban scale. Small towns – and similarly major cities in their early stages as small towns – are generally not protected from floods by substantial capital works. By implication, then, a city's flood protection infrastructure reflects the technology of its era of rapid urban growth. Furthermore, once set in motion, the reliance on technology for flood protection becomes a self-reinforcing strategy, difficult to reverse as more and more of the urbanized area becomes dependent on it.[70]

In the field of disasters research, a phenomenon known variously as the "levee effect" or the "safe development paradox" has long been observed. It is perhaps one of the earliest and most robust findings in natural hazards geography. The basic idea is that flood protection structures such as dikes and levees are built to reduce risk, but paradoxically, in the long run they actually increase risk by engendering a "false sense of security" that leads to ever more human settlement in hazardous areas. At some point, a catastrophic flood will occur that exceeds the capacity of the flood protection works, causing them to fail. The result is much greater loss than would have been suffered had the flood protection works never been constructed.[71]

[70] The economic rationale for Calgary's Glenmore Dam, built in the 1930s Depression era as a public works project for water supply, was related to providing jobs. See www.calgary.ca/planning/water/glenmore-dam-infrastructure-improvements.html.

[71] The concept of the levee effect was originally pointed out by geographer Gilbert White (1945). For discussion, see, for example, (Birkland et al., 2003; Burby, 2006; Haer et al., 2020).

The Vienna and Calgary cases provide two different vantage points from which to add nuance to our understanding of the levee effect. Its label notwithstanding, the levee effect need not be predicated primarily on actual flood levees; rather, it may apply more broadly to situations where constructed or technological solutions are utilized for flood protection. Moreover, it is questionable whether the levee effect is an unintended side effect of the construction. In Vienna, for example, structural flood mitigation was pursued precisely to extend the city into lands that would otherwise be uninhabitable due to flooding – the pressure from and potential for urban development are what make the economic case for the capital investment.

It is similarly questionable whether people and businesses moving into hazard lands are making decisions entirely out of a false sense of security. In Calgary, for example, studies found that most residents in high-risk areas reported being unaware of the risk when they moved in. Ignorance is different from feeling adequately protected by engineering works. One important factor may be the loss of collective memory about the flood risk as protective infrastructure prevents smaller flood events from occurring, thus reducing the more frequent, tangible reminders of the hazard. In addition, collective awareness of a city's flood hazard also declines during periods of rapid population growth, when many new residents arrive in town who are unfamiliar with the area and its hazards.

It is telling that in Calgary, when given the buyout opportunity after the 2013 flood (when neither ignorance nor a sense of security would apply any longer), most homeowners declined and chose to stay. Somewhere within the phenomenon of the levee effect there is also a degree of public acceptance of risk, considered in balance with the benefits of the location. After all, while a catastrophic flood large enough to overwhelm protective infrastructure is possible, it is unlikely within the timeframe of a person's mortgage or residency at an address. In comparison, the day-to-day benefits of the location – whether in terms of job access, commute time, access to amenities, social networks, or perhaps housing affordability, as the case may be – are immediate and tangible. Furthermore, risk is also tempered by expectations that after a disaster, assistance will be forthcoming from government (and/or insurance), however realistic or not that may actually be.[72]

Nor do other parties in the urban growth process have much incentive to consider the risk of floods that happen infrequently. Disaster sociologist Kathleen Tierney argues that the workings of the urban "growth machine" – a coalition of developers, city officials, local business organizations, and other players pursuing

[72] Research has highlighted many other factors that come into play in households' decision-making related to natural hazard risk. For example, households may be myopic with respect to risk, may not have adequate risk information, may perceive that "it can't happen to me," or may have strong place attachment. Importantly, their ability to relocate (e.g., financial resources) may be constrained. Federal government policies may also disincentivize individuals as well as state and local governments from investing in flood loss avoidance; see (Burby et al., 1999).

an agenda of urban growth – are a key part of the process of urban risk creation. For developers, the financial downside associated with selling property on the floodplain is minimal. In Calgary, for example, "home builders shoulder financial liability for one year after completion, part of a mandated warranty on new homes … After one year, financial risk is transferred to the homeowner." For municipal authorities, new development is helpful for generating tax revenues, not to mention providing housing for a growing population. Other city government goals may also entail trade-offs with floodplain development. In Calgary's case, increasing density in the older urban core was a key part of municipal strategies aimed at limiting sprawl, reducing greenhouse gas emissions, and improving quality of life – even though the older urban core was built on the floodplain.[73]

One of the notable themes in Calgary's flood history is the increasingly important role of government, especially municipal urban planning, in influencing flood exposure. Over the course of Calgary's postwar decades of rapid urbanization, the practice and profession of urban planning emerged, became institutionalized, and arguably exerted ever-greater influence on urban form and urban development processes. From initially coordinating and facilitating urban expansion and suburban sprawl, it shifted to an urban sustainability agenda that included promoting central city densification. On the one hand, this policy led to greater flood exposure. But on the other, by implementing river parks and prohibiting new development in the highest-risk area (i.e., the floodway), urban planning also mitigated potential flood exposure.

How does urban development affect flood *vulnerability*? Whereas flood exposure is relatively straightforward to conceptualize, flood vulnerability is more complex and ambiguous. Exposure is what is in harm's way – the people, buildings, infrastructure, and so on that could be flooded. Vulnerability is the propensity for those people and property to suffer damage, loss, or disruption should they be flooded. (Here, I consider the concept of capacity to be within the scope of vulnerability, recognizing that they are sometimes discussed separately.)

Differential vulnerability might relate to physical, social, or other attributes. An example of differing physical vulnerability would be a house constructed on stilts, spared when floodwaters flow under it, next to an identical house built at ground elevation that is severely damaged. Social vulnerability often relates to access, or the lack of access, to resources (e.g., money, social networks, knowledge) and power. Among the most well-established findings in the disasters literature is that low-income, socially marginalized groups are more vulnerable than high-income groups to adverse outcomes in disasters – injury, death, displacement, financial distress, difficulty in recovering. Social vulnerability to disasters is often measured

[73] For growth machine, see (Tierney, 2014, ch. 6). Quote is from (Haney, 2022, p. 24).

in terms of variables such as income, race/ethnicity, and housing tenure that serve as proxies for the propensity to suffer loss in a hazard event.

But it is not necessarily the case that the most vulnerable groups in society are always the populations most at risk of flooding. For example, at the time of Calgary's 2013 flood, many of the inundated residential neighborhoods had populations that were predominantly affluent, white, highly educated homeowners – "a wealthy class of individuals, living in a wealthy city." This profile reflects the relative economic value of property near the rivers at that time. But several decades previously, riverbank property in the inner city had been considered undesirable, supporting low-value uses, inhabited by lower-income populations, and priced accordingly.[74]

Had a flood the size of the 2013 event occurred in, say, 1980, those affected would have been primarily low- to middle-income households. It is unclear whether a flood warning and a mass evacuation order would have been issued, and it is likely that the number of people killed would have been higher. In comparison with the actual 2013 disaster, such a flood would have affected a much larger proportion of Calgary's area and population (as the city was smaller then) and imposed a much greater burden on its resources for recovery.

Viewed over the course of a city's history, it is not self-evident that vulnerability at the urban scale – separate from exposure – worsens over time. Yet it should be acknowledged that in some ways cities do tend to become more vulnerable over time. One that is apparent in both the Vienna and Calgary cases is that when flood frequency is reduced (due especially to flood protection infrastructure), there is loss of collective memory of the flood hazard. This leads to attrition in the population's awareness of and preparedness for flood disasters and translates into behaviors such as buying homes in hazardous areas.

On the other hand, other trends related to vulnerability, especially within society's institutions, may give some cause for cautious optimism. Not only have flood forecasting capabilities and warning systems improved, but emergency management has become more professionalized. Mechanisms for reducing vulnerability are increasingly being introduced into land-use planning, building codes and regulations, and more hazard-resistant infrastructure design.

And finally, in relation to the Urban Dynamics Framework, it is useful to examine the question of how flood disasters in turn influence urban development. Here, too, there is cause for cautious optimism in that learning and adaptation do take place after disasters. Scientific and technical knowledge about the risk typically improves substantially after a disaster. In Calgary, for example, the 2013 flood drew attention to groundwater flooding as a damage mechanism in riverine flood

[74] Quote is from (Haney, 2022, p. 28).

events, spurring the phenomenon to be studied and incorporated into the city's Flood Resilience Plan. Disasters may lead to learning on the part of how government and other institutions respond to a disaster, as well as more systematic strategies and investments for addressing the risk before the next event. Other institutional changes also occur that represent adaptations more broadly to a changing environment – for instance, in the Canadian case, the industry's offering of riverine flood insurance after the 2013 disaster.[75]

The Vienna and Calgary cases demonstrate how urban flood risk today and into the future have been shaped by long-term, evolving interactions between economy, landscape, and technology. From the specifics of these cases, a few key insights can be discerned regarding this dynamic: A city's risk retains the imprint of its founding era, when the town was originally sited in relation to the physical landscape and its associated hazards. Growth pressures during periods of major population increase may instigate flood protection investments to allow the city to expand into hazard lands. The self-reinforcing dynamic of urban development leads to a situation that becomes increasingly difficult to reverse, as persistence in the urban landscape entails not only durable physical structures but also vested interests, from homeowners in the floodplain to institutions charged with flood protection.

Flood disasters are characteristic of how a city has developed, as well as the physical landscape in which it is located. How a city deals with hazard events small and large is part of its history, and the responses to each event leave a legacy for the city's future inhabitants. Disasters do not fundamentally alter the processes of urban growth and change that give risk to risk; at least, this appears to be the case for disasters that are less than overwhelmingly catastrophic.

But can we really make all these claims on the basis of two cases of medium-sized riverine cities? Do these assertions stand up in the context of other hazards and landscapes and other types of urban areas? Chapter 4 investigates how urban development and disaster risk interact in relation to flooding in a different setting: coastal zones. It examines cities that have experienced catastrophe and explores how the narrative of evolving flood risk may differ between medium-sized cities and very large metropolises.

[75] Whether new flood insurance options actually reduce risk is unclear. Insurance uptake may be low, it may benefit the wealthy more than those in need, and it may encourage risk-taking such as further development in floodplains. On the other hand, insurance augments at-risk populations' resources for withstanding and recovering from a disaster. Insurance can in principle also be integrated with incentives to reduce risk at the property in return for lower premiums.

4

Cities and Coastal Flooding

4.1 Coastal Flooding

What happens where a river meets the sea? Anywhere that two complex systems meet, the outcome is likely to be: "It depends." At a basic level, a river mouth is where fresh water drains into the ocean, but even this simplistic characterization has multifaceted, intricate, and varying implications. The size of the river and the strength of currents along the shore, for example, are just two of myriad factors that affect the characteristics of a coastal river delta or estuary. The mixing of fresh and salt water has implications for plant, fish, and other life. Layer on top of this the effects of human settlement, from protective seawalls to port and harbor facilities, and the picture becomes substantially more complex. Yet appreciating the broad contours of this complexity is essential in order to understand the flood risk faced by coastal cities and how this risk is likely to change in future. It is not simply that rising sea levels will inundate more land.

Geomorphologists would say that where a river meets the sea, it loses its forward momentum and its ability to carry sediments. As it slows, the pebbles and larger particles drop out first, then sand grains, then the finer silt and clay particles further out from the shore. Meanwhile, the ocean side is active with the energy of waves, tides, and currents. Along some coasts, waves and currents are strong enough that river sediments are quickly washed away before they can accumulate. Salt water from the ocean extends up into the lower reaches of the river, so that the area is affected by tides and waves as well as riverine processes. But along other coasts where waves and currents are less strong, or where riverine processes dominate, the sediments build up and a delta forms at the mouth of the river. The deltas of large rivers such as the Mississippi comprise massive accumulations of sedimentary deposits; over time, as the main river channel through the delta becomes clogged with sediment, it may shift course: "This happens when an active part of the delta extends seaward so far that the river's route to the sea becomes so inefficient for the movement of sediment that the river shifts to a shorter and more efficient route."[1]

From the perspective of understanding the landscapes on which cities are built, as well as their implications for hazards, it is helpful to distinguish between estuaries and deltas as coastal settlement geomorphologies, as has been suggested by the Intergovernmental Panel on Climate Change (IPCC) in its 6th Assessment Report. Estuaries are defined as "a wetland receiving sediment from both fluvial and marine sources, which is affected by tide, wave and river processes," and deltas are "a wetland where fluvial sediment is supplied and deposited more rapidly than it can be redistributed by basin processes such as waves and tides."[2]

What happens where a river meets the sea also depends on the local topography, bathymetry, and the shape of the coastline. For example: "If the shore and offshore slope away gradually as in the form of a broad ramp, most of a wave's energy is spent in crossing this zone … The picture is quite different along coastal cliffs where deep water runs close to the shore. Here waves undergo little energy attenuation before reaching shore, and instead smack the shore nearly full-force." Furthermore, waves and currents that move along the shoreline are also continually shaping the landscape. Headlands, where land protrudes into the sea, tend to be exposed to greater wave energy and hence erosion; bays, meanwhile, are more protected and experience lower energy from the sea. Since "one is giving up sediment while the other is collecting it" along a shoreline, it is no coincidence that bays are often characterized by beaches.[3]

Sediment matters because it supports plant life along the coast, which in turn helps to stabilize the sediments as well as to support other forms of life. Estuaries are highly productive settings from a biological standpoint, and humans benefit in many ways. For example:

> Coastal marshes are valuable ecosystems. By providing refuge and forage opportunities for wildlife, fishes and invertebrates, marshes are the basis of the economic livelihoods of many communities. Shallow ponds and seed-producing vegetation provide overwintering habitat for millions of migratory waterfowl, and the role of wetlands in absorbing nutrients and reducing loading to the coastal ocean is widely recognised, as is their value for protecting local communities from flooding, either by damping storm surges from the ocean or by providing storage for riverine floodwaters.[4]

With so many physical processes intersecting, river mouth settings are highly dynamic landscapes. Even without the influence of humans, even without hurricanes and other storms, and even without sea-level rise, these settings would

[1] See (Marsh & Kaufman, 2013) for an accessible introduction to coastal geomorphological processes; quote is from section 21.5.

[2] (Glavovic et al., 2022, p. 2167).

[3] Quotes are from (Marsh & Kaufman, 2013, section 22.3).

[4] (Reed et al., 2009, p. 136).

be continually changing through processes such as delta formation or coastal land loss through erosion. Along some coasts, land may even be rising over geologic timescales due to processes such as mountain formation or glacial retreat. In storm events, high winds and powerful surge and wave action can cause substantial change to the landscape and ecosystems in a matter of hours. But over decades and centuries, human actions are powerful agents of change – in terms of modifying coastal areas, as significant as climate change impacts, or possibly more so.[5]

Examples of human impacts on coastlines are legion and familiar, even if their impacts may sometimes be surprising or at least unintended. Upstream dams can dramatically reduce the supply of sediment downstream and hence impede delta formation at the river's mouth. River channels and harbor areas often require regular dredging to maintain conditions necessary for navigation, to the detriment of fish habitat. Urbanization and groundwater extraction can cause land subsidence, which in coastal areas means a lowering of the land level relative to the sea and hence greater potential flooding. Counteracting coastal land loss often involves deliberate efforts to increase available land through reclamation, such as the filling in of coastal wetlands that might otherwise have helped to mitigate flooding.[6]

Even protective structures can have unintended consequences. Many coastal cities have built structures such as seawalls to protect the shoreline from wave action, groins (walls extending into the sea) to reduce beach erosion from along-shore sediment movement, or breakwaters to help shelter harbors from wave energy. Seawalls may reduce erosion in the short term, but by deflecting wave energy downward and away, they may cause scouring at the base that ultimately undermines the structure or may increase erosion on neighboring shorelines. Groins and breakwaters, by interrupting the movement of sediments along the shore, can cause beach erosion downshore. Over the long term, the unintended consequences of protective structures may very well include shoreline retreat.[7]

Flooding, for a coastal city situated at the mouth of a river, can take various forms. The city is at risk of floodwaters from the river itself, which may be caused by excessive rain in the upstream catchment area. Within the urban area, sudden heavy rains can overwhelm the capacity of stormwater drainage infrastructure; rapid runoff is exacerbated by impervious surfaces such as parking lots and streets that impede the ability of the ground to soak and retain the rainwater. This pluvial flooding can affect any city, not just one on the coast. From the ocean side, coastal flooding is often associated with hurricanes and other storms. In a hurricane, the

[5] (Blumberg & Bruno, 2018; Stive et al., 2009).

[6] (Marsh & Kaufman, 2013, section 22.7); see also (Blumberg & Bruno, 2018).

[7] See (Blumberg & Bruno, 2018, ch. 11).

low pressure at the center of the storm system causes a storm surge – a raising of the sea surface – that upon approaching the shore further grows in height and behaves like a wave. Together with the powerful winds and associated surface waves, the storm surge is extremely destructive when it hits the coast. But coastal flooding can also occur in some low-lying places when there is no storm, simply from high tides, especially where land has been subsiding and during the highest tides in the year. Sea-level rise related to climate change, superimposed on this picture, complicates the underlying dynamics.[8]

It is no accident that numerous cities around the world, including many of the largest, are situated along coastlines at the mouth of a river. Originally, such locations would have afforded numerous benefits for human settlement – fresh water, fishing grounds, transportation access both inland and over the sea, and flat land, to name a few. Sheltered locations with naturally deep harbors would have been especially suitable for ports. Throughout urban history, coastal cities have faced and adapted to the hazards inherent in this landscape.

This chapter focuses on the relationship between coastal flood risk and urban development by examining the environmental histories of two case study cities. As with the discussion of riverine flooding, this approach presumes that it is necessary to understand how a city has grown over time in order to clarify the underlying forces driving changes in its coastal flood risk. This involves examining urban development in relation to landscape, technology, and economy – and in response to disaster events.

The chapter focuses on two cities that have been extensively studied by other researchers, New Orleans and New York. New Orleans may very well be the single most richly chronicled urban case study in the hazards and disasters field. Researchers from many disciplines in the natural and social sciences have closely examined Hurricane Katrina (in 2005), its aftermath, and the long-term recovery. Not only that, but the story of New Orleans – in which hurricanes and coastal flooding feature prominently – has been told through multiple books by urban geographers and environmental historians. Urban scholars have extensively studied New York City, too, though prior to Hurricane Sandy (in 2012) there had been comparatively little attention paid to coastal hazards. This chapter draws on the abundance of documentation on these two cities to examine the question: How did coastal flood risk change over time?

Beyond their specifics, these two cases are also useful for drawing more generalized insights on disaster risk dynamics in the coastal context. The argument here is not that they are "typical"; both are indeed quite singular, and it is not

[8] Since tides are caused by the gravitational pull of the moon and sun, their heights vary throughout the day and year. At any coastal location, tidal height is also influenced by offshore water depth, coastal landforms, and other local factors; hence, tidal ranges are both highly predictable and very location-specific.

clear by what measure any city could be considered "typical." Rather, New Orleans and New York City provide contrast within a broadly similar framework. Both are US cities with similarly long histories, located in areas at risk of not infrequent coastal storms. However, they differ in three potentially critical ways: in urban size (and associated growth trajectory); in economy; and in setting, with New Orleans being on a major delta dominated by the Mississippi River and New York located on an estuary. Following the two case studies, the chapter will revisit the guiding questions of urban development and disaster risk in order to consider whether these coastal cases confirm, refute, or complicate the propositions suggested in Chapter 3.

4.2 New Orleans

The Mississippi River drains 3.2 million km^2 of land and about 40% of the continental USA; unsurprisingly, its delta is dominated by riverine processes. Over thousands of years, the river has deposited sediment at its mouth at a much greater rate than ocean waves and currents can remove them. Where the river meets the sea has thus moved substantially over millennia. As sedimentary deposits created new land, the coastline advanced outward. Over time, the river's main channel and distributaries, winding through the delta landscape, would shift course, sometimes abruptly: "Delta lobes formed as river channels elongated and bifurcated and were ultimately abandoned through a process of upstream avulsion in favor of shorter routes to sea level"; even then, the abandoned channels often remained connected, forming "a skeletal framework of interconnected distributary channels and natural levee ridges." Such ridge features in the landscape, while subtle, help to protect interior wetlands from storm surge, waves, and saltwater intrusion. On occasion, the river would break through a weak spot in a natural levee along its banks, forming a crevasse and depositing sediment atop land in the area. At its historic maximum, the Mississippi River delta comprised 25,000 km^2 of marshes, forested wetlands, shallow water bodies, and low-relief uplands.[9]

Prior to European colonization, the delta was inhabited by semi-nomadic, hunter-gatherer Indigenous populations who adapted to the landscape and its hazards in many ways. For example, "because flooding by the river and by hurricanes occurs in different seasons in Louisiana, and because the availability of migratory food sources is also predictable, native peoples found higher ridges of the delta to be good sites for villages and temporary camps." They "negotiated the watery semi-earth by shoring up elevations through middens and other anthropogenic

[9] (Day et al., 2019; Day & Hunter, 2022; Twilley et al., 2016). See also National Park Service: www.nps.gov/miss/riverfacts.htm. Quote is from (Day et al., 2019, p. 168).

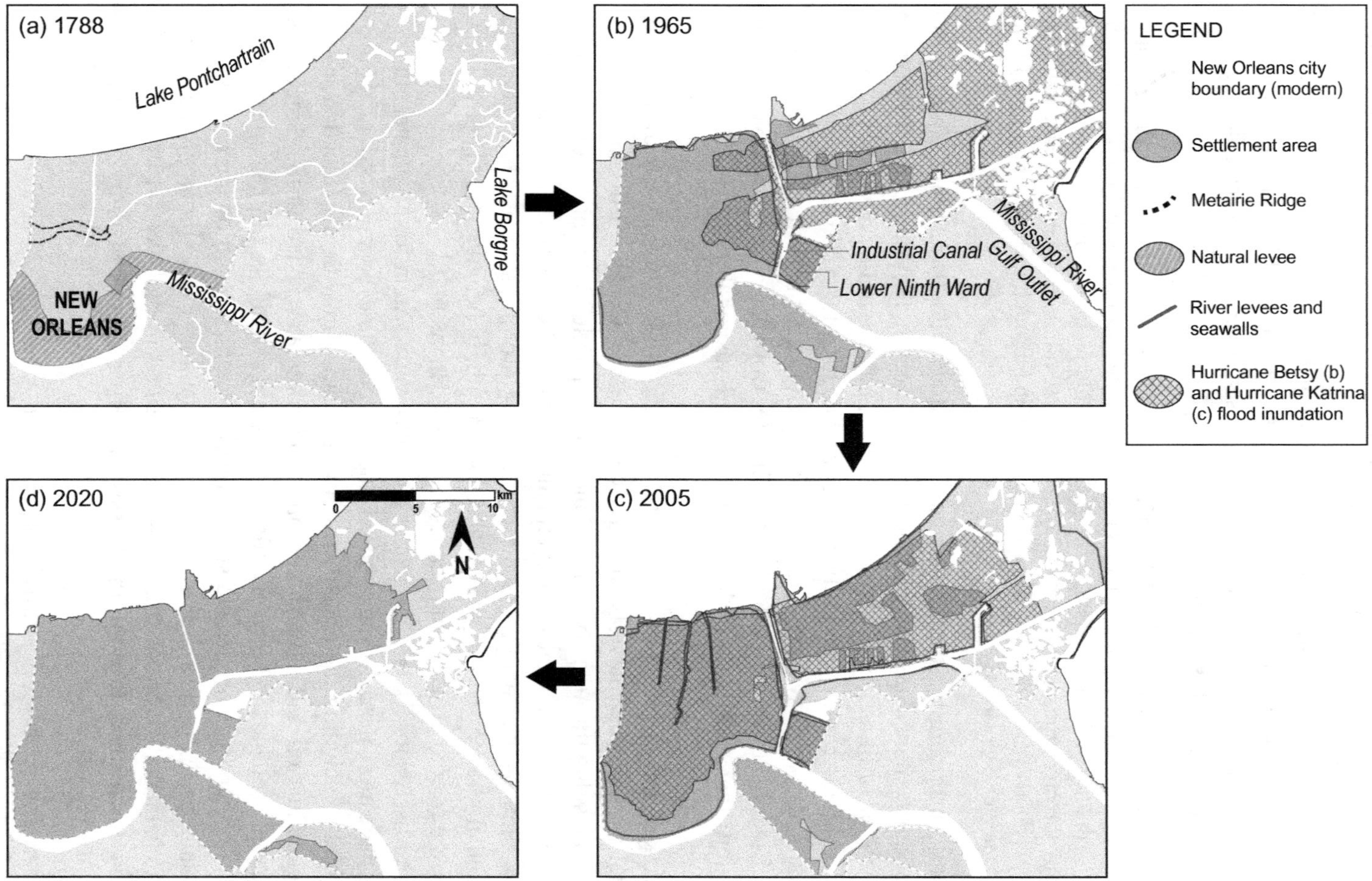

Figure 4.1 New Orleans, urban expansion 1788–2020. (Data based on: Campanella, 2010; Colten & Giancarlo, 2011; Colten & Sumpter, 2009; Halpin & Varuso, n.d.; Encyclopædia Britannica, Inc., 2024b; Kates et al., 2006. Maps by Charlotte Milne.)

topography, or adapting to the environment by shifting to higher ground when high water came."[10]

To sustain this vast deltaic landscape, ongoing supplies of sediment are needed to offset soil compaction and natural ground subsidence, which can be as much as 1.5 cm per year in parts of the delta, as well as sea-level rise. Riverine flood events play a major role in this replenishing:

> Historically, seasonal overbank flooding, crevasse formation, and minor distributaries introduced large amounts of river water with associated sediments and nutrients into the interdistributary basins of the [Mississippi River Delta] plain, forming and sustaining wetlands by directly promoting vertical accretion and providing nutrients that enhance vegetation productivity and result in organic soil formation through increased root growth and organic matter deposition.[11]

Perhaps surprisingly, storms also contributed to land formation. While storm surges during hurricanes can cause substantial erosion, they can also deposit large amounts of sediment onto coastal wetlands. Indeed, studies have found that on balance: "[Hurricanes] generally do not produce long-term detrimental impacts to unmodified coastal systems and they often provide net benefits (e.g., redistribution of sediments into interior areas, freshwater from heavy rains to offset salinity intrusion) that contribute to long-term wetland sustainability, habitat diversity, and vegetation productivity."[12]

The key here is "unmodified" coastal systems – the picture is very different for coastal wetlands that have been heavily altered and weakened by human activities. Canals dug through coastal wetlands, for example, focus high-velocity water flows during storms. Constructed embankments impede floodwaters from depositing sediments, hamper drainage after flooding, prolong saltwater intrusion, and, through all these effects, inhibit vegetation growth. In heavily altered coastal wetlands, the overall effect of hurricanes is indeed detrimental.[13]

The Mississippi River delta reached its maximum extent in the nineteenth century; thereafter, its dynamics shifted and the coastline began receding. Human activities – including the construction of upstream dams, flood protection levees, dredging, and oil and gas exploration – had cumulatively led to the degradation of coastal wetlands. The river today carries about half its prior sediment load. Instead of hundreds of active distributaries, large and small, flowing over the deltaic plain, there are now only two (the main channel of the Mississippi River and the Atchafalaya River). Wetland loss rates peaked in the 1960s–1980s and have slowed down since. Overall, the Mississippi River delta lost some 5,000 km^2 of

[10] Quote "because flooding …" is from (Day et al., 2019, p. 170). Quote "negotiated the watery semi-earth …" is from (Campanella, 2016, p. 3).

[11] (Day & Hunter, 2022, p. 8). [12] (Day & Hunter, 2022, p. 15). [13] (Day & Hunter, 2022).

coastal wetlands over the twentieth century – "coastal waters have submerged 25% of this productive delta, as the Gulf of Mexico moves slowly inland closer to human settlements that were developed in their present location nearly 300 years ago."[14]

* * *

New Orleans, the major urban settlement on the Mississippi River delta, does not front the open ocean. When French colonizers established the city in 1718, decades before the American Revolution in 1776, they chose a site some 150 km above the river's mouth. The site was strategically advantageous on several levels (Figure 4.1). Broadly speaking, "a city near the mouth of North America's greatest river positioned French colonials to defend and exploit the unknown riches of the vast Mississippi Valley from Spanish and English interests." The delta's position as a nexus for waterborne transportation along both river and ocean was clearly a paramount reason for founding a colonial city there. The specific upriver site that was chosen provided a relatively safe "back door" route for navigation: "Rather than sailing up a hundred treacherous miles of the lower Mississippi (the 'river route') amid fog and debris, against the current, and sometimes against the wind, voyagers could instead traverse the usually calm waters of the Mississippi Sound … into the protected waters of Lake Pontchartrain, and up a small rivulet" to a portage and the elevated natural levee on a sweeping bend of the river; moreover, this site also had "slightly upraised land, fine soils, a well-positioned perch for river defense, and deep water for the docking of ships." The specific town site thus reflected technological considerations of the age of sail.[15]

But while the location was strategically advantageous, it was also inherently problematic from a hazards standpoint. The land was low and the water table high, with abundant surrounding swamps. Moreover, the region was prone to flooding from the river and from storms. But these limitations were secondary considerations, outweighed by the commercial advantages of the city's strategic location.[16]

The original town site was established on the higher ground of a natural levee. Before the construction of artificial levees,

> floods regularly delivered huge amounts of sediment-laden water to the floodplain lining the river. As water escaped the river channel, it slowed, allowing coarser sands and sediments to settle near the channel. This process created a band of higher, well-drained ground, known as the natural levee, adjacent to the waterway – about 15 feet [5 m] above

[14] (Day & Hunter, 2022). Model-based analysis suggests that levees and resource extraction have been more important sources of land loss than dam construction (Edmonds et al., 2023). Quote is from (Twilley et al., 2016, p. 713).

[15] Quote "a city near the mouth …" is from (Campanella, 2016, p. 3). Quote "Rather than sailing …" is from (Campanella, 2010, p. 16), and "slightly upraised land …" is from p. 17.

[16] See (Campanella, 2016; Colten, 2005) and a more detailed discussion in (Campanella, 2010, ch. 5).

sea level in New Orleans … The overall topography of the city forces water to flow away from the river, towards the brackish Lake Pontchartrain, but the absence of slope and the intervening ridges created a massive wetland between the city and the lake.[17]

Topography in New Orleans is subtle, and the subtleties are critical from the perspective of both urban development history and flood risk.

New Orleans is an old city by American standards. In 1812, when Louisiana became a US state, the city had a population of 17,000. Within three decades, by 1840, it had over 102,000 people – making it the third largest city in the country, and the fourth largest commercial port in the world (after London, Liverpool, and New York). Its economy was tied to the trade and transport of agricultural goods, including cotton, rice, and sugar. In the era of steamboats, New Orleans flourished as the major port connecting river and sea transportation in the American south. By 1860, just prior to the Civil War, New Orleans' population had grown to 175,000 people. In 1910, it reached some 340,000. By that time, however, New Orleans' national importance had already been declining as water transport gave way to railroad; many other cities were also rapidly urbanizing, and New Orleans' relative rank among US cities had dropped to 15th.[18]

Through these decades, urban development in the city proceeded according to "a set of conditions and unwritten rules": "The first condition was immediate adjacency to an already urbanized area. The appeal to pedestrians of minimal walking distances encourage new developments to occur quite literally across the street from existing ones … Roads, canals, and railroads diminished the need for immediate adjacency, broadening the 'rule' to include accessibility."[19]

Beyond this, land "needed to be high and dry before urban development could occur":

For most of the city's first two centuries, this important topographic rule restricted it to the crescent-shaped natural levee of the Mississippi River and, to a lesser extent, the smaller Esplanade and Metairie-Gentilly ridges. The natural levee crested at 10 to 15 feet above sea level near the riverfront (the "front-of-town") and sloped downward to uninhabited swamp and marshland, which lay inches above sea level.[20]

To be converted to urban uses, the land also had to be legally and financially acquirable; for example, landowners would often sell plantation land to developers only when economic pressures had driven up land prices to a sufficiently profitable level. Areas tended to be developed for wealthier residents in the upstream direction, where there was broader terrain, proximity to affluent and amenity-rich

[17] (Colten, 2002, p. 241).
[18] For economy, see (Colten, 2005). For a detailed chronology of New Orleans' urban history, including population growth, see (Campanella, 2010). For connection to rail versus water transport, see (Zaninetti & Colten, 2012).
[19] (Campanella, 2010, pp. 36–38). [20] (Campanella, 2010, p. 38).

neighborhoods, and distance away from refuse dumped into the river. Meanwhile, areas close to "nuisances" – railroad tracks, swamps, dumps, high crime, and poverty – tended to be downstream, and these areas were developed for commercial and industrial uses or lower-income residences. In this direction, it was "no coincidence that the Lower Ninth Ward ended up as one of the city's poorest and most isolated neighborhoods, and among the slowest to urbanize."[21]

Throughout this period, the danger of flooding from both river and hurricanes was ever-present. After New Orleans' founding in 1718, the Mississippi River flooded in 1719 and a hurricane struck in 1722. The latter destroyed much of the nascent town, providing a "clean slate" for an improved realignment of its streets and land parcels. This restart was possible because at the time "there was so little invested in what was lost that bold new plans – for new flood control and orderly urban planning – were able to move forward in the aftermath."[22]

Many more hydrometeorological disasters followed. Tropical storms swept through frequently, on average more than once per decade, causing mainly wind damage but limited flooding, thanks to the buffering effects of healthy wetland expanses in that era. Damaging floods from the river and/or lake also occurred on average more than once a decade. In 1849, the largest of these flooded 220 city blocks; the city enacted a special tax to fund infrastructure repairs.[23]

One flood disaster that took place in 1871 was particularly instructive. Upstream of the city, the river had created a crevasse and discharged floodwater into the lake; however, unusual winds pushed the excess water back toward the city. Funneled into a navigational waterway, the New Basin Canal that had been built in the 1830s, the floodwaters caused levee failure and major flooding in the city – and served as "an early example of how ungated manmade canals can expose urban populations to flood hazards by inviting external waters into the metropolis, which was the essential circumstance of the Hurricane Katrina flood of 2005."[24]

In response to the persistent flood threat, for many decades, local levees were constructed and episodically enhanced. Over time, however, the scale of the problem and economic interest became great enough to involve the federal government. The US Congress enacted legislation, the Swamp Lands Acts of 1849 and 1850, that enabled Louisiana to "collect revenue from the sale of swamplands and apply it to levee improvements."[25]

> Over the next century, this law would lead to the reclamation of sixty-five million acres of wetlands, producing wealth but also luring people into flood plains and setting up for inevitable flood losses. In Louisiana, the act helped pave the way for extractive and developmental activity in wetlands and marshes, which created jobs and revenue but

[21] (Campanella, 2010); quote is from p. 41. [22] (Campanella, 2016); quote is from p. 6.
[23] (Campanella, 2016). [24] (Campanella, 2016); quote is from p. 15. [25] (Colten, 2005, p. 30).

also environmental losses through canal excavation and the impounding and drainage of swamps. As a result of these actions, the source of flood threat for New Orleanians would gradually shift from the Mississippi River to the Gulf of Mexico.[26]

The federal government also created the Mississippi River Commission in 1879, which was charged with working with the Army Corps of Engineers to develop a consistently designed levee system that could facilitate river navigation as well as flood control. Effectively, this shifted the cost and responsibility of building and maintaining levees away from state and local authorities to the federal government. By the 1890s, the Army Corps had adopted a "levees-only" policy and "proceeded to realign, heighten, and strengthen the earthen dykes, eschewing all forms of spillways and lateral water storage to the point of sealing off natural distributaries" – an approach that "largely severed the river from its deltaic distributaries and the adjacent wetlands." After these major engineering works, the hazard of river flooding seemed diminished for some decades.[27]

Among the city's population, the poor tended to be the most vulnerable to flooding. "Recent arrivals to the city, with few financial resources, generally occupied the least desirable districts, which were also the least expensive and lowest in elevation." Moreover, "improvements to the river levee system deflected flooding from the wealthy neighborhoods and concentrated inundations to the city's margins," for example, impacting subsistence populations on lakefront homes built on stilts.[28]

It is worth noting that flooding was not the only environmental hazard that New Orleans faced in the eighteenth and nineteenth centuries. Other types of threats could be even more catastrophic – yet the city recovered each time. An urban conflagration in 1788 burned 80% of the city to the ground; it was followed by a construction boom in what is today the city's central business district. A destructive 1794 blaze was followed by regulations requiring more fire-resistant construction materials. Disease outbreaks – cholera, malaria, dengue, yellow fever – were frequent, and epidemics could take thousands of lives. A yellow fever episode in 1853 killed as many as 10% of the city's residents. Indeed, the 1849 flood "may have actually saved lives. Only months earlier, cholera plagued the populace, but floodwaters and heavy rains had washed away filthy stagnant pools" and death rates were subsequently observed to have actually declined. In spite of all these hazards and disasters, the city remained and continued to expand.[29]

* * *

[26] (Campanella, 2016, p. 11).

[27] See (Colten, 2005). Quote "proceeded to realign …" is from (Campanella, 2016, p. 17). Quote "largely severed …" is from (Day et al., 2019, p. 171).

[28] (Colten, 2006, p. 732). [29] (Campanella, 2016); quote "may have actually saved lives …"is from p. 10.

According to the decennial census, the population in New Orleans continued to grow until it peaked in 1960 at some 627,000 people. In the early twentieth century, vast reserves of oil and gas were discovered under the coastal marshes of Louisiana, and an oil boom helped fuel economic growth from the 1920s. During this era of substantial growth, several important changes occurred that enabled the city to accommodate hundreds of thousands of new people – most notably (from the perspective of flood risk), changes to flood management infrastructure, the drainage of swamplands, and the development of municipal water and wastewater infrastructure systems. These were at one level technical projects, but they also entailed profound socioeconomic ramifications.[30]

In 1927, a catastrophic flood on the Mississippi River caused numerous levee failures and inundated over 70,000 km^2 of land across multiple states, displacing over a million people. The disaster effectively "destroyed the illusion of 'control' behind the levees-only policy, and replaced that ill-advised strategy with a more sustainable policy of accommodating the will of the river." It catalyzed a new approach that involved multiple tactics besides enhancing levees, in particular, dams and other structures to control and store excess water upstream, as well as floodways and spillways – emergency flood outlets – along the river. These large engineering works have been successful in preventing major riverine floods in New Orleans; however, the major floodways "have trapped a vast amount of sediment that would have otherwise reached coastal wetlands."[31]

Two major hurricanes that hit New Orleans during the first half of the twentieth century provide a window into how the underlying urban development patterns were altering the landscape of risk. The Great Storm of 1915 caused surges 5–7 m high on the Gulf coast and 2 m high on Lake Pontchartrain, along with levee breaks, lowland flooding in the city, wind damage to thousands of structures, and 275 deaths. Floodwaters for the most part receded naturally, but in areas surrounded by levees, the waters sat for days until pumped out. Yet considering the strength of the hurricane, "the marvel of the Great Storm of 1915 was not the extent of its damage, but its limit." The main response was further flood control measures along the lake.[32]

Another major hurricane struck in 1947. In the intervening decades, two navigational channels, the Industrial Canal and the Gulf Intracoastal Waterway, had been constructed to support the city's economically important shipping and shipbuilding industries. "Both manmade waterways allowed surge water to enter

[30] For oil boom, see (Horowitz, 2020).

[31] (Campanella, 2016); quote "destroyed the illusion ..." is from p. 21. Quote "have trapped a vast amount of sediment ..." is from (Day et al., 2019, p. 171). Over 100 dams were constructed in the upstream Missouri river basin through the 1950s and 1960s (Day et al., 2021).

[32] (Campanella, 2016); quote is from p. 20.

unimpeded from the north via the lake and the east via the Gulf." Despite 51 deaths and $100 million in damages, the primary response to this event was, as before, further enhancements of the flood protection levees along the lake and marshes.[33]

The most consequential changes in the early twentieth century for flood risk, however, were the city's initiatives to drain wetlands and to construct new water and wastewater infrastructure systems. A Sewerage and Water Board was established in 1899 to oversee drainage, potable water, and sewer service provision. Piped potable water replaced cisterns that had served as mosquito breeding grounds. By 1930, virtually the entire city was served by the municipal sewerage system. The public health benefits – for example, lowered mortality rates – were rapid and substantial. In terms of drainage,[34]

> the Sewerage and Water Board proceeded to build a world-class system. It used natural topography to collect runoff via an intricate system of gutters, pipes, and below-ground canals leading to massive lift pumps, which would propel the water through newly excavated and/or widened outfall canals and into Lake Pontchartrain or other adjacent water bodies. By the early 1900s, the system commenced removing impounded swamp water and lowering the ground water.[35]

At one point, levees were constructed "not along the shoreline of Lake Pontchartrain but 3,000 feet into the lake … to reclaim the land between the new levee and old lake shoreline for a series of new residential subdivisions (and later a branch of the state university and modern airport)." By 1925, the system drained an area of some 120 km^2.[36]

Draining the backswamps, a form of land reclamation, opened up substantial tracts of land for new development. "A land rush from the old riverside city into trendy, new lakeside suburbs ensued; assessed property value citywide grew during 1900–14 by 80 percent." Over time, New Orleans was transformed "from a compact riverside crescent in the late 1800s to a spread-eagled triparish conurbation by the late 1900s. Municipal drainage preceded every expansion." The new subdivisions were encouraged by "authorities who saw taxable real estate, developers who eyed lucrative house-building opportunities, bankers eager to lend mortgages, and upwardly mobile white middle-class families, who would settle into [racially] segregated subdivisions." More broadly, urban expansion responded to the pressures for new housing and infrastructure to accommodate population and economic growth.[37]

[33] See (Campanella, 2016; Youngman, 2015). Quote is from (Campanella, 2016, p. 16).
[34] For water and wastewater infrastructure, see (Colten, 2002). [35] (Campanella, 2016, p. 18).
[36] (Burby et al., 2006; Campanella, 2010). Quote "not along the shoreline …" is from (Burby et al., 2006, p. 55).
[37] Quotes "A land rush …" and "from a compact riverside crescent …" are from (Campanella, 2010, p. 76). Quote "authorities who saw …" is from (Campanella, 2016, p. 18).

Drainage, and the opening of new lands for development, also impacted racial segregation within the city, particularly for historically marginalized black populations. "The first population realignment in response to drainage was the expansion of Blacks into low-lying areas to the rear of the city." At the same time, newly drained lakefront areas became almost entirely populated by whites, an outcome of city policies and discriminatory real estate practices (eventually outlawed in the 1950s). The overall effect was the establishment of "racially segregated districts in areas vulnerable to hurricane-driven storm surges." Moreover, "in general, the poor remained in the city and often occupied low areas vacated by those leaving for the newer suburbs."[38]

The major infrastructure improvements of this era of substantial growth also had the unplanned effect of aggravating the risk from hurricanes and floods:

> Until the late 19th century, New Orleans was still almost completely above sea level, albeit by only a few meters. Over the course of the 20th century, the city spread into adjacent wetlands as they were leveed, large pumps were put in place, and the wetlands were drained. As a consequence, the city expanded from the relatively high natural levees adjacent to the river out to the edge of Lake Pontchartrain as well as up and down river from the original footprint of the city. Unfortunately, this had two unintended and ultimately catastrophic consequences. First, wetlands, especially baldcypress swamps, that served to reduce hurricane surge and waves were lost to urban development. Second, the draining of highly organic wetland soils exposed them to oxidation and subsidence. Because of this, the city is now up to 5m below sea level.[39]

The population became increasingly dependent on the system of pumps and levees for flood protection.

* * *

In the decades between 1960 and 2005 (the year of Hurricane Katrina), the population of New Orleans declined – by over 170,000 people to 455,000 residents. These figures pertain to New Orleans proper (Orleans Parish), and much of the city's loss reflected an exodus to nearby suburban parishes in the metropolitan area, which continued to grow overall. For the city itself, the population loss "had the effect of shifting fiscal and political power outwardly into suburban parishes, while leaving disinvestment, a lower tax base, deprived populations, and deteriorating infrastructure in the inner core … [B]y the 21st century, New Orleans ranked as the thirty-first largest city in the nation – and among its poorest." Many of the suburbanizing populations were white, so that New Orleans' racial composition

[38] Quote "The first population realignment …" is from (Colten, 2002, p. 253). Quote "racially segregated districts …" is from (Colten, 2006, p. 732). Quote "in general, the poor remained …" is from (Kates et al., 2006, p. 14654).

[39] (Day et al., 2021, p. 15).

shifted from about 70% white to nearly 70% black over the course of the twentieth century. The mobility patterns further reflected income and wealth differentials, as "those with means moved to new suburbs, and the poor remained within the core city, generally in the low-lying locations." Economic stagnation, particularly after a downturn in the oil sector in the 1980s, also contributed to New Orleans' long-term decline.[40]

Within New Orleans proper, overall population decline was also accompanied by spatial redistribution in ways that exacerbated flood vulnerability. "Within the city, segregation became much more pronounced … and with it increased vulnerability among the poor black citizens. What had been poor white neighborhoods became poor black neighborhoods, and many were in low areas. The city's Ninth Ward exemplifies this situation."[41]

Middle-class black households "mostly moved lakeward to the neighborhoods east of City Park and thence into the subdivisions of eastern New Orleans." There was a broad pattern of people relocating from higher to lower ground in this period; moreover, since many parts of the suburban parishes are also low-lying, the net effect was an increase in populations vulnerable to hurricane impacts across the metropolitan area.[42]

A key factor in these urbanization trends was Hurricane Betsy in 1965 – or more to the point, the ways in which society responded to that disaster. Betsy, a category 3 storm, was the country's first "billion dollar hurricane." It destroyed over 27,000 houses and displaced more than 300,000 people from their homes. Within New Orleans, over 40% of the land area was inundated. Most of the flooding occurred along three navigation canals that had been constructed in the preceding few decades – the Industrial Canal, Gulf Intracoastal Waterway, and Mississippi River–Gulf Outlet (MR–GO).[43] "Water filled sections of the Seventh, Eighth, and Ninth wards, racially mixed working-class neighborhoods … Hardest hit of all was the Lower Ninth Ward. A series of Industrial Canal levee breaches plus overtopping deluged the poor, mostly black section … Only the streets closest to the Mississippi River – … a majority-white working-class area at the time – evaded the deluge."[44]

[40] Population figure is from (Campanella, 2016). Others have estimated the pre-Katrina population at 437,000; see (Kates et al., 2006). Quote "had the effect of shifting …" is from (Campanella, 2016, p. 25). For racial composition shift, see (Colten, 2006). Quote "those with the means …" is from (Kates et al., 2006, p. 14654).

[41] (Colten, 2006, p. 732).

[42] Quote "mostly moved lakeward …" is from (Campanella, 2016, p. 25). For increase in hurricane-vulnerable population, see (Colten & Sumpter, 2009).

[43] The US National Weather Service estimates that Hurricane Betsy caused $1.42 billion in damages, in 1965 dollars (not adjusted for inflation). Adjusted for inflation, it was the 10th most costly hurricane in the country's history, as of 2010 (Blake et al., 2011). For storm impacts, see (Colten & Sumpter, 2009; Kates et al., 2006).

[44] (Campanella, 2016, p. 24).

Society responded to the disaster by intensifying prior strategies of flood protection. The 1965 Flood Control Act put the federal government "in the business of storm protection" and included provisions for the Lake Pontchartrain and Vicinity, Louisiana, Hurricane Protection Project. In general,[45]

> federal, state, and local efforts proceeded to strengthen levees around the basins flooded by Betsy, expand residential developments into them, augment the very canals that ushered Betsy' surge inland, and design new levees to standards that Betsy demonstrated to be obsolete. The project was never fully funded and only partially executed, but enough flood-protection devices were installed to greenlight urbanization into ever lower-lying and far-flung areas.[46]

Twice as much land was now protected by the expanded levee system in New Orleans, available for development. Notably, this territorial expansion was not incidental; rather, it was central to the project's business case:[47]

> These levees would help prevent a recurrence of the losses experienced from Hurricane Betsy, and, more important, they would facilitate continued urbanization of this very hazardous region. In fact, protection of *existing development* accounted for only 21 percent of the benefits needed to justify the project. An extraordinary 79 percent were to come from *new development* that would now be feasible with the added protection provided by the improved levee system.[48]

Development followed, with some of the fastest growth in the city in these newly protected areas; what's more, "construction of higher levees after Betsy exaggerated the bowl-like qualities of the encircled urban area … As the city drained the newly fortified suburban tracts, land surfaces sank from near to well below sea level."[49]

Soon after Hurricane Betsy, the US Congress passed key legislation in the form of the 1968 National Flood Insurance Act. Previously, insurance companies had for the most part refused to include flooding in standard policies, having "retreated from the market following the great 1927 Mississippi River flood." The availability of flood insurance may have served as another factor underlying households' willingness to move into low-lying areas. By the time Hurricane Katrina hit, New Orleans had one of the highest flood insurance rates in the country, at 67%.[50]

In brief, then, societal response to Hurricane Betsy served to intensify risk: "Although the city proper lost population between 1965 and 2005, the urban region experienced new development and population growth directly into areas flooded

[45] (Campanella, 2010, p. 109). [46] (Campanella, 2016, p. 24).
[47] For land protected by expanded levee system, see (Kates et al., 2006).
[48] (Burby, 2006, pp. 174–175). See also (Horowitz, 2020). [49] (Colten & Sumpter, 2009, p. 361).
[50] Quote "retreated from the market …" is from (Knowles & Kunreuther, 2014, p. 327). For insurance and household behavior, see discussion in (Burby, 2006). For insurance rates at the time of Hurricane Katrina, see (Horowitz, 2020).

by Betsy, and concurrent loss of population density in areas that experienced the least flood damage in 1965 … Population movement into low areas offset structural projects to reduce hurricane impacts."[51]

* * *

In 2005, Hurricane Katrina struck as a category 3 storm with severe winds, record rainfall, and an extreme storm surge. Water in Lake Pontchartrain rose by 3 m and in New Orleans' canals by 4–5 m. The MR–GO and Gulf Intracoastal Waterway funneled surge into the Industrial Canal, where a floodwall failed, leading to inundation of much of the Lower Ninth Ward. Floodwalls were also damaged along other canals, "allowing water to surge into ~80% of the city and essentially fill the bowl to depths ranging from 5 cm to 5 m." Some 1,200 people died as a direct result of Hurricane Katrina, mostly in New Orleans. While perhaps 1 million residents in the metropolitan area had evacuated before the storm, within the city of New Orleans, roughly 100,000 had stayed. Many lacked the means to evacuate. Low-income populations, who were disproportionately black, were especially hard hit: "Not only did many live in low-lying areas, but evacuation plans relied on private automobiles that left many poor residents to endure the impact of the hurricane-induced flooding."[52]

Katrina was by far the costliest hurricane in US history up until that point, causing over $108 billion in property damage (in 2005 dollars). In the city of New Orleans, over 70% of homes were damaged. While damage in the historic district, situated on the higher ground of the natural levee, was "mostly wind driven and repairable," in neighborhoods developed in the twentieth century near the lake and eastward, flood damage was "utterly devastating."[53]

Hurricane Katrina accelerated New Orleans' population decline. The number of residents shrank not only in the city proper but in the metropolitan area as a whole. A few months after the storm, around one-third of the population in the metropolitan region – and approximately two-thirds in the city proper – had been displaced. Recovery was slow. Population loss was experienced not only in areas that had been flooded but also in some others that had not, due to loss of jobs. The most

[51] (Colten & Sumpter, 2009, pp. 360–361).

[52] For storm impacts, see (Campanella, 2016; Gramling et al., 2011). Quote "allowing water to surge …" is from (Kates et al., 2006, p. 14654). Early estimates put the death toll in Louisiana at 1,570; see (Kates et al., 2006); the revised figure of 1,200 is from (Blake et al., 2011). Quote "not only did …" is from (Colten, 2006, p. 731).

[53] Storm damage figures are from (Blake et al., 2011; Olshansky et al., 2008). The cost figure is for Hurricane Katrina as a whole and is not limited to New Orleans. One early estimate for New Orleans indicated "an aggregate monetary loss of around $40–50 billion in Orleans Parish including direct property losses ($20–22 billion), still ongoing economic losses ($4–8 billion), and emergency assistance ($16–20 billion)" (Kates et al., 2006, p. 14655). Quotes "mostly wind driven …" and "utterly devastating" are from (Campanella, 2010, p. 152).

socially vulnerable population groups, including the poor, elderly, and minorities, tended to have the lowest rates of return. The only part of the metropolitan area that saw population growth after Katrina was a suburban parish located on the north shore of Lake Pontchartrain, outside of the Mississippi delta. In the ensuing decade, a number of older, lower-income, flooded neighborhoods in the city gentrified, as reflected in post-Katrina increases in housing prices and residents' educational levels.[54]

Compared with 455,000 before the storm, New Orleans' population had rebounded to 384,000 by 2020, or around its level in 1920, a century earlier. The footprint of the urbanized area remained, however, so that, overall, the flooded neighborhoods became less densely populated. The depopulation shifts following Katrina "resulted in a less flood-prone settlement pattern" in the ensuing years, from the perspective of the absolute number and share of people living below sea level: "Katrina has pushed population growth towards higher ground and concentrated the population loss in the neighborhoods that suffered inundation due to the higher costs of restoring damaged properties."[55]

Reconstruction and recovery following Hurricane Katrina proceeded in a largely unplanned fashion. Prior to the disaster, the city had not only weak urban planning institutions but also low public trust in planning. For example, the city had no comprehensive plan (a long-range policy document to guide urban development) and its zoning ordinance was outdated. Its city planning department focused on procedures rather than on shaping the direction of the city's future; developers "took their proposals directly to the city council … A history of bribery and corruption marred the entire planning process." Scholars have noted:[56]

> Following a disaster is not the ideal time to initiate planning. Without a basic planning infrastructure in place, post-disaster planning is more challenging and takes much longer. The best preparation for recovery planning is to have active planning processes beforehand, including networks of well-established community organizations, lines of communication, and a variety of planning documents and tools. This was not the case in New Orleans.[57]

The first effort at a recovery approach, the Bring New Orleans Back (BNOB) plan, suggested "shrinking the footprint" of the city – concentrating reconstruction on higher ground and buying out properties in heavily damaged, low-lying areas in order to restore wetlands that could serve as buffers for storm surge. While rational from a flood risk reduction standpoint, it encountered strong public resistance, and

[54] (Campanella, 2016; van Holm & Wyczalkowski, 2019; Zaninetti & Colten, 2012).
[55] Population figures are from www.census.gov and (Campanella, 2010). For less flood-prone settlement pattern, see (Zaninetti & Colten, 2012); quotes are from pp. 691–692.
[56] For urban planning and post-Katrina recovery, see (Olshansky et al., 2008). Quote "took their proposals …" is from (Blakely, 2012, p. 119).
[57] (Olshansky et al., 2008, p. 278).

"advocates for the city's low-income population came out in force to denounce the BNOB Plan and all planning as the work of the city's power elite to seize the land of the poor."[58]

Subsequent recovery planning efforts did not seek to restrict where rebuilding might be allowed. As noted by urban planner Edward Blakely, who subsequently led the mayor's Office of Recovery Management, "The contest and controversy in planning in New Orleans begins with determining the problem we are trying to solve: floods or social inequality … New Orleans had deep problems prior to Katrina" and "hurricanes are not the central feature that is shaping how the citizens view their future. Local policymakers and citizens see social problems as a larger and more menacing threat to the city's future than floods and levees." Moreover, the federal government's updating of flood insurance maps "sent a message of actuarial encouragement for status quo resettlement" and its homeowner compensation program "provided grant money to do exactly that."[59]

Katrina did instigate further large-scale investments in hurricane protection. By 2011, the Army Corps of Engineers had constructed a $14.5 billion Greater New Orleans Hurricane and Storm Damage Risk Reduction System to protect from a 1 in 100 year storm:

> Unique in the nation, the system comprises closable gates and bypass pumps on the outfall canals, a rock-barrier closing of the MR-GO, an immense, Dutch-style 2.8-kilometer-long barrier across the "funnel" formed by the GIWW and MR-GO, sector and sluice gates on various navigation and drainage canals, the world's largest pumping station … plus heightened and strengthened levees … and floodwalls with deeper-driven sheet piling.[60]

The system performed well in hurricanes that struck the region in 2008 and 2012. In the meantime, lessons had been learned from Hurricane Katrina's failed evacuation efforts, and subsequent evacuation and emergency response planning was more successful.[61]

Outside the city, the state of Louisiana also initiated a Coastal Master Plan in 2007 "to articulate a clear statement of priorities to achieve comprehensive coastal restoration and risk reduction goals" and created the Coastal Protection and Restoration Authority to implement projects and regularly update the plan. In this $50-billion, 50-year program, conventional flood control structures such as levees and pumps would be implemented alongside the restoration of natural processes that would create wetlands and sustain ecosystems in the delta; "the two most important restoration activities are river diversions and marsh creation for land

[58] (Blakely, 2012, p. 123).
[59] Quotes "The contest and controversy …" and "hurricanes are not the central feature …" are from (Blakely, 2012, pp. 122, 123). Quote "sent a message …" is from (Campanella, 2016, p. 30).
[60] (Campanella, 2016, p. 31). [61] (Campanella, 2016).

building in the coastal zone." Projects are selected after model-based analysis of a 50-year future with each potential project in place compared with a future without it; analysis considers project benefits for both reducing land loss and mitigating risk from storm surge. Large-scale sediment diversion projects are planned "to nourish and maintain existing wetlands and to create coastal wetlands over time, in much the same way as southeast Louisiana was originally built by the Mississippi River before levee construction."[62]

4.3 New York City

New York City is located on an estuary at the complex confluence of several waterways where freshwater meets the ocean (Figure 4.2). From the north, the Hudson River drains into the sheltered Upper New York Bay, then southward through a channel, The Narrows, into Lower New York Bay on the coast. The Lower Bay is more exposed to the Atlantic Ocean but partly protected by two barrier spits, Sandy Hook and Rockaway. From the west side, several smaller rivers also join the estuary. On the east side, Upper New York Bay is connected by the East River to another major water body, Long Island Sound, that adjoins the Atlantic Ocean. Daily tides thus flush New York Harbor from both the east and south, and indeed, "the rivers surrounding Manhattan are not exactly rivers as such; the East and Hudson rivers are more like extensions of the sea, rising and falling with the tides … Waters coming up the East River from the harbor meet waters coming through Long Island Sound … As a consequence, there are some very odd tides around Manhattan." Prior to urbanization, the region was a vast archipelago comprised of numerous islands, bays, inlets, and coastal lagoons. Even today, the city's complex coastline is some 840 km long. Of New York City's five boroughs, only the Bronx is situated on what was originally the mainland; the rest of the city was built on islands.[63]

Along the margins of the Lower Bay, the city's southernmost shores largely comprise a low-lying landscape with sandy beaches and dunes. These areas, including the 18 km long Rockaway Peninsula, the Coney Island Peninsula, and the East and South Shores of Staten Island, are especially at risk from storm surges and coastal flooding. The Rockaway Peninsula, which "acts as a barrier shielding

[62] Quote "to articulate a clear statement …" is from (Coastal Protection and Restoration Authority of Louisiana, 2023, p. 2). Ironically, "the first meaningful funding for the Coastal Master Plan" derived from legal settlements after the 2010 BP Deepwater Horizon oil spill in the Gulf of Mexico, most of which were designated for the Coastal Protection and Restoration Authority (Horowitz, 2020, p. 192). Quote "the two most important restoration activities …" is from (Day et al., 2019, p. 172). For project selection, see (Coastal Protection and Restoration Authority of Louisiana, 2023); quote "to nourish and maintain …" is from p. 37. The Mid-Bataria Sediment Diversion project received a key permit in 2022 to proceed with construction.

[63] (City of New York, 2013; O'Neil et al., 2016; Sanderson, 2009). The Hudson River drains an area of 12,800 km^2 (4,940 square miles) (Tarr, 2021). Quote "the rivers surrounding …" is from (Sanderson, 2009, p. 85).

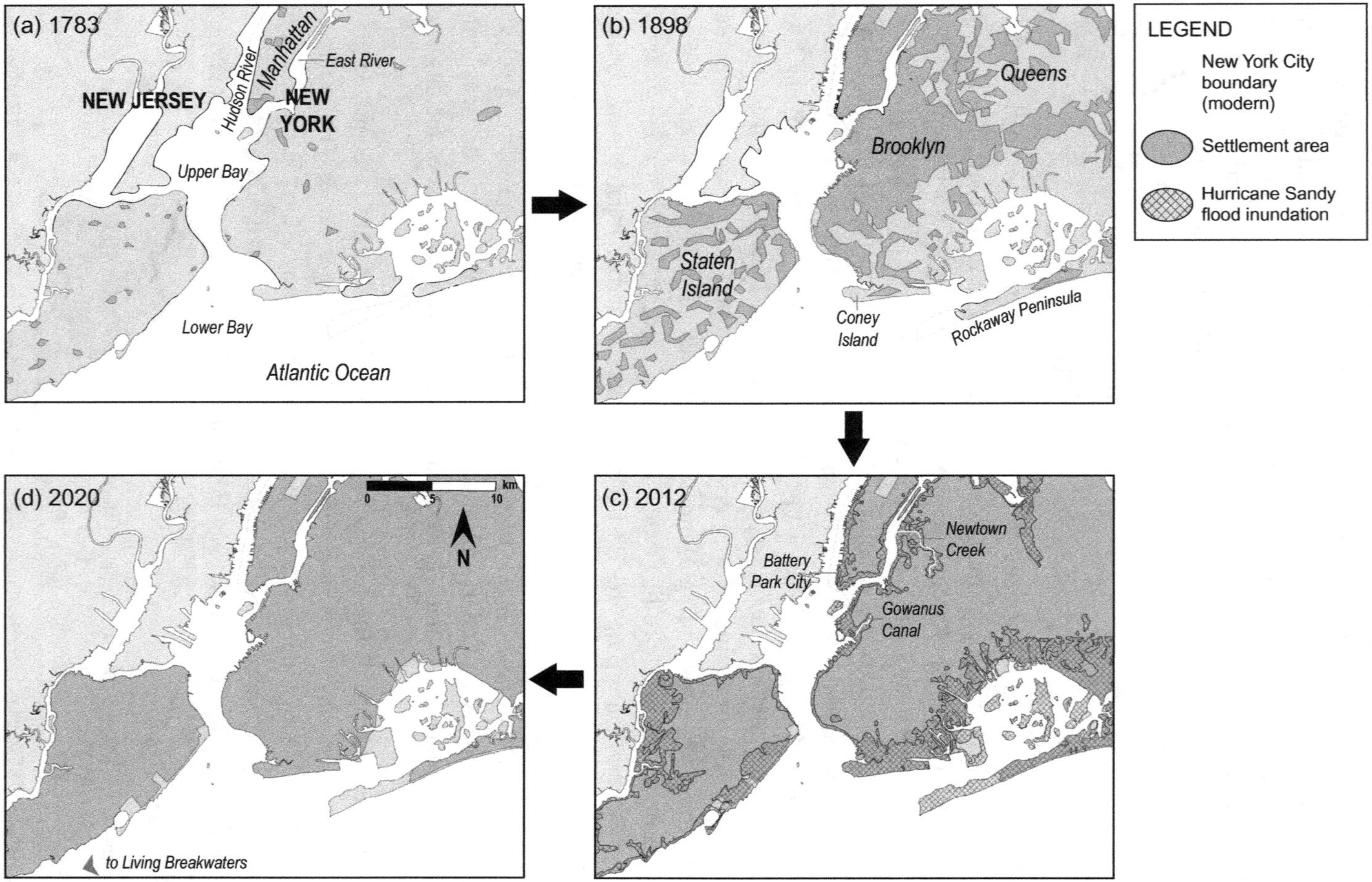

Figure 4.2 New York City, urban expansion 1783–2020. (Data based on: City of New York, 2013; Encyclopædia Britannica, Inc., 2024c; Steinberg, 2014; The New York Public Library, 1776; Wei & Miselis, 2022. Maps by Charlotte Milne.)

the areas lying inland from it, once itself was partially shielded by smaller barrier islands to the south. Over time, though, those smaller islands disappeared, leaving the Peninsula completely exposed to the ocean." Moreover, the landscape is continually evolving: "The natural movement of sediment from east to west along the Rockaway Peninsula over the course of the twentieth century formed what is today the community of Breezy Point – an area built on land that literally did not exist just a short time ago." The Coney Island Peninsula "was once an actual island … reachable only at low tide. The entire area was a collection of wetlands, tidal marshlands, bays, inlets, creeks, and barrier islands." The East Shore of Staten Island was "a vast swath of marshes and swamps" while the South Shore had some hillier ground.[64]

The shoreline along the Upper Bay was, before urbanization, characteristically steeper in topographic profile. Glaciers had carved the fjord-like valley of the Hudson River. "When the last ice sheet began its retreat about twelve thousand years ago, a ridge of rock and sediment was left behind spanning Staten Island and Long Island. Meltwater from the retreating glacier eventually perforated the ridge to produce a narrow channel," The Narrows. At the end of the last ice age, sea levels rose and submerged the low-lying lands, so that the New York Harbor area is sometimes described as a "drowned estuary." The water was deep – over forty feet just offshore of lower Manhattan – and since the Hudson River in its lower reaches around New York City "has no gravity flow …, it has not built up a floodplain."[65]

In this saline environment, tides provide a natural flushing of the waters that once enabled the growth of massive reefs of filter-feeding oysters. A single oyster can filter up to 50 gallons (189 liters) of water per day, and this filtering action benefits the ecosystem by improving water quality. Oyster reefs several meters high once blanketed some 900 km^2 of the estuary, providing important habitat for fish and other shellfish. The rich biodiversity in the waters, as well as on land, provided important food sources for the Indigenous Leni Lenape inhabitants in the region. Moreover, the oyster reefs protected the shoreline by reducing the energy of incoming waves.[66]

* * *

European settlers began colonizing the estuary in the early seventeenth century, with the Dutch establishing an outpost called New Amsterdam on the southern tip of Manhattan in the 1620s. The particular site seems to have been selected for

64 (City of New York, 2013); quotes are from pp. 304, 303, 337, 271. See also (Coch, 2015).

65 See (City of New York, 2013). Quote "when the last ice sheet …" is from (Steinberg, 2014, pp. 3–4). For glacial extent and terminal moraine location, see also (Stanford et al., 2021). Quote "drowned estuary" is from (Steinberg, 2014, p. 3). Quote "has no gravity flow …" is from (Tarr, 2021, ch. 1). For water depth, see (Sanderson, 2009) and (City of New York, 2013).

66 (Brandon et al., 2016; O'Neil et al., 2016; Sanderson, 2009). The "salt front" in the estuary varies seasonally but is generally located north of Manhattan (Sanderson, 2009).

reasons of defensibility, while the estuary as a whole provided deep waters and sheltered harbor on a major navigable river. The region was also rich in plant and animal life; "To the Lenape, the estuary was a gift of simple abundance. To the Dutch, who judged any land in relation to its rivers and bays, New Amsterdam was God's gift to maritime commerce, an activity at which the Dutch had come to excel by the middle of the sixteenth century." The location provided access to the beaver pelt trade of the North American interior, and the town became increasingly important in the transatlantic trading network. New Amsterdam emerged as a "convenient entrepôt for the slave trade in North America and a source of vital supplies for the plantation economies developing to the south."[67]

The Dutch settled on the low-lying wetlands of a hilly, densely forested landscape with abundant streams and springs for fresh water. While centered on the southern part of Manhattan Island, they also colonized other marshlands in areas known today as Gowanus, Flushing Meadows, and Jamaica Bay, as well as New Dorp near Great Kills wetland on Staten Island. In southern Manhattan, they transformed streams into canals to both drain the marshlands and allow small boats access to the town. Along with technologies of town-building, they brought over the colonial institution of land ownership – "the legal right to sell, lease, and bequeath the land." By the time the Dutch ceded the territory to the British in 1664, New Amsterdam was a small town of some 2,500 people.[68]

Renamed New York by the British, the town grew into a prosperous city, the second largest in the American colonies (after Philadelphia), with some 18,000 people by 1760. The British filled in the canals and expanded the shoreline outward, creating new land for city-building and transforming southern Manhattan. A new institutional arrangement, the designation of underwater land as a form of saleable property, enabled this build-out:[69] "The filling of land around the once narrow tip of Lower Manhattan began during colonial times with the sale of water lots. Wharf entrepreneurs could purchase water adjacent to land from the City.

[67] The Dutch purchased the site for 60 guilders from the Lenape in 1626. For discussion, see (Gurwitz, 2019; Steinberg, 2014). For defensibility, see (Steinberg, 2014). Other features of the harbor were also advantageous: It is generally ice-free, has a relatively small tidal range, and can be accessed from both the Lower Bay and Long Island Sound. The in- and out-flow of the tides also helped sailing ships when winds were not favorable. See (Glaeser, 2005; Gurwitz, 2019; Steinberg, 2014). Quote "to the Lenape …" is from (Steinberg, 2014, p. 16). Quote "convenient entrepôt …" is from (Burrows & Wallace, 1999), cited in (Steinberg, 2014, p. 17).

[68] Sanderson (2009), in a detailed reconstruction of the landscape ecology before the imprint of European colonization, estimates that Manhattan Island had 573 hills, 300 springs, 66 miles of streams, and more than 20 ponds. Broad Street and Canal Street today roughly trace two of the Dutch canals (Sanderson, 2009; Steinberg, 2014). Quote "the legal right …" is from (Steinberg, 2014, p. 12). Population figure is from (Gurwitz, 2019).

[69] In New York, this practice began with the 1686 Dongan Charter; at the time, a similar ordinance already existed in Massachusetts (Steinberg, 2014). Underwater land from the Dongan Charter was exhausted within a few decades, and in 1731, "the Crown turned around and made yet another gift of underwater land to the City of New York. This time the grant involved land under water 'four hundred feet beyond low-water mark'" (Steinberg, 2021, ch. 13).

(The City owned "the land" between low and high tides.) After filling the lot with garbage and earth, owners could build wharves into the East River."[70]

Constructing this new land benefited maritime commerce by extending the shoreline into deeper water, thereby allowing larger ships to dock, and by providing more space for warehousing. By the time the American colonies declared independence in 1776, some 30 ha (74 acres) of former marsh or open water had been filled in to create new land in southern Manhattan – almost as much area as had been densely settled in 1695 – but the urban population was still concentrated on just 3% of the entire island.[71]

* * *

In the initial decades after American independence, New York emerged as the leading port and largest city in the country. Its economy was based on maritime trade, both regionally and internationally: "New York City was where consignments of furs, food, wood products, and iron ingots produced in the backcountry were consolidated, insured, documented, and loaded onto seaworthy and adequately manned vessels. It was also where imports destined for purchase by City and hinterland residents were unloaded, inspected, taxed, and dispatched on their way down the regional supply chain."[72] Population tripled between 1790 and 1810, from about 33,000 to over 96,000.[73]

Over the course of the nineteenth century, New York transformed from a mercantile port city to an industrializing metropolis. Transportation technologies were changing rapidly, with the advent of steam power, canals, and railroads; for New York City, the 1825 opening of the Erie Canal was pivotal. The canal provided a water route across upstate New York between Lake Erie and the Hudson River, thereby greatly lowering the cost of transportation between the continent's interior and global markets. Within 15 years of the canal's opening, the port of New York was handling more cargo than rival ports Boston, Baltimore, and New Orleans combined; by 1860, it accounted for nearly half of the nation's grain exports and 60% of total national imports.[74]

New York emerged as a major manufacturing center, specializing in a number of sectors that were related directly or indirectly to the port:[75] "The rise of New

[70] Quote is from (Sanderson, 2009, p. 81). See also map on that page. The fill material comprised "everything imaginable, from sunken ships to stones and trash – anything that could conceivably create solid ground" (Steinberg, 2021, ch. 13).

[71] (Steinberg, 2014). [72] (Gurwitz, 2019, p. 93). [73] (Steinberg, 2014).

[74] For economic transformation, see (Baics & Meisterlin, 2016). For impact of Erie Canal, see www.canals.ny.gov/history/history.html; (Gurwitz, 2019). Shipping channel improvements in New York harbor were also important to the port's viability (Steinberg, 2014). Changes in early nineteenth-century shipping technology, such as larger and specialized vessels, led to the emergence of a hub-and-spoke transportation system, favoring New York as a central port (Glaeser, 2005).

[75] (Gurwitz, 2019).

York's three great manufacturing industries in the 19th century, sugar refining, publishing and the garment trade, depended on New York's place at the center of a transport hub. In all three cases, manufacturing transformed products from outside of the U.S. into finished goods that would be sold within the country."[76]

As these manufacturing sectors grew over time, the city's advantages became self-reinforcing, for example, by attracting skilled workers in those sectors. By the end of the nineteenth century, New York State was producing nearly half of all men's clothing and two-thirds of women's clothing in the country, mostly in New York City. In the latter half of the century, the city's continuing growth "owed at least as much to its role as the entryway for immigrants into the U.S." Commercially, the city emerged as America's financial center. In the 1880s, New York became the first city in the world with a centralized electric power system. The population ballooned, expanding by 50% in nearly every decade. By 1875, New York City had 1 million residents.[77]

Supporting this burgeoning economy and population required major changes to municipal infrastructure services, particularly water supply. With local ponds and streams inadequate and contaminated, the city began looking farther afield for potable water, and "the natural features of the island diminished in importance." In 1842, the new Croton aqueduct system, "one of the great engineering feats of the era, nearly on a par with the Eric Canal," began conveying fresh water to the city from a new dam and reservoir in the mountains over 65 km away. Water consumption soon outpaced supply, however, and a New Croton Aqueduct was constructed in 1890, only to "set the stage for yet more domination over distant waters" as the city's water use continued to escalate.[78]

City-building in the nineteenth century spread out spatially from lower Manhattan northward across the entire island. Early urban development had been constrained: "New York was trapped by water. A pond and broad, sodden marshlands unfolded north of southern Manhattan's dense settlement." As population pressures mounted, city officials issued the consequential Commissioner's Plan of 1811, laying out a gridiron street plan for Manhattan that would shape the city's future physical expansion. With 12 north–south avenues and 155 cross streets, it embodied a highly ambitious vision for urban growth. The 1811 plan served to "prepare Manhattan's vast unbuilt landscape for development and construction, turning it over to speculative real estate markets … New York City became a builder's paradise, offering a largely unrestricted real estate market where (for better or worse) land could be put to its most profitable use." On the plan map, the

[76] (Glaeser, 2005, p. 3).
[77] (City of New York, 2013; Glaeser, 2005; Gurwitz, 2019; Steinberg, 2014; Tarr, 2021). Quote "owed at least as much …" is from (Glaeser, 2005, p. 3).
[78] (Steinberg, 2014); quotes are from pp. 50, 115, 156.

linear route for Twelfth Avenue was superimposed in part over the Hudson River. Building out the city along the lines of the 1811 grid would transform Manhattan's topography, "leveling rugged terrain …; burying rippling streams, glistening ponds, and green marsh; and creating one gargantuan drainage dilemma."[79]

The nineteenth-century expansion of the city was also enabled by technological innovations in mass transit – horse-drawn omnibuses, horsecars, and ultimately electric streetcars – that reduced travel times and costs to get from outer neighborhoods to the downtown core. Streetcar transportation technology thus encouraged suburbanization, often by design: "In many cases, transit companies held real estate interests along the urban fringe, which they connected via streetcar to spur development, even if the line itself was unprofitable." Electric streetcars thus "exacerbated trends that began with the horsecar … In essence, this entailed the general separation between major commercial activities in the downtown and districts of residences and other activities, such as manufacturing, in less dense areas surrounding the core and along the urban fringe. The American walking city … came to an end." As the city expanded northward, by mid century, lower Manhattan had evolved into a well-defined central business district where high land values, commercial specialization, and rising rents drove out residential and industrial activities.[80]

As the city expanded northward, so too did its urbanized shoreline. In the older area of southern Manhattan, the waterfront was dominated by port-related commercial activities; further northward, the shores of the East and Hudson Rivers accommodated industrial uses. The spatial pattern reflected the nineteenth-century shift from a mercantile to an industrial economy, "dynamics by which certain industries no longer located in the central areas but sought out more peripheral lands further north and especially along the rivers. Typically, these included industrial plants with larger spatial demands or those directly benefitting from water access" such as ironworks, meat-packing plants, or shipbuilding.[81]

Urban development also began to take off across the East River in Brooklyn, where the population expanded between 1810 and mid century from 4,400 to 97,000, and by 1880 exceeded half a million people. With space limited on Manhattan, Brooklyn served "as a giant warehouse for various bulk commodities such as lumber, coal, and grain." Here, too, the waterfront was extended out into the river by making new land:[82]

[79] Quote "New York was trapped …" is from (Steinberg, 2014, p. 42). Quote "prepare Manhattan's vast unbuilt landscape …" is from (Baics & Meisterlin, 2016, p. 1155). For Twelfth Avenue, see (Steinberg, 2014). Quote "leveling rugged terrain …" is from (Steinberg, 2021, p. 42).

[80] For technological innovation in urban transportation, see (Young, 2015); quotes are from p. 7. For lower Manhattan, see (Baics & Meisterlin, 2016).

[81] (Baics & Meisterlin, 2016); quote is from p. 1160.

[82] Quote "as a giant warehouse …" is from (Steinberg, 2014, p. 81).

European settlers purchased much of this sprawling land from the Lenape people in the 1630s. At that time, the Waterfront largely consisted of marshlands, marked by navigable creeks and small islands. Eventually property owners and government filled in the marshes and extended and regularized the area's coastline, paving the way – literally – for development, which began in earnest in the 19th century, when the area became a center of shipbuilding, manufacturing, and waterborne commerce. Through this industrial boom, thousands of homes – mostly attached row houses – were built along or near the water to provide shelter to those whose labor was powering the businesses that dotted the area.[83]

Newtown Creek, which runs between present-day Brooklyn and Queens boroughs, began to be heavily industrialized from the 1830s. Its wetlands were filled in, the watercourse channelized and stabilized, and its nature altered "from a natural drainage condition to one … governed largely by engineered and institutionalized systems." With over 50 industrial facilities – "oil refineries, petrochemical plants, fertilizer and glue factories, sawmills, and lumber and coal yards," the creek became heavily polluted. A little further south, marshlands along the Gowanus Creek were replaced by the 1.8-mile-long Gowanus Canal, which allowed vessels inland access from the bay. Opened in 1854, the canal was at one point "among the busiest industrial and commercial inland waterways in the United States," and it, too, came to be severely polluted. The Brooklyn–Queens waterfront that took shape in the nineteenth century was characterized by many low-lying, flood-prone areas.[84]

In the early centuries of New York's urban development, little attention was paid to coastal flood risk, despite settlement on and the making of new low-lying, flood-prone lands. Epidemics of yellow fever, cholera, and other diseases were much more deadly than floods. After a major fire in 1835, real estate boomed and "led inevitably, given the waterfront's importance to commerce, to still more development in the floodplain."[85]

Several damaging hurricanes and storms did occur, but these were infrequent during the period of intense nineteenth-century urban development. A nor'easter came through in 1723 when the city had some 7,000 people. A hurricane estimated at category 3 struck New York in 1788, and another similar-sized one in 1821. These two storms, it turned out, were the largest coastal flooding events that New York City experienced until Hurricane Sandy in 2012. In the 1788 hurricane, flooding caused substantial damage, including "destruction of the Battery seawalls, many wharves, several bridges, and a filling in of many cellars on Lower Manhattan streets." The 1821 hurricane caused similar damage, and reports indicated that "Manhattan was [briefly] cut into two islands along Canal Street … Winds sank or

[83] (City of New York, 2013, p. 239).

[84] Quote "from a natural drainage condition …" is from US Environmental Protection Agency, cited in (Zimring, 2021). Quote "among the busiest …" is from (City of New York, 2013, p. 242).

[85] See (Baics & Meisterlin, 2016; Steinberg, 2014). Quote is from (Steinberg, 2014, p. 80).

de-masted most of the ships in the Harbor. Roof slates and broken glass swept the street, and tree destruction was massive." No major storms struck the city for the next few decades until 1893, when a category 1 hurricane hit the city directly. By this time, New York was a metropolis; the storm caused some damage to high-rise buildings, downed telegraph wires, and disrupted business in the financial center. Damage was most dramatic, however, in the outlying beach areas of the region, where the storm surge "completely destroyed Hog Island, a barrier island that once existed seaward of Rockaway Beach," along with a resort complex on the island.[86]

* * *

New York continued its rapid growth in the decades leading up to World War II. In 1898, the city expanded to its current boundaries by absorbing Brooklyn and the boroughs of Queens, the Bronx, and Staten Island. This consolidation formed a metropolis of some 3.4 million people. In the 1920s, it surpassed London to become the largest city in the world; by 1940, population had further grown to 7.5 million.[87]

Much of New York's critical transportation infrastructure dates to this era of major expansion:

> Over time, as New York City grew, it became increasingly important to link the soon-to-be consolidated boroughs more effectively. Accordingly, in the late 19th and early 20th centuries, the City undertook a major program of bridge-building, completing some of the city's most iconic spans, including the Brooklyn and Manhattan Bridges over the East River. With the same goal in mind, New York City also … open[ed] the first subway line in 1904. The subway system has since expanded to become the largest in the world … As the city continued to expand through the 20th century, [transportation agencies] built four bridges, and two tunnels connecting New Jersey to New York City, and seven bridges and two tunnels within the city.[88]

The region's airports were also constructed in the prewar years of major urban expansion. Much of this infrastructure was built in low-lying districts: "Most area rail and tunnel entrance points and airports lie at elevations of 3 m or less."[89]

After World War II, the city's overall growth trajectory slowed, and for a time declined, in the face of numerous compounding structural challenges. The mass popularization of the automobile and the construction of auto-focused transportation infrastructure were crucial contributors: "By the 1950s, the United States had

[86] (Coch, 2015; Orton et al., 2016; Steinberg, 2014). Given limited historic records, there is disagreement in the literature regarding the size of these events; the 1821 hurricane has also been reported as category 1 or 2 (Coch, 2015; Steinberg, 2014). Quote "destruction of the Battery seawalls …" is from (Orton et al., 2016, p. 8916). Quote "Manhattan was …" is from (Coch, 2015, p. 199). Quote "completely destroyed Hog Island …" is from (Gornitz et al., 2002, p. 66). The 1893 storm has also been estimated as a category 2 hurricane (Coch, 2015).

[87] (NYC Department of City Planning, n.d.; Zimring & Corey, 2021).

[88] (City of New York, 2013, p. 176).

[89] (Gornitz et al., 2002, p. 65).

become 'car country'" with increasingly sprawled suburbs. The rise of trucking sharply lowered the cost of transporting goods and allowed industrial activities to spread out; access to waterways became less important, and manufacturing activities left the city. New York City lost over 600,000 manufacturing jobs in this period. Technological change in the shipping industry, namely containerization, further aggravated the city's deindustrialization trend: "Just as other radical changes in transportation turned the tables of local comparative advantage, so the container encouraged the development of new manufacturing and distribution centers at the expense of old ones" like New York City. Urban challenges compounded, with rising crime rates, deteriorating infrastructure, poor city management, and financial crisis: "Deindustrialization and suburban white flight had left much of the city in a state of impoverishment and reduced tax revenues. By early in 1975 the city was unable to meet its financial obligations" and was going bankrupt. Between 1970 and 1980, the population declined from 7.9 million to 7.1 million. Brooklyn, formerly a leading manufacturing center, was particularly hard hit and suffered a 14% drop in population in this decade.[90]

Deindustrialization was, however, accompanied by the rise of other sectors – most notably, finance, management, and related business services – so that the city's economy turned around in the late 1970s. New York "reinvented itself … as a service city that has become increasingly oriented around finance and corporate management." This transformation was particularly pronounced in Manhattan. For example, between the mid-1960s and 2000, the occupancy of midtown Manhattan office space shifted from 50% corporate headquarters, primarily of manufacturing companies, to mainly financial and law firms. By 2000, the city's population had grown to 8.0 million.[91]

On September 11, 2001, disaster struck in the form of a terrorist attack that caused over 2,700 deaths at the World Trade Center in lower Manhattan. Three large office buildings were destroyed and numerous others damaged – nearly a third of total office space in the downtown area. Citywide, over 300,000 jobs were lost. Yet for the large business service firms that had been clustered in lower Manhattan, "whether the benefits are a wide and deep labour market, proximity to clients and suppliers, or knowledge spillovers from interactions among suppliers, clients and competitors or all three, relocating outside Manhattan was apparently

[90] Quote "by the 1950s …" is from (Young, 2015). Other large and older American cities experienced similar trends. In New York's case, a further aggravating factor was the curtailment of immigration as a result of national policy in the 1920s (Glaeser, 2005). For manufacturing jobs, see (Fainstein & Fainstein, 1987). Quote "just as other radical changes …" is from (Levinson, 2006b, p. 80). Quote "deindustrialization and suburban white flight …" is from (Steinberg, 2021); see also (Glaeser, 2005). For population decline, see (NYC Department of City Planning, n.d.) and (Levinson, 2006b).

[91] (Fainstein & Fainstein, 1987; Glaeser, 2005). Quote "reinvented itself …" is from (Glaeser, 2005, p. 28). For midtown office space, see (Drennan, 2018). Population figure is from (NYC Department of City Planning, n.d.).

not an attractive option." Over 95% of the business and government offices survived by relocating elsewhere within Manhattan or, to a lesser extent, elsewhere within the metro region.[92]

In the decades leading up to Hurricane Sandy in 2012, New York City's coastal land and land uses changed substantially in concert with the city's broad urban economic trends. As far as implications for coastal flood risk are concerned, three patterns are particularly noteworthy: the creation of new land through landfilling; the demise of New York harbor's working docklands; and housing and urban redevelopment along the waterfront.

Through the mid twentieth century, the practice of sanitary landfilling – incorporating solid waste (garbage and other discarded material) in engineered fill – was used to reclaim land in many of the city's low-lying coastal areas, including most of its tidal marshes. This created space for urban infrastructure, development, and amenities: highways, housing, parks, and LaGuardia and Kennedy airports, among others. Between 1935 and 1947, for example, an area of salt marshes equivalent in size to all of Manhattan was reclaimed through sanitary landfilling. By the late twentieth century, of the vast expanses of wetlands that once extended throughout the New York Harbor estuary, only some 20% remained.[93]

Meanwhile in the working harbor areas, the waterfront was being dramatically reshaped by the advent of containerization: "The container got its start in New York Harbor, and within a decade it rendered New York Harbor all but unrecognizable." The old port facilities were by now obsolete and in poor condition, inadequate to the demands of the new technology. Instead, the port authority invested in purpose-built facilities on reclaimed tidal marshlands across the Hudson River in New Jersey, at Port Elizabeth – "a massive construction project: a nine-thousand-foot channel, eight hundred feet wide and thirty-five feet deep …; thousands of feet of wharf frontage; rail lines; and roadways up to a hundred feet wide." The scale of the project could not have been implemented in New York City, where the waterfront was already densely built up. As containerization took off, shipping lines switched en masse to berthing at Elizabeth; "By the middle of the 1970s, the New York City docks were mostly a memory." In the latter twentieth century, large sections of the city's working coastline "fell into disuse and disrepair."[94]

Coastal housing and urban development trends also reflected changing economic conditions and government strategies of urban renewal. Notably, "for

[92] See (Drennan, 2018; Rose, 2017). Quote "whether the benefits …" is from (Drennan, 2018, p. 14). In terms of jobs and business revenues, the impact of 9/11 was felt disproportionately by nonwhite low-wage workers and businesses employing them (Gotham & Greenberg, 2014).

[93] (Steinberg, 2021). Similar loss of marshland occurred across the bay in New Jersey (Squires, 1992). See also (Gornitz et al., 2002; Peabody, 2021; Steinberg, 2014).

[94] For containerization impact, see (Levinson, 2006a); quotes are from pp. 50, 64, 73. Quote "fell into disuse …" is from (City of New York, 2013, p. 40).

much of the 20th century, the urban waterfront was not considered a luxury asset … So many buildings belonging to the New York City Housing Authority wound up on the water precisely because the land was flood-prone and thus of low value." Analysts have identified concentrations of public housing in the coastal floodplain, much of which was built in the 1940s–1960s; for example, Manhattan's low-lying Lower East Side has "26 public housing developments with more than 30,000 residents, nine owned by the NYC Housing Authority (NYCHA), exposing ~21,000 low income and predominantly people of color to the floodplain." Government urban renewal programs in the 1950s–1960s supported public–private initiatives to redevelop some of the city's older districts, "emphatically including urban waterfronts as sites for high-end residential districts." From the 1970s, state law allowed greater private development along the waterfront, while the city's Public Development Corporation (PDC) "developed plans for thirteen waterfront projects that involved platforms extending out into the surrounding waters."[95]

The layering of these trends can be vividly seen in how the southern tip of Manhattan evolved in the decades preceding Hurricane Sandy:

> As maritime activity along the Manhattan shoreline declined, especially after World War II, waterfront buildings and piers fell into disrepair, as did many adjacent inland areas, which were occupied by dilapidated commercial buildings, vacant warehouses, and run-down tenement buildings. In time, the Southern Manhattan shoreline entered an area of transition. Civic leaders recognized that the waterfront could once again become a valuable asset, as a home for parks and new residential and commercial office development.[96]

Battery Park City, a major housing and commercial development project on the western waterfront of Lower Manhattan, was constructed in the 1970s by building new land out into the Hudson River with fill that included excavated soil from the World Trade Center construction site. (With this last major land expansion, in total, nearly 40% of Southern Manhattan is built on some 365 ha or 900 acres of landfill.) For the most part, the waterfront here is a hard edge, "rimmed by a bulkhead wall, which generally fronts on public space."[97]

The devastation of 9/11 in 2001, and the subsequent rebuild, accelerated the pace of change in Lower Manhattan: "The idea to transform LM/BPC [Lower

[95] Quote "for much of the 20th century …" is from (Bellafante, 2022); "26 public housing developments …" is from (Herreros-Cantis et al., 2020, pp. 21–22); "emphatically including urban waterfronts …" is from (Platt, 2013, p. 2); "developed plans …" is from (Steinberg, 2021, ch. 13). For PDC, see also (Fainstein & Fainstein, 1987).

[96] (City of New York, 2013, p. 367).

[97] For Battery Park City, see (Steinberg, 2021, ch. 13). For area of landfill, see (City of New York, 2013). The shoreline at the time of Dutch arrival in 1686 was 3–4 blocks inland from where the waterfront is today (Steinberg, 2014). Quote "rimmed by a bulkhead wall …" is from (City of New York, 2013, p. 368); see also (Gornitz et al., 2002).

Manhattan/Battery Park City] into a tourist destination and a diverse, live/work district was hardly new … but it would take a series of crises – first the recession of 1989–1992, and then 9/11 – to make the idea a reality." In the 2000s, postdisaster redevelopment assistance and economic incentives led to a construction boom in luxury housing in the area; Lower Manhattan/Battery Park City more than doubled its housing stock and experienced the fastest population growth in the city, shifting from a mainly financial district into a mixed-use residential area. In sharp contrast, the Lower East Side and Chinatown – "known for their large, low-income populations, working-class jobs, and the dense concentration of subsidized and relatively affordable housing" – stagnated or declined in the decade following 9/11, in a pattern of uneven redevelopment that analysts have attributed to a range of disaster recovery programs.[98]

Across the East River on the Brooklyn–Queens waterfront, coastal land uses were changing along with the expansion and decline of major industrial activities. In some areas, public housing projects were built in the mid twentieth century. The largest in Brooklyn, Red Hook Houses, was located on a site that was "lightly populated and of little economic value"; "That industry had already started to abandon these areas offered an opportunity that the housing authority could exploit." By the latter half of the twentieth century, many industries such as petroleum and shipbuilding had closed or left the area. In the 2000s, the City rezoned some blocks, and new high-rise buildings were developed in waterfront neighborhoods such as Williamsburg.[99]

> [In 2005], in an effort to reactivate vast stretches of Williamsburg's industrial waterfront, which had fallen into disuse, … the City rezoned much of the northern part of the neighborhood. This rezoning allowed the construction of much-needed new housing, including significant numbers of affordable housing units … After the rezoning, high-density waterfront development and mid-rise development farther inland took place. This development has resulted in some of the few buildings along the waterfront that were built to modern resiliency standards.[100]

Further away from the central city, coastal areas also changed over the twentieth century through suburbanization. In Southern Brooklyn, for example, the tidal strait separating Coney Island from the mainland was filled in, along with other marshlands and waterways, to allow for suburban development: "The coastline was extended into the ocean and [bays], subsuming smaller barrier islands. By the mid twentieth century, summer bungalow communities had largely become year-round neighbourhoods." Numerous public housing projects were also developed there. In

[98] (Gotham & Greenberg, 2014); quotes are from pp. 139, 143.

[99] For Red Hook Houses, see (Bloom, 2008); quotes are from pp. 46, 70–71. For industries closing, see (City of New York, 2013; Zimring, 2021).

[100] (City of New York, 2013, p. 243).

South Queens, the extension of road and mass transit networks spurred residential development on the Rockaway Peninsula, a long barrier spit with a mean elevation less than 2 m above sea level.[101] "In the 1950s, a new wave of development began, this time focused primarily on the Peninsula. There, the public sector and private developers began constructing nursing homes, public housing developments, and affordable housing projects … This trend continued through the 1960s and 1970s, resulting in high concentrations of disadvantaged populations in certain parts of South Queens."[102]

The Rockaway Peninsula "became the epicenter of public housing in Queens." The area was prone to coastal erosion, and major beach nourishment projects were implemented over the decades; however, high costs eventually led to deferred maintenance and "the area's beaches have continued to erode, reducing their ability to protect the neighborhoods along the Peninsula." One neighborhood, however, was distinctive:[103]

> [The Arverne] community historically consisted of bungalow housing that was cleared as part of an urban renewal project in the 1960s. After laying fallow for many decades, the area began to spring back to life in recent decades with the construction of Arverne by the Sea, a 117-acre mixed-use development … which opened in 2008. The City not only required that the new development be constructed on an elevated site, it also called for a wide planted dune system facing the ocean.[104]

Staten Island also saw rapid suburbanization after the opening of the Verrazzano–Narrows Bridge connection to Brooklyn. "On the East Shore, some development occurred on land in close proximity to, and sometimes within, wetland areas. On the South Shore, development also moved closer to the shoreline."[105]

In the century or so of major urban expansion preceding Hurricane Sandy, New York City experienced only a few storms and coastal flooding events; however, scientific awareness of the risk was growing. A category 3 hurricane in 1938 made landfall in Long Island. Hurricane-force winds caused extensive tree damage, and severe coastal flooding occurred in the city. The Rockaway Peninsula, at the time "covered largely by private homes," was "overwashed" by a 3 m storm surge. A major storm also struck in December 1992:[106]

> Flooding of lower Manhattan, together with near hurricane-force wind gusts led to the almost complete shutdown of the metropolitan New York transportation system …

[101] (City of New York, 2013); quote "The coastline was extended …" is from p. 337. See also (Steinberg, 2014). Elevation figure is from (Gornitz et al., 2002).
[102] (City of New York, 2013, p. 304).
[103] Quote "became the epicenter …" is from (Soll, 2021). Quote "the area's beaches …" is from (City of New York, 2013, p. 309).
[104] (City of New York, 2013, p. 306).
[105] (City of New York, 2013, p. 271). See also (Wagner et al., 2016).
[106] (Babson et al., 2020; Coch, 2015; Gornitz et al., 2002). Quote is from (Coch, 2015, p. 201).

> The December 1992 storm revealed the vulnerability of the metropolitan New York – New Jersey – Connecticut transportation systems to major nor'easters and hurricanes … Flood levels of only 0.30–0.61 m above those of the December 1992 storm could have resulted in massive inundation and loss of life.[107]

Hurricane Irene in 2011 led to some flooding and beach erosion in the metro region. Analysts developed increasingly sophisticated understanding of the risk, for example, identifying that "the right angle bend between the New Jersey and Long Island coasts funnel surge waters toward the apex – the New York City harbor"; models indicated that the "area outlined by the 10-ft contour (3 m) in New York City and environs could have a likelihood of flooding once in 50 to as often as every 5.5 years, on average, by the 2080s."[108]

But with relatively few damaging storms, interest in flood protection was episodic, and the city did not develop a concerted, effective strategy to reduce coastal flood risk. The response following the 1938 hurricane was to construct coastal engineering structures (e.g., sea walls, groins, and jetties) to widen beaches, but as these interfered with the natural movement of sand along the coast, they had the unintended effect of aggravating coastal erosion. Passage of the 1968 National Flood Insurance Act paradoxically contributed to a situation of increasing risk:[109]

> The real estate and building industries, which were committed to market-driven land development, fought implementation of the legislation and, as a result, many communities in especially hazardous areas did not take action to restrict development but instead took their chances with the hazard on the assumption that the US government would bail them out in the end with disaster-relief payments.[110]

Indirectly, however, changes to building codes in the 1960s, designed to improve fire protection, may have effectively reduced flood risk by encouraging construction in heavier materials (steel, concrete, masonry) that are less vulnerable to flood damage: "Over time, older, light-frame buildings in central portions of the city tended to be replaced by bigger, heavier buildings, while light-frame, low-density buildings remained more common on the edges of the city."[111]

Modern flood protection standards were incorporated into the city's building code from 1983, when the Federal Emergency Management Agency (FEMA) released maps indicating the 100-year floodplain. In older parts of the city such as Southern Manhattan and the Brooklyn–Queens waterfront, some 90% of buildings predate this code change. Even in newer areas such as the East and South Shores of Staten Island, nearly 60% of houses were constructed before the 1983 flood

[107] (Gornitz et al., 2002, p. 65). [108] (Coch, 2015); quotes are from (Gornitz et al., 2002, pp. 66, 85).
[109] For lack of effective strategy, see (City of New York, 2013). For response after 1938 hurricane, see (Coch, 2015).
[110] (Steinberg, 2021, ch. 13). [111] (City of New York, 2013, p. 71).

protection standards were incorporated into code. In 2009, the city's Office of Emergency Management released a natural hazard mitigation plan that emphasized "technocratic measures such as using fiber optics to improve communication during flood disasters and updating the hundred-year floodplain maps … No serious consideration was given to measures that might impinge on economic growth … [such as] managed retreat." However, hazard mitigation efforts did include further building code upgrades and efforts to begin restoring wetlands.[112]

Prior to Hurricane Sandy, a few initiatives had been undertaken to address the risk of major coastal flooding events – "beach nourishment in Coney Island and Brighton Beach, dune restoration at Rockaway Peninsula, elevated structures at Battery Park City, and some constructed wetlands with elevated edges …" – however, these efforts "had not been made at the required scale."[113]

* * *

Hurricane Sandy, also referred to as Superstorm Sandy, struck New York on October 29, 2012. Although technically downgraded to a post-tropical cyclone by the time it made landfall, it was nonetheless a massive storm that caused catastrophic damage. Its wind field, or the extent of tropical storm-force winds, was three times as large as Hurricane Katrina's. The storm's powerful winds, low pressure, angle of approach, and timing – "Sandy arrived during a full moon, when Atlantic tides were at their highest" – combined to generate a record-breaking storm tide of 4.3 m (14 feet) above Mean Lower Low Water (roughly, the low tide line) at the Battery in Lower Manhattan. Southward-facing coastal areas of the city were especially battered by Sandy's massive storm surge and wave action.[114]

Coastal flooding was extensive, reaching across 132 km^2 or 17% of the land area of New York City, vastly exceeding the 100-year floodplain delineated on the FEMA flood maps. Many areas were inundated by well over a meter of water above ground level – as much as 3.4 m on the Coney Island peninsula, for example, and 4.3 m on the southern coast of Staten Island. With the storm surge came powerful, destructive waves. In addition to direct flooding from the sea, the storm surge also caused inundation more indirectly: "The city's many bays, inlets, and creeks functioned as 'backdoor' channels, funneling ocean waters inland" in areas

[112] (City of New York, 2013). The Flood Insurance Rate Maps were associated with construction design requirements and eligibility to participate in the National Flood Insurance Program. Quote is from (Steinberg, 2021, ch. 13).

[113] (Rosenzweig & Solecki, 2014, p. 398).

[114] (Steinberg, 2014; City of New York, 2013). Hurricane Sandy impacted a much broader area than just New York City, including several countries in the Caribbean and areas of the US mid-Atlantic and northeast; in particular, "the extent of catastrophic damage along the New Jersey coast was unprecedented in the state's history" (Blake et al., 2013, p. 17). Quote "Sandy arrived …" is from (City of New York, 2013, p. 11). Peak water levels were also aggravated by sea levels that had risen 1.64 feet in the period 1800–2000 (Orton et al., 2016). Storm tide reflects the level of storm surge plus astronomical tide (Blake et al., 2013).

such as Southern Brooklyn, the Rockaway Peninsula (via Jamaica Bay), Newtown Creek, and the Gowanus Canal, and flooding also occurred where the city's storm-water drainage system was overwhelmed.[115]

In New York City, the flooded areas included over 443,000 residents and nearly 90,000 buildings (9% of the city's building stock), as well critical healthcare, utility infrastructure, and transportation facilities. There were 43 deaths, around half occurring on Staten Island. Across the city, some 6,500 patients were evacuated from hospitals and care facilities, and nearly 2 million people lost electric power. The storm destroyed close to 800 buildings and damaged thousands more. Losses were estimated at some $19 billion. Overall, the storm was the second most expensive in US history up until that point, after Hurricane Katrina.[116]

Patterns of building damage reflected not only the physical flooding but also construction types and age. Damage intensity was much higher in areas that experienced strong wave action than in neighborhoods with stillwater flooding, and also higher among buildings constructed prior to a 1961 land-use zoning resolution and/or adoption of the 1983 Flood Insurance Rate Map standards. These older buildings comprised the overwhelming majority of structures in the 100-year floodplain. The most physically vulnerable structures were pre-1961, one-story, light-frame buildings such as bungalows: This type represented 18% of the building stock but 73% of severely damaged or destroyed buildings in the flooded area. High-rise buildings, by contrast, tended to experience loss of basement mechanical equipment, which could also make them uninhabitable.[117]

The storm caused considerable disruption to the city's infrastructure. Damage to electric power and steam systems, in particular, was unprecedented:

> One-third of the city's electric generating capacity was temporarily lost. Five major electric transmission substations in the city flooded and shut down. Parts of the natural gas distribution network were inundated. And four of six steam plants in the city were knocked out of service. By the time the storm passed, more than 800,000 customers (representing over 2 million New Yorkers) were without power and 80,000 were without natural gas service. A third of the buildings served by the city's steam system – including several major hospitals – were without heat and hot water.[118]

Some 6 hospitals and 26 nursing homes had to close. Over 400 public housing buildings lost electric power, elevator service, heat, or hot water. Many wastewater

[115] (City of New York, 2013); quote is from p. 43. See also (Blake et al., 2013).

[116] (City of New York, 2013). Less than 20% of homes in the flooded area were covered by the National Flood Insurance Program (City of New York, 2013). Including insured and uninsured losses across the USA, Hurricane Sandy cost an estimated $65 billion in 2012 dollars, or $88.5 billion in 2024 dollars, after adjusting for inflation (National Centers for Environmental Information, 2024). The early estimate of $19 billion for New York City may not be entirely comparable in scope and methodology to these later figures.

[117] (City of New York, 2013). Some 72% of buildings in the 100-year floodplain were constructed before 1961, and 85% before 1983.

[118] (City of New York, 2013, p. 107).

treatment facilities were temporarily offline. In some of the hardest-hit areas, utility outages continued for weeks. Roads, railroads, airports, and ferry terminals were flooded, as were many subway and vehicular tunnels under the Hudson and East Rivers – "nearly every element of New York's transportation system shut down" for up to 2 to 3 weeks. Damage to waterfront industrial facilities such as oil refineries and storage terminals led to a shortage of gasoline for weeks, which also impeded emergency response.[119]

Along the city's coastline, several areas were particularly hard hit. In Southern Manhattan, the worst flooding occurred on the East River side, where a bulkhead was breached, surge waters extended inland for several blocks, and flooding spread across older, low-lying areas built on fill. On the Hudson River side, storm surge overtopped the bulkhead and flooded one to two blocks inland; however, "along Canal Street, a former waterway that was filled in during the city's northward expansion, water traveled nearly a half-mile inland." Notably, very little damage was experienced at Battery Park City, which though on landfill had been built at a raised elevation:[120]

> Around Lower Manhattan, most historic landfill was created to expand maritime activity. Though well-suited for their original purpose, as these areas transitioned from maritime to other uses, the land was never raised to higher elevations. By contrast, Battery Park City was planned for housing and commercial space from the start – one of the first examples of landfill being added to Manhattan for a non-maritime purpose. Therefore, the elevation of the site was not dictated by the need to access the water … [T]he engineers who designed the development relied on then-existing flood hazard information to inform their planning. As a result, the buildings at Battery Park City generally sit approximately seven feet higher than the elevation of the former island edge.[121]

Within Lower Manhattan, as the city recovered from the storm, disparities became apparent between wealthier and poorer districts:

> The New Lower Manhattan – wealthier, more heavily insured, with superior infrastructure, and more well-connected politically than ever – was able to withstand the storm's initial impact better than most and then repair and rebuild with remarkable speed … [T]he entire Financial District and Battery Park City were to get essential services like electricity, heat, and hot water back within days, and 99 percent of that area's commercial, residential, hotel, and retail inventory "back to business" within weeks. This stood in stark contrast to poorer storm-affected neighborhoods throughout the city, including those in the towering co-ops and public housing of the "old" Lower Manhattan in the Lower East Side and Chinatown, whose buildings lacked basic services for weeks.[122]

Along the Brooklyn–Queens waterfront, the storm surge inundated waterfront areas and traveled up the Gowanus Canal and Newtown Creek, damaging properties in

[119] (City of New York, 2013); quote is from p. 175. [120] (City of New York, 2013); quote is from p. 373.
[121] (City of New York, 2013, p. 373). [122] (Gotham & Greenberg, 2014, p. 237).

inland areas as well. Overwhelmed sewers led to sewage backups and spillage of contaminated water. The Red Hook neighborhood was severely flooded, and the Red Hook Houses lost electric power, heat, and in some cases potable water for weeks. Williamsburg, by contrast, experienced comparatively little flooding and damage, an outcome attributable in part to the higher elevation of new buildings in the neighborhood.[123]

While these older, central urban areas in Southern Manhattan and the Brooklyn–Queens waterfront were primarily impacted by storm surge, suburban communities located along the more exposed Lower Bay and facing the Atlantic were impacted by both storm surge and destructive wave action. Southern Brooklyn, South Queens (including the Rockaway Peninsula), and the East and South Shores of Staten Island accounted for some 90% of buildings in the inundation zone. In Southern Brooklyn, some communities were partially buffered by beaches that had been augmented, or nourished, for flood protection purposes; however, inundation was still extensive, "much of it caused by flooding originating not from the ocean but from the area's bays, creeks, and inlets" such as Coney Island Creek – "inundation that occurred via inland waterways, and historic creeks and marshland that had been paved over decades before." On the Rockaway Peninsula, in addition to destruction from wave action and inundation, major fires broke out and spread as flooding impeded emergency response. One bright spot, however, was the neighborhood called Arverne by the Sea, "where the dune system on the beach in front of the new development absorbed the impact of waves, while the elevated sites and special drainage features in the development kept most housing units free of water." On Staten Island, "peak storm tides reached 16 feet – almost five feet higher in Tottenville than at the Battery in Manhattan." Most buildings in the flooded area were older, low-rise, wooden structures, and East and South Shore communities on Staten Island accounted for as much as 23% of all seriously damaged or destroyed buildings in Hurricane Sandy citywide.[124]

Following Hurricane Sandy, with increased awareness of the importance of addressing climate change, coastal flooding and climate change risks were explicitly included in the rebuilding considerations. An electric power complex in Manhattan that had been inundated with seawater was repaired to withstand even more severe flooding; hospitals moved critical equipment out of their basements; the public transit authority installed submarine doors, mechanical gates, and other

[123] (City of New York, 2013). Reconstruction and recovery were also very slow: "At the Red Hook Houses, … residents had to wait nearly five years for repairs to boilers and roofs to even begin" (Bellafante, 2022, p. 4).

[124] (City of New York, 2013); quotes are from pp. 337, 341, 310, and 275. Beaches were also severely eroded by the storm. See also (Kilgannon, 2012). Some 23% of buildings tagged yellow or red by building safety inspectors were located on the East and South Shores of Staten Island.

devices to prevent flooding of the subways, learning the lesson from Sandy when "the only defenses the subway system had were plywood and sandbags."[125]

The city government issued a $20 billion recovery and coastal protection plan called *PlaNYC: A Stronger, More Resilient New York*. Adopting resilience as its guiding theme, the city declared that "a resilient city is one that is: first, protected by effective defenses and adapted to mitigate most climate impacts; and second, able to bounce back more quickly when those defenses are breached from time to time … We *can* embrace our coastline … The city cannot, and will not, retreat." Thus while focusing many risk reduction initiatives on vulnerabilities revealed by Hurricane Sandy, the city largely maintained its predisaster approach of adapting to the hazard in ways that would accommodate continued urban growth: "Rather than change the flexible adaptation pathway approach initially developed in New York City, the experience of Hurricane Sandy has grounded, reinforced, and expanded it. Sandy and its aftermath have actualized it from a generalized heuristic to a specific trajectory with milestones." In 2014, the city instituted higher standards for flood-resistant construction in the 100-year floodplain, applicable to new buildings. In 2021, it adopted zoning provisions for coastal resilience to encourage, as well as remove barriers to, more flood-resilient design in construction and future postdisaster recovery.[126]

Compared to before Hurricane Sandy, more areas of the city became subject to flood resilience regulations and plans as the risk became better understood. The year after the storm, FEMA released new maps that updated the obsolete 1983 Flood Insurance Rate Maps. The new maps delineated a much larger 100-year floodplain for the city than had previously been determined, which meant that the number of existing buildings falling within the 100-year floodplain area nearly doubled. Analysts further projected that with sea-level rise, in the coming decades, the 100-year floodplain would extend even further and "today's 100-year flood will become more frequent, occurring on average every 28–71 years in the 2050s, and every 8–59 years in the 2080s"; moreover, even without a storm event, monthly tidal flooding would become increasingly problematic in many low-lying areas.[127]

Besides building and land-use regulations, various government entities also proposed a number of large-scale, capital-intensive projects to address coastal flood

[125] (City of New York, 2023a; Rosenzweig & Solecki, 2014). Quote is from (McGeehan & Hu, 2017).

[126] Quote "a resilient city …" is from (City of New York, 2013, p. 7). Quote "rather than change …" is from (Rosenzweig & Solecki, 2014, p. 406). See also (Steinberg, 2021). Observers have noted, for example, that in New York City after Hurricane Sandy, "resilience has been improved, but public decision-making was not definitively transformed" (Mitchell, 2022, p. 10). In 2023, the City created a new Bureau of Coastal Resilience, housed in the Department of Environmental Protection, to lead and coordinate its flood resilience efforts (City of New York, 2023a; 2023b). For flood resilience provisions, see (Bellafante, 2022; Bureau of Policy and Research, 2022; City of New York, 2023a).

[127] (City of New York, 2013; Rosenzweig & Solecki, 2014). Quote is from (Orton et al., 2019, p. 100).

risk. With their size, complexity, controversy, and funding requirements, however, as of some 10 years after Hurricane Sandy, many of these remained in planning or incomplete states. For example, the US Army Corps of Engineers led a major effort to study options for flood protection at the regional scale, encompassing not only New York City but also the larger New York–New Jersey metropolitan area. In 2022, it proposed a $52.6 billion plan comprising "dozens of miles of floodwalls, levees and berms along the shoreline and 12 storm surge barriers – arrays of movable gates – across entrances to waterways throughout the region … by far the most expensive project ever proposed by the Corps," but the plan drew controversy and additional requirements for further study.[128]

Along the shoreline of southern Manhattan, a series of contiguous flood resilience projects – also referred to as the BIG U – has been planned to extend from Battery Park City on the Hudson River side down to the Battery and up the East River side (to East 25th Street). Cost-shared between the city, state, and federal governments, the projects were in various stages of planning, design, and initial construction a decade after Sandy. Their designs involved combinations of parks elevated with fill, floodwalls, berms, sliding floodgates, "deployable flip-up barriers along the waterfront," and improved drainage systems to protect against future flood events.[129]

In the more peripheral areas of the city, the post-Sandy recovery period opened up opportunities for new types of flood mitigation approaches. One of the most notable was the Living Breakwaters project, an initiative to reduce coastal erosion and attenuate wave action by constructing a series of artificial, carefully designed reefs – "partially submerged rubble mound structures" with "ecologically enhanced concrete armor units" on which oysters would eventually be cultivated – offshore of Tottenville in South Staten Island. The vision for the project reflected acknowledgment of the vast oyster reefs that once helped to provide coastal protection in New York Harbor:[130] "Tottenville was once protected by a wide shelf and series of oyster reefs, which in turn supported a robust oyster farming industry. Over time, due to siltation, overharvesting, channel dredging, and human pathogens in the water, the once abundant oyster reef collapsed …

128 (Bureau of Policy and Research, 2022). The effort is known as the New York & New Jersey Harbor & Tributaries Feasibility Study. Quote is from (Yaro & Gutman, 2023). See also (Stormwater Solutions, 2023; U.S. Army Corps of Engineers [USACE], 2022).

129 (Bureau of Policy and Research, 2022; City of New York, 2023a; Lewis, 2023; Rebuild by Design, n.d.). Quote is from Rebuild by Design website (https://rebuildbydesign.org/work/funded-projects/the-big-u/).

130 Living Breakwaters and the BIG U were both winners of the Rebuild by Design competition run by the US Department of Housing and Urban Development after Hurricane Sandy to spur innovative design solutions for regional resilience. In addition to flood risk reduction, Living Breakwaters was also designed to provide ecological and social benefits and involved elements such as shoreline restoration and educational programming. Quote is from https://hcr.ny.gov/living-breakwaters-project-background-and-design. See also (Governor's Office of Storm Recovery, 2022); www.hud.gov/sandyrebuilding/rebuildbydesign; and critique in (Wakefield, 2020).

Without these natural systems, the shore of Staten Island remains exposed to wave action and coastal erosion."[131] Some 10 years after Hurricane Sandy, Living Breakwaters was under construction with financing from federal and state government sources.[132]

On the eastern shore of Staten Island, a sizable program of managed retreat was implemented in Oakwood Beach and other communities that had experienced substantial damage from storm surge, which had been as high as 6 m in Hurricane Sandy. As an alternative to rebuilding, New York State implemented a voluntary buyout program that ultimately purchased some 500 properties in these communities in order to relocate residents away from highly vulnerable shorelines and turn the areas into green space.[133]

> In neighborhoods like Oakwood Beach … homes were built around wetlands a century ago and have been susceptible to flooding for decades. Oakwood Beach, in particular, was initially developed as a vacation community in the 1920s and transformed into a year-round community after World War II, when beach bungalows were winterized to accommodate returning soldiers looking for housing. Even before Sandy, Oakwood Beach residents experienced severe flooding in connection with multiple Nor-Easters.[134]

Ten years after Sandy, the buyout program on Staten Island had been completed. It represented an exception, however, in the context of coastal development across the city, where the prevailing sentiment was that

> given the scale of New York's building stock in the coastal area, the fact that buildings can be constructed to address the flood risks faced in the vast majority of coastal neighborhoods, and the limited alternative options for a growing population in New York City and the region, wholesale abandonment of or retreat from the city's waterfront is simply not a practical option. The City, therefore, proposes an approach pursuant to which buyouts would be a tool in the City's tool kit, but one that would be used sparingly and, where used, would most commonly be used with the goal of redeveloping acquired properties in a more resilient fashion.[135]

Overall, then, coastal flood risk increased in the years after Hurricane Sandy and is anticipated to continue doing so. As of 2015, nearly one-sixth of New York City's land and 400,000 of its residents fall within the 100-year floodplain. With sea-level rise and continuing urban development, more land, people, and property

[131] Quote is from https://hcr.ny.gov/living-breakwaters-project-background-and-design. Analysts have shown through computer simulations that oyster beds could have significantly reduced wave heights and energy from Hurricane Sandy in New York Harbor (Brandon et al., 2016).

[132] (Governor's Office of Storm Recovery, 2022).

[133] (McGhee et al., 2020; Rosenzweig & Solecki, 2014). The communities were Oakwood Beach, Graham Beach, and Ocean Breeze. Whether the buyouts ultimately reduced the former residents' vulnerability is unclear; one study found that nearly all of the buyout households relocated to areas of higher poverty and over 20% moved to locations that were still at risk from coastal flooding (McGhee et al., 2020).

[134] (Governor's Office of Storm Recovery, 2022, p. 26). [135] (City of New York, 2013, p. 79).

will become exposed to coastal flooding. By one estimate, in the 10 years after the storm, "market rate values of real estate in the 100-year floodplain have increased to over $176 billion – a 44% increase since Superstorm Sandy"; by the 2050s, with sea-level rise, the expanded floodplain would bring an additional 38% increase in the total property value at risk. The share of NYCHA's public housing buildings in the 100-year floodplain is estimated to grow from 17% (in 2022) to 26% in the mid-2050s. Even though more stringent flood resilience standards have been implemented in the building code, they apply only to structures built from 2014 onward – or just some 3.5% of buildings in the 100-year floodplain.[136]

Observers have commented that the city government and development industry have no real incentive to reduce flood exposure, especially in densely developed parts of the city. For one, properties in the coastal floodplain were generating some $2 billion per year in property tax revenue for the city. Hurricane Sandy did not seem to dampen people's demand for housing, even in areas that the storm demonstrated to be flood-prone. The availability of flood insurance effectively subsidizes development on the floodplain, and enrolment in the National Flood Insurance Program increased by some 50% in the decade following Hurricane Sandy.[137]

> It seemed … that New Yorkers would finally retreat from the harbor. But that is not what happened. Over the past decade, we have gone in a very different direction, populating the waterfront even more enthusiastically, especially along the East River in Brooklyn and Queens. According to the city's Department of Buildings, 225 permits have been issued for new apartment buildings in flood zones since Jan. 1, 2013.[138]

Hurricane Sandy was among the costliest natural hazard events in US history up until that time, second only to Hurricane Katrina, yet on the whole it seemed to have had little long-term impact on New York City's population growth and overall urban development. From the vantage point of 10 years after the storm, analysts reflected: "It takes a systemic disruption to have a systemic effect. It is possible that the coastal and urban New York and New Jersey counties had such considerable assets and resources, reasonably efficient and effective government, and robust and redundant critical infrastructure, that even a massive storm such as Sandy did not fundamentally disrupt the systems for more than a year."[139]

Nor, it should be acknowledged, was Sandy the most devastating event in New York City's recent history. By many measures, the COVID-19 pandemic was much more disruptive, causing over 45,000 deaths. The pandemic "initiated an unprecedented shock to New York City's economy" and recovery lagged in some areas

[136] (City of New York, 2023a) and (Bureau of Policy and Research, 2022); quote is from p. 4 of the latter. See also (Abramson et al., 2022; Herreros-Cantis et al., 2020).

[137] (Bellafante, 2022; Bureau of Policy and Research, 2022; City of New York, 2023a; Herreros-Cantis et al., 2020).

[138] (Bellafante, 2022). [139] (Abramson et al., 2022).

such as tourism and office vacancy rates. In the initial months of the pandemic in 2020, the city's population shrank by over 5% (468,000 residents), including some 420,000 who moved away from the city.[140]

4.4 Urbanization and Coastal Flood Risk

Hurricane Katrina and Hurricane Sandy were two of the most destructive disasters in US history, topping the list of the country's "billion-dollar weather and climate disasters" at #1 and #5, respectively. Viewing these events through the lens of urban history, from colonial times to the present, clarifies why New Orleans and New York City suffered the damage that they did and how the disasters themselves contributed to the continuing evolution of flood risk in those cities.[141]

In many ways, the two cases present more contrast than similarities – in their population size (455,000 v. 8.2 million at the time of the storms), their physical setting (river delta v. complex estuary), the proximate causes of flooding (failure of flood protection infrastructure v. coastal inundation), and long-term postdisaster situation (population decline v. growth), to name a few of the more striking differences. Yet probing more deeply into the backstory reveals remarkable similarities in terms of how urbanization processes set the stage for disaster outcomes.

Following the Urban Risk Dynamics framework, the lessons of New Orleans and New York can be considered through a series of questions: How did urban development affect the hazard? How did it influence exposure and vulnerability? And how did the disasters themselves trigger adaptations that in turn influenced future coastal flood risk?

In standard risk framings, the hazard is thought of as being exogenous to the human system at risk, but the New Orleans and New York cases make clear that – as with riverine flooding in Chapter 3 – urbanization does affect the coastal flood hazard at the local level in terms of attributes such as flood depth, wave energy, and the extent of inundation.

Specifically, urbanization in coastal cities often entails the filling in, paving over, and building atop of marshes and other wetlands that naturally characterize landscapes where rivers meet the sea. In both New Orleans and New York, extensive tracts of wetlands were transformed to accommodate population expansion, particularly during eras of rapid growth. As wetlands are lost, so too are their protective benefits against coastal flooding. Without this buffering from storm surge and wave action, waterfront development is more exposed to a more intense flood hazard.

[140] Mortality data from New York City: www.nyc.gov/site/doh/covid/covid-19-data-totals.page. See (City of New York, 2023a; Quealy, 2020; Schmahmann et al., 2022). Quote is from (City of New York, 2023a, p. 144).

[141] Rankings reflect adjustments for inflation, as of June 2024. Data source: (Smith, 2020).

Urbanization can be implicated in the loss of other natural features offshore as well that would otherwise provide some degree of coastal protection. In New York's case, massive oyster reefs had once blanketed broad expanses of the estuary. Their loss was not due to direct paving over, clearly, but related to urbanization nonetheless in the form of overharvesting of the oysters themselves, pollution, channel dredging, and other mechanisms of habitat destruction.

A second way in which urbanization aggravates coastal flood hazard is through the construction of navigational waterways that in a coastal storm serve, inadvertently, to funnel the surge. Whether in the form of modified streams or entirely human-constructed waterways, these channels were built to allow maritime traffic to access urban areas, particularly in the earlier presuburbanization decades in a port city's history when shipping-related and industrial activities were located closer to the urban center. Examples include the Industrial Canal, Gulf Intracoastal Waterway, and MR–GO in New Orleans, and the Gowanus Canal and Newtown Creek in New York. As powerful floodwaters are funneled into these channels in a storm, the floodwalls and other protective structures lining the waterways can fail or be overtopped, as happened with severe localized consequences in Hurricane Sandy and catastrophically in Hurricane Katrina.

And third, urban development also shapes the local topography along the shoreline, directly influencing the area of land at risk of inundation in a coastal flooding event. This is most striking in the case of New York, where many of the low-lying coastal areas flooded in Hurricane Sandy – especially in the older urban core in Manhattan and Brooklyn – comprised not only filled-in wetlands but also entirely "made" land, where various fill materials over the centuries had been deposited into open water to create new space for wharves, warehouses, apartment buildings, and other urban uses. Moreover, many former water channels that had been filled in and paved over as the city developed remained low-lying and were also readily flooded. In New Orleans, too, urban development in some areas encroached into places that had previously been covered with water. Perhaps more significantly, however, urban development processes – including flood protection processes that reduced Mississippi River sediments, drainage infrastructure, and building on former wetlands – aggravated land subsidence. The city sank with a bowl-like profile over the course of the twentieth century, from being slightly above to sitting slightly below sea level. In these ways, urban development effectively expanded the floodplain.

While it is unsurprising that urban development increases flood exposure, the New Orleans and New York cases illustrate that this is especially so for coastal cities, where occupying the land at the water's edge is central to the urban economy – indeed, to its economic reason for being.

For port cities like these, the historic urban core is located where early settlers found both convenient access to navigable waters and some degree of relative protection, whether on the raised land of the Mississippi River's natural levee or a defensible island in New York's more protected Inner Harbor. As population grew over time, the urbanized area expanded into some of the more hazardous lands in the area (from the perspective of coastal flooding) – the backswamps in New Orleans, for example, or the Rockaway Peninsula and the East and South Shores of Staten Island – when these areas became economically viable through drainage technology or new modes of intraurban transportation access. As a proportion of the total city, the people and buildings exposed to flooding may have declined in some periods, since much of the total urban expansion may have taken place outside the floodplain (e.g., suburban growth in inland areas). Nonetheless, considered in terms of absolute numbers of people and property, flood exposure would have increased as urbanization proceeded.

What is remarkable is how urban expansion into flood-prone lands was at times intentionally enabled by the construction of flood protection structures. In New Orleans in particular, the expansion of the levee system following Hurricane Betsy in 1965 was financially justified by the new potential development that the levees would make feasible. In contrast, New York did not expand with such dependence on flood protection structures, and it is worth noting that not only does the city have a more favorable topography (from the perspective of avoiding flood losses) but it also did not experience frequent destructive hurricanes during its periods of major urban expansion.

The dynamics of urban growth and change are also reflected in long-term shifts in coastal flood vulnerability. In both cases, the hurricanes revealed the relationship between physical vulnerability and periods of rapid urban expansion. In Hurricane Katrina, it was not New Orleans' old historic core that suffered the worst damage but rather flooded neighborhoods such as the Lower Ninth Ward that had been developed later. In the Hurricane Sandy inundation zone, pre-1961 light-frame buildings accounted for a small minority of the building stock but a large majority of the damaged or destroyed buildings, and they were disproportionately represented in areas such as Staten Island; in New York, flood resilience provisions in the building code were only instituted from 1983 onward. Moreover, in the case of New York, at least, older maritime waterfront areas and the low-lying neighborhoods behind them were also highly vulnerable, but tracts of newer development such as Battery Park City, which were designed not for maritime commerce but for residential and commercial use, fared well compared to adjoining older areas. Thus physical vulnerability across the urban landscape varied in ways that reflected when different parts of the city were initially developed and/or redeveloped.

One broad constant regardless of era, however, was that the least economically valuable land was occupied by the most socially vulnerable populations. In New Orleans, the least desirable districts were typically also the "least expensive and lowest in elevation," and flood protection works at times benefited wealthy neighborhoods at the direct expense of marginal ones. In New York, public housing developments for low-income populations were often located on low-cost, flood-prone lands. Disparities extended to the postdisaster recovery period: The most socially vulnerable groups in New Orleans tended to have the lowest rates of return after Hurricane Katrina, and in New York, many poorer neighborhoods suffered substantially longer infrastructure disruption than wealthy areas in Hurricane Sandy.[142]

Overall, the two cases also reinforce the importance of contextualizing the severity of a disaster in relation to its long-term urban history. Predisaster trends in metrics such as population numbers reflect underlying forces giving rise to these trends, such as a city's economic competitiveness, social conditions, and government capacity. Hurricane Katrina accelerated New Orleans' population loss trend. New York had experienced periods of decline prior to Hurricane Sandy, in the 1950s and most notably in the 1970s when the city faced population loss and bankruptcy; however, the situation turned around as the economy restructured, and the city was on a long-term growth curve on the eve of Sandy, having also recovered (in overall terms) from the 9/11 terrorism disaster in 2001.[143]

Finally, it is interesting to consider how catastrophic events like Hurricanes Katrina and Sandy may trigger adaptations in modern cities and influence the evolution of future risk. Several broad trends can be observed. First, many lessons are identified and learned in relation to the more visible failures in the event – planning for the evacuation of vulnerable populations; preventing subway tunnels from flooding; moving electrical equipment from basements to higher floors; and the like. Scientific understanding advances regarding the hazard and risk, both current and future. Flood maps may be updated, and resilience standards in building codes raised, as in New York. These adaptations undoubtedly improve preparedness and mitigate losses, at least at the margins, from future flood events.

Catastrophic hazard events also draw sizable new funding from state and federal levels of government. They open opportunities for large-scale interventions to reduce risk in the long term (such as Louisiana's coastal protection and restoration efforts, New York–New Jersey's regional-scale flood protection, and Manhattan's BIG U), even though such capital-intensive initiatives may stall or take many years to come to fruition. For the most part, however, such large-scale efforts seek to protect existing urbanized areas rather than alter urban development itself; they thus reinforce ongoing urbanization trends and patterns. Even innovative efforts at nature-based solutions such as Living Breakwaters are fundamentally about protecting cities from flood hazard.

[142] Quote is from (Colten, 2006, p. 732).
[143] For long-term population numbers and forecasts, see (City of New York, 2023a).

Catastrophic events provide strong signals regarding which areas of a city are most at risk of future flooding. Yet radical changes to existing urbanization patterns, however risky they might be, do not occur, as demonstrated in public resistance to the idea of "shrinking the footprint" of New Orleans in order to focus reconstruction on higher ground. In flood-prone areas that are already densely developed and where real estate values are high, as in New York's older urban core, adaptations tend to rely on technology and capital to provide enhanced flood protection. It is in lower-density neighborhoods that have experienced repeated flooding, where such approaches may be too cost-prohibitive, that localized initiatives to strategically retreat from flood-prone coastal areas may succeed – as shown by the home buyout program on Staten Island.

So far, the four urban case studies have demonstrated some commonalities between riverine and coastal cities in terms of how urban development interacts with disaster risk over time. Comparisons further suggest some ways in which city size, as well as the scale of a disaster or catastrophe, may influence these dynamics. Chapter 5 examines whether these themes are particular to floods or might resonate with other types of hazards and how they manifest in cities outside of Europe and North America.

5

Cities and Earthquakes

5.1 Earthquakes

What do earthquakes have to do with floods? At first glance, these hazards may seem to be entirely disconnected. Earthquakes are classified as geohazards and floods as hydrometeorological phenomena. Human activity does not influence seismicity (with some minor exceptions), whereas extreme rainfall, storms, and flooding are being exacerbated by climate change. Earthquakes occur on seismic faults; floods, along waterways. Earthquakes strike without warning, but flood conditions can be monitored and anticipated. Earthquakes cause damage from ground shaking, while floods destroy through inundation.[1]

Yet some earthquakes generate tsunamis, which are a form of coastal flooding. In the 2011 Great East Japan triple disaster, more lives were lost and property destroyed by tsunami than from the seismic shaking and Fukushima nuclear power plant accident combined. Around the world, many coastal cities are located in seismic zones.

And more fundamentally, as with flooding, how earthquakes impact cities is related to the physical landscape. To clarify the significance of landscape, this chapter first provides a basic description of earthquake phenomena with an emphasis on what makes a seismic event dangerous. It is not just earthquake magnitude that matters – relevant factors also include other seismic source characteristics, ground motion attenuation and amplification, site effects, ground failure, and attributes of buildings and other structures that affect their response to shaking.

The largest magnitude earthquakes are not necessarily the most damaging ones. Magnitude is a measure of the amount of energy released in the earthquake. This energy dissipates with distance from the seismic source. From the perspective of a city, what matters more than magnitude is intensity – how severe the shaking will

[1] Human activities such as the rapid filling of dam reservoirs, mining, and fracking have been found to increase local seismicity (Doglioni, 2018; McGarr et al., 2002).

be when the energy released by the earthquake reaches the city. Intensity can be measured quantitatively (e.g., peak ground acceleration (PGA)) or qualitatively (e.g., along the categorical Modified Mercalli Intensity [MMI] scale).[2]

Generally speaking, earthquakes that are larger, nearer, and shallower (i.e., with hypocenter closer to the ground surface) are more dangerous. Globally, the largest magnitude earthquakes occur at the boundaries of tectonic plates that comprise the earth's crust, where one plate is subducting under another; when these events occur under the sea, they can generate major tsunamis. For some earthquake-prone cities, these subduction zone megaquakes (potentially up to about magnitude 9) pose the most serious threat; for many other urban areas, however, other types of faults that produce smaller earthquakes but lie closer to the city are the dominant hazard. Even moderate magnitude earthquakes can be highly damaging if they are close enough to produce high intensity shaking. Moreover, not all earthquake faults have been identified and mapped – there can be surprises.

When the energy waves from an earthquake reach a city, ground shaking intensity will be stronger in some areas than in others. This is not only because some areas lie closer to the fault but also due to local soil conditions. Soft soils such as sands and clays, for example, amplify earthquake ground shaking. This means that in the same earthquake and at the same distance from the epicenter, sites on soft soils such as a riverbank generally experience stronger shaking than those on, say, rocky hilltops. Moreover, some cities are built over deep sedimentary basins; these types of geologic structures can greatly amplify earthquake ground motions, especially the longer wavelength motions. (An earthquake releases energy across a spectrum of wavelengths.) This matters because longer wavelength ground motions are especially damaging to certain kinds of structures, such as high-rise buildings and long-span bridges. In the 1985 Mexico City (Michoacán) earthquake, basin amplification effects contributed significantly to the collapse of hundreds of high-rise buildings in the part of the city that was built on an old lakebed.[3]

When shaking intensity is high, some types of ground are also prone to liquefaction, a phenomenon whereby solid land briefly loses its coherence. Liquefaction occurs in water-saturated, loosely consolidated sediments – typically, ground comprised of sandy soils where the water table is high, such as along riverbanks or coastlines. When water that is sufficiently pressurized by earthquake shaking separates the sand grains, the ground liquefies. Although the change is transient, it causes damage to whatever structures have been built on top of, or buried in, the ground.

[2] For large earthquakes, moment magnitude (M_w) is commonly reported as a measurement of size.

[3] For 1985 earthquake, see (Beck & Hall, 1986; Flores-Estrella et al., 2007). Mexico City was also struck by a less devastating although still severe earthquake in 2017. The fault mechanisms and epicentral distances differed between the 1985 and 2017 earthquakes, and consequently damage was concentrated in different urban zones in the two events (Diaz-Fanas et al., 2020).

The physical impact of earthquakes derives not only from ground motion and ground failure but most importantly from the properties of buildings and other structures that govern how they respond to the shaking. Unreinforced masonry buildings, for example, are designed to carry vertical loads such as the weight of the structure itself; the brick-and-mortar construction has little ability to withstand horizontal forces and can readily collapse in an earthquake. Even reinforced concrete (RC) buildings can suffer serious damage if their design (e.g., details of their steel reinforcement) does not allow sufficient ductility in how the building responds to shaking.

This chapter considers how urbanization processes affect seismic risk. Risk arises from the interaction between hazard, exposure, and vulnerability. This chapter examines what these interactions look like in the context of earthquakes. It pays particular attention to how risk changes over time and the role of urban development processes – especially the influence of economic forces, technology, and landscape – in this evolution. Two cases are presented: Kobe, Japan; and Christchurch, New Zealand. Both have experienced major seismic disasters (in 1995 and 2010–2011, respectively), and in the earthquake field, they are often thought of synonymously with these events. It is useful, however, to step back and view the disasters within the longer arc of the cities' urban development histories.

5.2 Kobe

The city of Kobe, Japan, occupies a narrow strip of coastal land roughly 30 km long by 2–4 km wide, backed by the Rokko Mountains on the north side and facing Osaka Bay to the south (Figure 5.1). The land drops sharply beneath the water, forming a naturally deep harbor. As many as 36 small rivers run down from mountains to the sea; being short and steep, they are prone to flash flooding during heavy rains. To the east of this narrow coastal strip, the landscape opens up to the broad alluvial plain on which the city of Osaka has been built up over centuries.[4]

Toward the end of Japan's feudal era in the 1860s, when Osaka was a "mega-castle town" and major economic center with a population of over 300,000, the precursor to present-day Kobe – a town called Hyogo situated toward the western end of the coastal strip on a deepwater harbor – contained perhaps 10,000 residents. A trading port had developed in the area as early as the eighth century CE but had remained small throughout the ages. In addition to the port, the region was also known for its production of rice wine (sake) in Nada on the eastern part of the coastal strip. Breweries there benefited from the local water quality, rice

[4] The reported length of the coastal strip differs between sources – for example, 20 km in (Yamasaki et al., 2010) and 30 km in (Economic Bureau, Kobe City Government, 1994; Edgington, 2010). For natural harbor, see (Yamasaki et al., 2010). For many small rivers, see (Tsu, 2005).

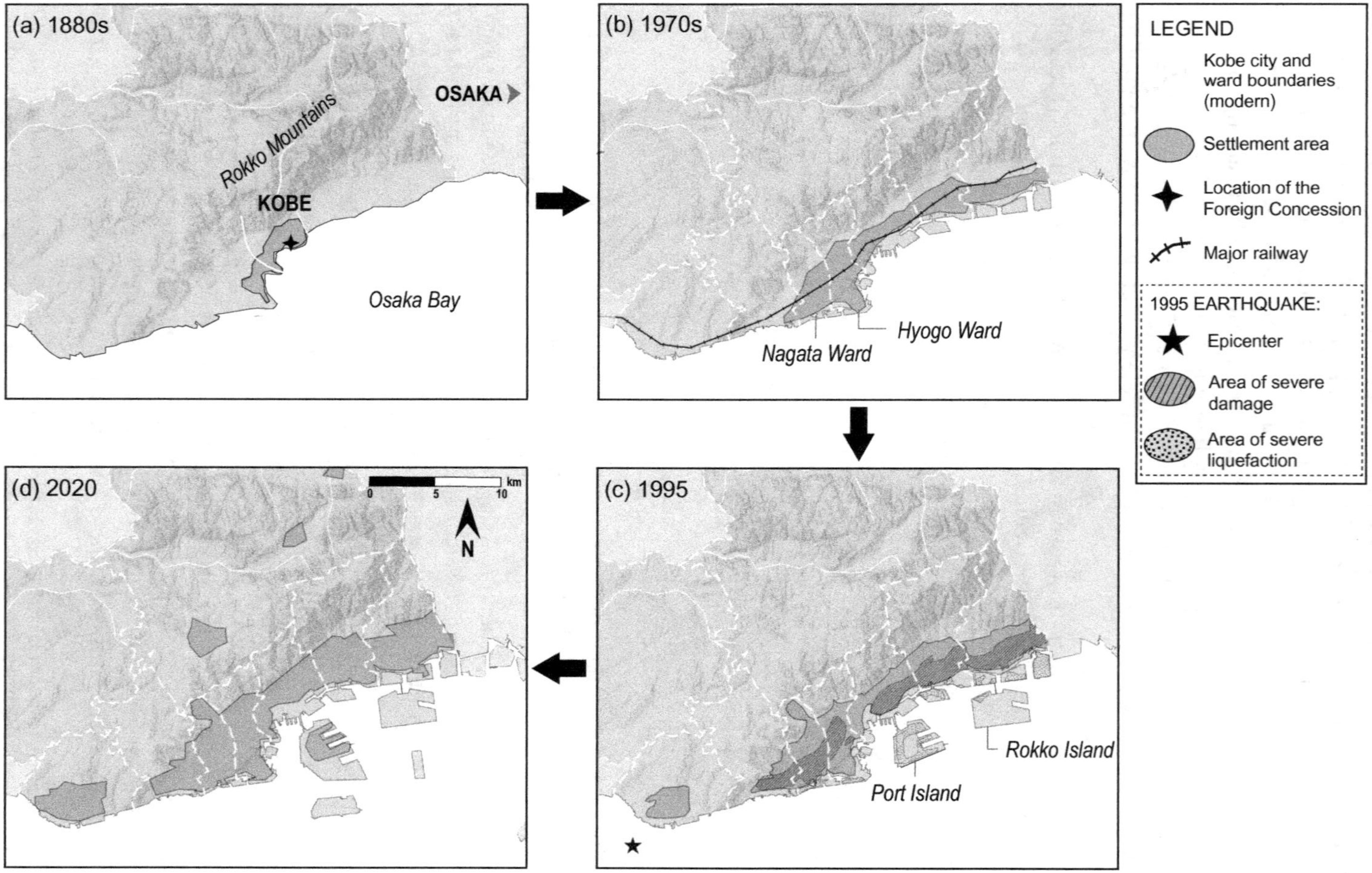

Figure 5.1 Kobe, urban expansion 1880s–2020. (Data based on: Edgington, 2010; Ennals, 2014; Hamada & Wakamatsu, 1996; Menoni, 2001; Yamasaki et al., 2010. Maps by Charlotte Milne.)

supply, and shipping access, as well as watermills along the rivers that powered the polishing of large quantities of rice.[5]

* * *

Kobe emerged as a city during the Meiji period (1868–1912), an era of rapid and profound societal change over the course of which Japan transformed "in a single generation from a closed feudal society to an industrialising and modernising nation which rapidly incorporated Western technologies, industries and organisational forms." The modernization drive was motivated in large part by national self-protection: "Exposure to Western military power, industrial technology, and international domination quickly persuaded the Meiji elite of the superiority of Western science and learning and the need to learn from the West. Meiji leaders believed that only by building Japan's military and industrial capacity could they defend themselves against Western colonisation." Rapid industrialization was accompanied by institutional reforms such as the abolition of feudal territorial domains and the creation of a capitalist system of property ownership.[6]

The opening of Japan to the West involved establishing several treaty ports where free trade was allowed to be conducted; among these, Kobe (Hyogo) was opened in 1868. A Foreign Concession district was created to accommodate the trading activities – not within the existing Hyogo town but "grafted" onto it on a new site about 3.5 km to the east, on the outskirts of a small fishing village called Kobe. The Foreign Concession covered a low-lying area of about 1,000 ha or 10 km^2; on this was superimposed a gridiron street plan ("a standard element in Euro-American town planning of that era") with 22 town blocks divided into lots that were auctioned off to foreigners from the treaty countries. "Except for continuing Kaigan-dori (literally: Seafront Avenue) along the harbourfront, the plan made little attempt to accommodate itself to the pattern of streets of what came to be called the 'Native Town,' which abutted it on the west," the latter comprising a "dense warren of existing Japanese buildings and land uses." The treaty port arrangement lasted for only three decades, but the imprint of the Foreign Concession remains today in the streets and site layout of Kobe's central business district (CBD).[7]

[5] Tsukada (2012) mentions Osaka's peak population as a "mega-castle town" to be 400,000. Rozman (1986) notes that Osaka's population had been declining in the latter part of the Tokugawa period. Hanley (1987) reports Osaka's population in 1858 as 314,370. For population of ancient Hyogo, see (Ennals, 2014). The trading port was known as Owada no Tomari in the Nara period (City of Kobe, 2019). Located at a river mouth, it ultimately silted up, and the port was moved to the Hyogo site in the twelfth century (Yamasaki et al., 2010). For a regional history of the sake brewing industry, see (www.gov-online.go.jp/eng/publicity/book/hlj/html/202104/202104_12_en.html). See also (City of Kobe, 2019; Tsu, 2005).

[6] For background on societal transformations and rapid industrialization in the Meiji era, see (Sorensen, 2004) and (Jansen, 1989). Quote "in a single generation …" is from (Sorensen, 2004, pp. 45–46); "Exposure to Western military power …" is from p. 48. See also (Beasley, 1989).

[7] Quotes are from (Ennals, 2014, ch. 2 and ch. 6). See also (City of Kobe, 2019; Yamasaki et al., 2010).

From the time it was established as an open port, Kobe grew quickly to become one of the early centers of Japan's industrializing economy. In the early Meiji era, the country's urban patterns began to modernize: "Prior to 1885 there was little railroad construction, buildup of factory production, or granting of municipal self-government. All these factors became important in the next period, when urbanization quickened," a period when Kobe and other new ports "led the way in urban growth." Kobe's deepwater harbor enjoyed site advantages over nearby Osaka, whose own port had opened to foreign trade in the same year: At Osaka, the extant harbor was unsuitable for international shipping because "large vessels could not navigate along the rivers due to accumulation of silt." Kobe, meanwhile, "attracted an influx of capital and foreign investment and grew rapidly. Large European firms established branches around its port ... and a range of domestic industrial activity began, including shipbuilding ... It was an early center of heavy industry. [Major shipyards] employed tens of thousands of workers by the 1920s." By 1914, Kobe's port was handling as much as half of the nation's imports and a third of its exports.[8]

New urban infrastructure systems accompanied this rapid industrialization. The central government prioritized railway construction in its modernization efforts and Kobe was an early beneficiary, connecting to Osaka by rail in 1874 and to Tokyo by 1889. Within Kobe, this railway line ran east–west along the coastal strip and passed a little to the north of the Foreign Concession, where a station was built at Sannomiya. Major expansions were made to Kobe's port facilities in the early twentieth century. Kobe was one of the first two Japanese cities to construct infrastructure such as suburban commuter railway, a natural gas system, and electric streetlights. As the city spread outward, transportation infrastructure, including a street railway system, reinforced the Foreign Concession area as the city's CBD. Private rail transportation companies, influenced by the example in Western countries where private railways participated in land speculation, actively engaged in urban development along the new suburban routes, including building new housing and amusement parks.[9]

In the decades between Kobe's establishment as a treaty port and World War II, the city's population expanded rapidly. By 1889, Kobe had 130,000 residents; by 1920 some three decades later, it had over 600,000, and by 1940 about

[8] Quotes "Prior to 1885 ..." and "led the way ..." are from (Rozman, 1986, pp. 320, 339). Quote "large vessels could not navigate ..." is from (Black, 2022, p. 84); see also (Kornhauser, 1977). Quote "attracted an influx of capital ..." is from (Tokyo Development Learning Center, 2018, p. 9). Import/export statistics are from (City of Kobe, 2019).

[9] For rail connection to other cities, see (Rozman, 1986; Sorensen, 2004). For Sannomiya Station and street railway system, see (Ennals, 2014). For urban infrastructure adoption, see (Tokyo Development Learning Center, 2018); the other early adopter was Yokohama, also a treaty port. Quote "influenced by early private railways ..." is from (Black, 2022, p. 161). For rail companies and urban development, see (Saito, 1997).

1 million – making it the fifth largest city in the country. The city's land area also increased, but more modestly (from 21 to 83 km^2 between 1889 and 1940).[10]

Rapid industrialization and urbanization invariably modified the landscape. One early example was the relocation of the Ikuta River, which originally flowed near the eastern edge of the Foreign Concession:

> During the first years of settlement, it was recognized that the river's banks were in such poor condition that they frequently collapsed. Flood was a serious concern … Another concern was that the extremely wide river bed would present an engineering challenge when it came to constructing a railway bridge that would link the region with Tōkyō. In 1871 the Japanese authorities decided to relocate the Ikuta River about 400 metres farther to the east; this would be accomplished by digging a straight channel from near the river's headwaters … right down to the sea.[11]

The old bed of the river was transformed into a wide road, and "now that the river had been moved and stabilized, the tracts of land immediately to the east of the settlement could be used for economic and recreational activities that could not be accommodated within the Concession." Another example was deforestation in the Rokko Mountains, which led to rapid runoff, mudslides, and flooding – and in turn to efforts at reforestation – within the space of a few decades. Land reclamation also altered the shoreline with new port facilities: "One consequence of this was that the Bund [Kaigan-dori] … ceased to be the 'water street.' When the shoreline was shifted seaward by some 100 metres, the Bund became an inland street."[12]

During this early era of rapid urban growth, flood hazard became more destructive as increasing numbers of people and property came to be at risk. The Hanshin Deluge of 1938 marked a turning point in flood management. Torrential downpours in that event caused sediment-laden flooding that "paralyzed the city, damaging some 15,000 buildings and claiming over 600 lives."[13]

> Once the rivers breached their dikes, this dreaded *yama-tsunami* or "mountain tidal wave" … bulldozed almost everything in its path, toppling buildings and crushing people to death … Thus, nearly 60 per cent of the city's low-lying areas were immediately submerged … Altogether, 72 per cent of the city's households were affected … Property loss alone was twice the municipal government's budget for that year.[14]

The disaster spurred the construction of hundreds of erosion control dams and other projects that prevented similar disasters from occurring in later decades. For example,

[10] Population statistics are from (City of Kobe, 2019; Yamasaki et al., 2010) and Table 2–18 in (Statistics Bureau of Japan, 2020). Land area is from (Yamasaki, 2010).

[11] (Ennals, 2014, ch. 6).

[12] (Ennals, 2014); quote "now that the river had been moved …" is from ch. 6 and "One consequence …" is from ch. 8. For maps of land reclamation over time, see (Yamasaki, 2010, Figure 9.2).

[13] (Tsu, 2005, p. 205).

[14] (Tsu, 2008, p. 202). For a map, see www.kkr.mlit.go.jp/rokko/disaster/history/s13/s13-index.php.

extreme rainfall events comparable to 1938 occurred in 1967 and 2018 but were much less destructive, with the latter causing minimal property loss and no fatalities.[15]

Within a few years of the great flood, Kobe again suffered catastrophe, this time in World War II. As an industrial center, it was targeted by Allied firebombing, which destroyed more than half of the city. Over 70% of the city's housing was lost. Kobe's industrial production in 1945 fell to just one-sixth of prewar levels. With large-scale evacuation during the conflict, by 1945, the city's population had plummeted from 1 million to 400,000 people.[16]

* * *

Kobe recovered rapidly after the war. Its population rebounded to 1 million by the mid-1950s and continued to expand, albeit at slower and slower rates. By 1980, the city had 1.4 million residents, close to what the population would be when the catastrophic earthquake struck in 1995. The city's land area similarly grew rapidly in the initial postwar decades and more slowly thereafter – from 83 to 420 km^2 between 1940 and 1950 to 545 km^2 in 1990 – mainly by absorbing neighboring towns and villages but also through land reclamation.[17]

While manufacturing led the economic recovery in the initial postwar decades, over time the economy diversified away from heavy industry. For example, major manufacturers expanded from producing ships, aircraft, and steel to also making robots, motorcycles, and machinery. The synthetic shoe industry emerged as a newly important sector after the war, and Nagata ward on the city's west side developed a cluster of small-scale factories that became the center of the nation's shoe production sector. But as global and national economic conditions continued to change over the decades, Kobe's economy also had to evolve in order to remain competitive:[18]

> By the late 1970s Kobe realized that its "smokestack" industries based around the port (steel and shipbuilding) had ended their growth cycle and that the city's economic future needed to be rethought. During the fifteen or so years before the earthquake the city took steps to shift its image from that of an industrial port toward that of an "urban resort"; this entailed a campaign to attract tourists … [and] restructuring the economy toward consumer- and service-oriented industries (e.g., fashion-oriented companies and the urban convention business).[19]

[15] (Hayashi et al., 2022) and www.mlit.go.jp/river/sabo/jirei/h30dosha/H30koukajirei_rokkou_jigyo.pdf. See also (Edgington, 2010; Tsu, 2005).

[16] Firebombing information is from (City of Kobe, 2019; Yamasaki et al., 2010). Housing loss is from (Prion & Filiatrault, 1996). Industrial production is from (City of Kobe, 2019). Population loss is from (Yamasaki et al., 2010); see also (City of Kobe, 2019).

[17] Population statistics are from (Statistics Bureau of Japan, 2020). Land area is from (Yamasaki et al., 2010). Reclaimed land accounted for 4% of the city's territory at the time of the 1995 earthquake (United Nations Centre for Regional Development [UNCRD], 1995).

[18] For manufacturing, see (Tokyo Development Learning Center, 2018).

[19] (Edgington, 2010, pp. 41–42).

In the postwar decades, Kobe's city government was heavily involved in urban development projects to spur economic growth – so much so that it became known as "Kobe, Inc." The City actively applied land readjustment tools, allowed by national reform in the 1950s, that "enabled local governments to slice portions off existing land owners' plots and swap the plots if this were deemed necessary to upgrade or build new infrastructure," such as for widening roads through densely built-up areas. In the 1960s in particular, "land readjustment in Kobe reorganized much of the Sannomiya central business area as well as suburban streets in the eastern wards."[20] "From the postwar period onwards, Kobe built deep expertise in urban development projects. Many of these were executed at a profit, through affiliated organizations … [that] spanned the gamut from railway companies to hotel developers … Such development accelerated after the first major reclamation project in 1966, and the city came to be known as a 'public developer.'"[21] Projects included an industrial park in the mountains, an underground shopping center in the CBD, and extensive land reclamation to provide space for the port as well as for new urban development. The city and national governments also constructed three highways connecting Kobe with Osaka, including the Hanshin Expressway that opened in 1970.[22]

Land reclamation figured prominently in Kobe's development. Rapid growth in a landscape constrained by mountains and sea created pressure for new land. The vast majority of the city's population and economic activities is concentrated on just 10% of the land area, along the coastal strip. Land reclamation had been pursued by the city government since the beginning of the twentieth century, but in the postwar era, it came to be implemented on an ever-increasing scale. Reclamation projects in the 1950s and 1960s focused on building out waterfront port and industrial zones. Later projects created entirely new islands in the bay: Port Island (436 ha) was completed in 1980, Rokko Island (580 ha) was finished in 1992, and Port Island Second Stage (390 ha) was under construction at the time of the earthquake; plans had also been made to build another island for a new airport. In total, Kobe built out some 2,300 ha of reclaimed land. (This strategy was not unique to Kobe: During the same era, Tokyo and Osaka were reclaiming even larger expanses from their respective bays.)[23]

[20] For Kobe, Inc., see (Edgington, 2010; Tokyo Development Learning Center, 2018). Quote "enabled local governments …" is from (Tokyo Development Learning Center, 2018, p. 10). The legislation was the Land Readjustment Act of 1954. Quote "land readjustment in Kobe …" is from (Edgington, 2010, p. 40).

[21] (Tokyo Development Learning Center, 2018, p. 9).

[22] For projects, see (Tokyo Development Learning Center, 2018). For highways, see (Edgington, 2010; Okimura et al., 1996).

[23] For concentration on coastal strip, see (City of Kobe Development Bureau, 1993). For land reclamation, see (City of Kobe Development Bureau, 1993; Edgington, 2010). The figure for total reclaimed land area is from (UNCRD, 1995). For Tokyo and Osaka, see (Shiozaki & Malone, 1996).

Port Island First Stage was designed with modern container and other port facilities built around its perimeter and commercial uses, recreational facilities, and housing for 20,000 residents in the interior; Rokko Island followed a similar design. Construction was a major undertaking. The fill – 292 million m^3 of material altogether for Port Island (both stages) and Rokko Island – came from the Rokko Mountains: "So much mountain was removed that an industrial park … could be built in the newly flattened area." The excavated material was transported down to the shore on a 14 km long underground conveyor belt, loaded onto barges, and dumped into the sea. Quay walls consisting of large concrete caissons formed the perimeters of the artificial islands. One road bridge and a light-rail line linked Port Island to the mainland; Rokko Island was similarly connected. These large-scale projects required participation by many parties: "The central government built the sea wall. The city moved the earth and did all the land reclamation. Housing was provided by the central government, the city, and private developers."[24]

Land reclamation is expensive, and various economic considerations drove these successive phases of major capital investments. For one, by the late 1950s, congestion at the port was presenting a bottleneck in the country's economic development. Moreover, the massive influx of population into the city after the war was causing excessive crowding in the inner city. In this context, "the idea of an artificial island just off the city emerged as the most promising solution, since it could solve both problems." Technological advances also made the idea appealing, as containerization was emerging in the 1960s and required deep-sea berths and extensive tracts of land. By the mid-1980s, Kobe was competing intensely with other cities to attract and retain companies, and the city needed more land to maintain a competitive edge.[25]

In addition to the artificial islands, the built-up area of Kobe also spread into new towns in the mountainous areas of the city's outlying suburban wards, developed as part of the city's urban planning policy. With housing investment channeled to the suburbs, these policies contributed to drawing middle- and high-income households away from the inner city. Younger families were also attracted to the suburbs by the availability of better planned, more spacious housing.[26]

In the midst of all this expansion, older areas in the urban center declined: "The city poured tremendous energy into relatively easy-to-develop suburbs in

[24] Island layout is from (Yamasaki et al., 2010). For fill material, see (City of Kobe Development Bureau, 1993). Quote "So much mountain …" is from (Tokyo Development Learning Center, 2018, pp. 10–11). For conveyor belt, see (Shiozaki & Malone, 1996). For quay walls, see (Iai et al., 1996; Okimura et al., 1996). Island connections are from (Shiozaki & Malone, 1996). Quote "The central government …" is from (Yamasaki et al., 2010, p. 257).

[25] Quote "the idea of an artificial island …" is from (Yamasaki et al., 2010, p. 256). For containerization and competition, see (Shiozaki & Malone, 1996; Tokyo Development Learning Center, 2018).

[26] (City of Kobe Development Bureau, 1993). For suburban demographics, see (Edgington, 2010; Hirayama, 2000).

the northern wards and reclaimed islands along the coast, but it could not (or would not) do much at all about the old and congested industrial and residential districts of its inner city." These inner-city areas suffered from multiple interrelated issues: "Housing investment was stagnant and dilapidated houses, frequently of wooden structure, were densely crowded. Many of the residents belonged to the low-income strata and the proportion of low-quality private rental housing was high." Out-migration of younger families had left the inner city with a high proportion of seniors. The building stock was old – some areas had pockets of housing that had survived the wartime bombings and were by then deteriorating. These issues were particularly concentrated in Hyogo and Nagata wards in the old city core on the west side of the CBD, which had "distinct neighbourhoods of blue-collar workers and senior citizens [who] were taking advantage of lower rents in pre-1960s wooden housing, much of it built in districts that had been laid out before modern building and planning codes had been introduced." In these areas, streets were narrow (4 m wide or less) and density high; for example, Nagata ward had a predisaster population density of 11,000 persons/km^2, compared with about 2,500 persons/km^2 across the city as a whole. Economically, the inner city had numerous small factories affiliated with heavy industries, especially synthetic shoe manufacturing. Among the city's nine wards, Hyogo and Nagata had the highest proportions of old housing (built pre-1960) and low-income residents. In contrast, the eastern wards of the coastal strip tended to be more white-collar, with residents often commuting to jobs in Osaka.[27]

In the postwar decades, the initially rapid pace of economic growth eventually slowed, influenced in part by the broader macroeconomic context:

> After the early 1990s, … an overheated ("bubble") economy at the local and national level cooled suddenly, which struck Rokkō and Port Island hard … Moreover, in the years leading up to the earthquake, the economic recession in Japan – together with declining land values – was making it difficult to encourage private-sector investment … Consequently, much of the reclaimed land in the second stage of Port Island was still unsold at the time of the quake.[28]

By this time, the shoe manufacturing cluster in the inner city was facing growing competition from low-cost producers in other Asian countries, and "overall the city's economic structure looked much the same as it had several decades earlier."[29]

[27] (Edgington, 2010); quote "the city poured …" is from p. 48 and "distinct neighbourhoods of blue-collar workers …" is from p. 30. Quote "housing investment was stagnant …" is from (Hirayama, 2000, p. 112). Street width is from (Edgington, 2010). Density numbers are from (UNCRD, 1995). Hyogo and Nagata demographic profiles are from (Hirayama, 2000).

[28] (Edgington, 2010, pp. 42–43).

[29] (Tokyo Development Learning Center, 2018, p. 11). See also (Hirayama, 2000).

Changes at the Port of Kobe mirrored in some ways the dynamics of the city's overall economy. Kobe was an early player in the containerization revolution in global shipping. It began receiving container traffic in 1967, at a time when few other Asian ports had the facilities required for accommodating the large ships. In 1976, it ranked second among container ports globally – after only New York–New Jersey. Over time, however, other competing ports within Japan as well as across Asia built up their capacity, so that even as Kobe's traffic volumes continued to grow, its relative position steadily slipped. At the time of the earthquake, it ranked sixth among container ports in the world.[30]

Broadly speaking, then, Kobe city just prior to the earthquake exhibited three important characteristics from the perspective of disaster vulnerability. First, it had developed extensive areas of reclaimed land along the waterfront and on the artificial islands. Second, there were concentrations of physical and social vulnerability in the inner-city wards west of downtown. And third, its built environment reflected a trajectory of rapid growth in the 1950s–1970s, followed by a slowdown in the years preceding the earthquake. The latter point is significant because of what was simultaneously happening with disasters, earthquake engineering, and public risk perceptions over this timeframe.

* * *

Despite being in a seismically active region, prior to 1995, Kobe city had never experienced a major earthquake. According to common perception, "during the 1,500 years that earthquake occurrence has been recorded in Japan, not once has Kobe been directly hit by an earthquake and it has always had the image of being a city safe from earthquakes." According to seismologists, "historically, only 2 earthquakes (M>7 in 868, M≈6 in 1916) have occurred in the vicinity of the Kobe earthquake." (Scientists later found paleoseismic evidence of active faults in the eastern Rokko Mountains, with the most recent major event before 1995 being a M≈7.5 event occurring four centuries prior, in 1596.) In any case, the risk of earthquakes in Kobe was perceived to be relatively low, and local disaster mitigation efforts had largely focused on flooding, typhoons, and landslides.[31]

Nonetheless, Japan as a country has extensive experience with earthquakes and has had regulations regarding seismic design of buildings from as early as 1919. As scientific knowledge advanced, especially with lessons learned from destructive earthquakes around the country, building standards were periodically revised.

[30] (Chang, 2000). Container traffic start year is from (Yamasaki et al., 2010).

[31] Quote "During the 1,500 years ..." is from Hideki Kaji, UNCRD Director, quoted in (UNCRD, 1995, p. 1). Quote "Historically, only 2 earthquakes ..." is from (Kanamori, 1995, p. 6). For active faults in eastern Rokko Mountains, see (Lin et al., 1998). UNCRD (1995) notes three historic earthquakes in the region, occurring in 868 CE (M ≥ 7, Himeji [west of Kobe]), 1579 (M 6.0, Osaka), and 1916 (M 6.1, Kobe). For risk perception and disaster mitigation, see (Edgington, 2010; UNCRD, 1995).

For example, the Building Standard Law adopted in 1950 (after the 1948 Fukui earthquake) increased the seismic loads that a building needed to be designed to withstand. In 1981, a major overhaul to the seismic design code was implemented with numerous improvements in design requirements.[32] Broadly speaking, "most major buildings constructed in the 1960s and 1970s were designed to resist earthquake forces corresponding to a peak ground acceleration or seismic coefficient of 0.1g using working stress design. In 1981, the building code was changed and the design peak acceleration was increased to about 0.3g."[33]

For highway bridges, similarly, earthquake provisions were first introduced soon after the 1923 Great Kanto Earthquake and subsequently revised several times. The 1971 Guide Specifications represented a major improvement: Among numerous changes, it incorporated consideration of soil liquefaction, which had been extensively observed in the 1964 Niigata earthquake. Consequently, "seismic safety was considerably upgraded in the highway bridges designed after 1971." Further methodological improvements were made in updated specifications issued in 1980 and 1990. In addition to design standards, seismic inspection programs of older highway bridges led to the identification of vulnerabilities in the Kobe area, and in some locations, concrete piers were seismically reinforced with steel jackets. But recall that Kobe's period of rapid growth took place in the 1950s–1970s, prior to many of these scientific and building code advances.[34]

* * *

The earthquake that struck on January 17, 1995, caused widespread devastation. Over 6,200 people in the region died, including over 4,500 fatalities within Kobe city. The earthquake's magnitude (M_w 6.9) was sizable but not extraordinary; from a seismological standpoint, it was considered a "typical shallow intraplate earthquake … [with] nothing particularly unusual in its source characteristics." The epicenter was located some 15 km southwest of Kobe, with focal depth at about 14 km. Surface fault rupture was observed in a rural area on Awaji Island southwest of Kobe, but not within the city itself. Yet "the propagation of the buried fault through the urban centre exposed the city to near-field motions over an extensive region," and the directivity of the ground motion, together with amplifying "basin edge effects" caused by local geologic conditions, combined to create a large zone of Japan Meteorological Association (JMA) intensity 7 ground shaking – the highest level on the JMA scale (equivalent to MMI XI–XII). This "damage strip" of severe

[32] Earliest date of seismic regulations is from (UNCRD, 1995). Building standard revisions are from (Mitchell et al., 1996; Nakashima & Chusilp, 2003).

[33] (Byrne et al., 1996, p. 776).

[34] (Bruneau et al., 1996; Kawashima & Unjoh, 1997). Quote "seismic safety was considerably upgraded …" is from (Kawashima & Unjoh, 1997, p. 508).

ground shaking, roughly 25 km long by 1.5–2 km wide, ran west to east straight through the most populated areas of Kobe and adjoining cities, where density was around 6,800 persons/km^2. Ground motions (0.3 g–0.8 g PGA) were much higher than levels considered in engineering design practice at the time. From a societal standpoint, the seismic event was indeed unusual – it was a direct hit by a severe earthquake on a densely populated urban area.[35]

The Kobe earthquake (which impacted a broader region beyond Kobe city and is also known as the Hanshin–Awaji great earthquake disaster or the Hyogoken–Nanbu earthquake) was the costliest disaster in the world up until that time. Since then, it has only been exceeded by the 2011 Great East Japan earthquake, tsunami, and nuclear disaster. Direct damage in the Kobe earthquake was estimated at 9.9 trillion yen, equivalent to US$100 billion at then-current exchange rates. For comparison, this was equivalent to six times the prefectural government's annual budget; by one estimate, damages amounted to nearly 1% of the total value of private and public infrastructure in the entire country. The earthquake generated 15.5 million m^3 of debris.[36]

Kobe lost about 15% of its building stock in the earthquake. Around 40% of businesses in the city were partially destroyed or worse. Over 67,000 houses and other buildings completely collapsed and another 55,000 partially collapsed. Dozens of fires broke out, eventually spreading over 500 ha and destroying another 7,000 structures. Many of the neighborhoods that burned were in the inner city – "densely built two-storey wooden housing areas … the very areas that had been untouched by bombing during the Second World War" that had been left "unimproved, and their streets unwidened, as their populations grew in the 1950s and 1960s." Some 39% of housing units in Nagata ward were lost in the earthquake, compared with 24% overall for the urban wards (i.e., those along the coastal strip) and 15% across the city as a whole, including the suburban areas.[37]

[35] Casualty numbers are from (City of Kobe, 1998; Edgington, 2010). The magnitude of the earthquake has been variously reported as moment magnitude M_w 6.9 and JMA magnitude M_J 7.2. Kanamori (1995) explains that the difference derives from the magnitude calculation method. Quote "a typical shallow intraplate earthquake …" is from (Kanamori, 1995, p. 10). Fault rupture is from (UNCRD, 1995). Quote "the propagation of the buried fault …" is from (Finn et al., 1996, p. 778). For correspondence between JMA and MMI scales, see Figure 2.8 in (UNCRD, 1995). For directivity and basin edge effects, see (Nakashima & Chusilp, 2003; Pitarka et al., 1998). The maximum ground accelerations in the Kobe earthquake were roughly double the levels of the 1923 Great Kanto earthquake (Okimura et al., 1996). For damage strip, see (Edgington, 2010). Ground motions and engineering design are from (Byrne et al., 1996).

[36] Cost comparisons with other disasters are based on data in EM-DAT, The International Disaster Database, www.emdat.be. Comparison is in terms of total damages, in inflation-adjusted dollars; the three costliest disasters caused by natural hazard events are the 2011 Great East Japan triple disaster (i.e., earthquake, tsunami, and nuclear disaster) (2021 US$273 billion), the Kobe earthquake (2021 US$192 billion), and Hurricane Katrina (2021 US$187 billion). The 9.9 trillion yen figure is from (UNCRD, 1995); numbers are from Hyogo Prefectural Government, cited therein. Relative damage figures and debris are from (Edgington, 2010).

[37] Housing share loss figure is from (Edgington, 2010). Business damage is from (City of Kobe, 2019). Over two-thirds of businesses suffered some degree of damage and disruption, and 20% were destroyed

Because the earthquake occurred in the early morning hours, the deaths were mostly caused by damaged and collapsed homes. Older, traditionally designed wooden houses were especially prone to collapse because of their heavy tile roofs – a protective measure against typhoons – and structural weaknesses, as well as wood rot in their beams and columns. Indeed, as a result of "significant evolution in design and construction practices" from the 1960s to 1980s, more recent wood construction performed significantly better than older vintages, and "it was common to see relatively new houses standing nearly intact among old houses that had collapsed." Roughly 50% of older housing units dating from before 1965 were lost in the disaster, in contrast with just 6% of those built after 1976.[38]

Fatalities, too, occurred disproportionately among older residents. Some 58% of those who died were aged 60 or older:[39]

> Official reports attributed the large number of deaths among the elderly to the greater number of younger people living in the city's outer suburbs, which were less affected by the quake; to the fact that many elderly people lived alone in the quake-stricken districts, especially women; and to the large number of houses in these areas that had been built before or immediately after the Second World War and that were of poor quality.[40]

Commercial and institutional buildings also suffered extensive damage and, had the earthquake occurred in the daytime, large numbers of people would have been killed in them. Ground motions were so strong that "even modern buildings designed in accordance with the present Japanese seismic design code might suffer fatal damage in such large shaking." Heavy damage was sustained in a third of the city's shopping districts and half of its markets, as well as some 50% of the sake breweries and 80% of synthetic shoe factories.[41]

Many reinforced concrete (RC) buildings suffered "weak-story" failures. Numerous concrete buildings in the Sannomiya CBD suffered mid-height story collapses including, for example, an eight-story City Hall building that pancaked at the sixth floor. The phenomenon likely derived from older construction practices in which the building's structural system and column strength transitioned abruptly at mid-height; "inadequate strength distribution along the height and poor detailing of reinforcement, among other causes, were found to be responsible for such failures." Buildings designed to the 1981 code generally performed

(Tokyo Development Learning Center, 2018). Over 33% of the city's 8,900 commercial premises were heavily damaged (Okimura et al., 1996). Collapse statistics are from (City of Kobe, 2019). Fire damage statistics are from (City of Kobe, 2019; Edgington, 2010). Quote "densely built two-storey wooden housing areas …" is from (Edgington, 2010, p. 50). Nagata and ward comparisons are from (Hirayama, 2000).

[38] For casualties and building damage, see (Nakashima & Chusilp, 2003; Prion & Filiatrault, 1996). Quote "significant evolution …" is from (Nakashima & Chusilp, 2003, p. 8). Housing loss by construction vintage is from (Edgington, 2010; Hirayama, 2000).

[39] (City of Kobe, 1998). [40] (Edgington, 2010, p. 7).

[41] Quote "even modern buildings …" is from (Nakashima & Chusilp, 2003, p. 5). Damage statistics are from (City of Kobe, 1998).

well, with the exception of those with soft first stories (often accommodating parking at that level).[42]

Among engineered buildings, damage was particularly prevalent in buildings that had been constructed before the 1981 code changes. For RC structures, the percentage of buildings experiencing serious damage or collapse was 1% for those built after 1981, but 4% for those under the previous (1971) code and 8% for those predating 1971. Among steel-frame buildings, too, older structures experienced much higher rates of serious damage and collapse than newer ones, an outcome attributed to changes from the early 1980s in both seismic design codes and construction practices. Subsequent detailed investigations did, however, find substantial evidence of hidden damage in steel structures.[43]

Disruption to transportation and utility infrastructure vastly compounded the disaster's impacts. The earthquake caused extensive damage to highways and railways throughout Kobe. For example, hundreds of bridge piers were damaged along the elevated Hanshin Expressway Route 3, a major connection between Kobe and Osaka that had opened in 1970, and several spans collapsed catastrophically. Much of the damaged transportation infrastructure had been built to older design codes. But even on Route 5 (Bay Shore route, opened in 1994), a new bridge failed – mainly due to liquefaction and lateral spreading at the foundations – and had to be closed for months. Rail systems, the primary mode of urban commuting, experienced damage to elevated sections, tunnels, and stations.[44]

> Since the earthquake caused especially severe damage in an area running parallel to the coast, many rail and expressway transport structures were destroyed, fragmenting the local transport networks and isolating local communities. By way of example, the collapse of the east-west Hanshin Expressway robbed the relief forces of their main transportation artery and threw emergency operations into disarray … Furthermore, the two artificial islands, Port Island and Rokkō Island, were completely cut off from the mainland when their new transit systems and connecting bridges were destroyed.[45]

Overall, the rail system required 8 months to restore, and the highway system, 20 months. Consistent with the geographic pattern of damage, transportation service disruption was much greater in the coastal wards of the city than in the mountainous suburban areas.[46]

[42] (Mitchell et al., 1996; Nakashima & Chusilp, 2003). Quote "inadequate strength distribution …" is from (Nakashima, & Chusilp, 2003, p. 6).

[43] Damage rates for RC buildings are from (Fukuyama & Sugano, 2000). For those with soft first stories, the rates were higher – around 2% for post-1981 buildings and 12% for pre-1981. For steel buildings, see (Nakashima & Chusilp, 2003). Detailed investigations after the 1994 Northridge (LA) earthquake had similarly found hidden damage in steel-frame buildings that was not immediately apparent.

[44] (Anderson et al., 1996; Bruneau et al., 1996; Chang & Nojima, 2001; Finn et al., 1996; Kawashima & Unjoh, 1997; Okimura et al., 1996).

[45] (Edgington, 2010, p. 50). [46] (Chang & Nojima, 2001).

Other lifeline infrastructure services – electric power, natural gas, water, wastewater, and communications – were also extensively disrupted. Immediately after the earthquake, Kobe lost nearly all its water supply due to the failure of its two major transmission pipelines (built in the 1950s) and widespread damage to buried water mains. Restoration was also delayed by the loss of the head office of the Water Works Bureau, located in the collapsed floor of the City Hall building. Restoration of water and natural gas service took several weeks. Transportation and lifeline infrastructure outages led to a host of compounding and cascading impacts. In the case of fire suppression, for example, not only was there a severe loss of pressurized water for fire-fighting but debris and traffic congestion impeded access by fire trucks.[47]

Liquefaction occurred extensively on the reclaimed lands of Kobe's waterfront, both along the original coastline and on the artificial islands. This damaged not only buried infrastructure and bridges but also a wastewater treatment plant, industrial facilities, warehouses, and port structures. (Liquefaction also occurred sporadically inland, where old reservoirs and irrigation ponds had been filled in to build schools and other public facilities.) Around the perimeters of Port Island and Rokko Island, caisson quay walls shifted outward by 2–3 m and the ground behind them dropped by 1–2 m.[48]

> The Port suffered extensive ground failure … that damaged all of its container berths and almost all of its non-container shipping berths. Gantry cranes, warehouses, all bridges to Rokko and Port Islands, and utility lines carried by these bridges all suffered major damage. The Port was essentially shut down as a result. Damage was estimated at 1 trillion yen (US$10 billion) … [T]he scale of damage was so great that repairs were not completed until March 1997, over two years after the earthquake.[49]

A few berths that had been seismically designed did survive, however, and damage was relatively light in the center of the islands where ground had been densified as part of site improvements. But full repairs required over two years, and by that time, Kobe's ranking among international container ports had dropped from 6th to 17th as it lost traffic to its competitors.[50]

* * *

Kobe eventually recovered from the catastrophe. Disaster recovery is complex, multifaceted, nuanced, differentiated, and nonlinear; moreover, the reference point is often unclear. The picture often varies depending on considerations such as: recovery compared with predisaster or without disaster, recovery to prior trends or

[47] (Chang & Nojima, 2001; Kuraoka & Rainer, 1996; Nojima & Kameda, 1996).
[48] (Finn et al., 1996; Hamada & Wakamatsu, 1996; Okimura et al., 1996). [49] (Chang, 2000, p. 53).
[50] For damage and repairs, see (Chang, 2000; Finn et al., 1996). Rankings are from (Chang, 2000).

to a "new normal," and recovery by whom. In terms of overall population trends, the city lost about 100,000 residents after the earthquake but reattained predisaster levels (1.52 million) within 10 years, by 2005. By that time, one study found that 25% of residents surveyed did not have any personal experience of the disaster, having been living elsewhere or not yet born at the time. Population grew modestly thereafter (to a peak of 1.54 million) before beginning a slight decline after 2012, mirroring broad trends in the country as a whole.[51]

The city's economy, "which was already faltering in the mid-1990s due to the challenges of industrial restructuring," was initially spurred by the postdisaster reconstruction stimulus. In the longer run, however, it settled into a new normal that was sometimes described as an "80% recovery" – a pattern of long-term losses related not just to the disaster itself but also to Kobe's ongoing economic challenges and broader macroeconomic conditions of Japan's "lost decade."[52]

And what happened to the physical city in the years following the earthquake? Within a few months of the disaster, the local government issued its Kobe City Reconstruction Plan and the prefecture issued its Hyogo Phoenix Plan for redeveloping the disaster area. The ideas contained in these plans did not represent a radical departure from previous practices: "Except for a new emphasis on housing, many of Kobe's pre-earthquake economic development ideas were being carried forward to these post-quake plans." For example, the reconstruction plans included a number of "symbolic projects" for assisting in the long-term recovery – many of which "had been 'on the drawing board' in some form or another long before the earthquake and had simply been transferred to the 1995 Reconstruction Plan once it became clear that national government funding might be available to implement them." Planning priorities largely aligned with those underlying the city's fourth master plan, which had been completed just before the earthquake:[53]

> This plan prioritized decentralization of the city's commercial activities on a metropolitan basis and earmarked twelve new suburban nuclei based around shopping centres, as well as two subcentres in the areas of JR (Japan Railways) Rokkō-michi Station (in the east) and JR Shin-Nagata Station (in the west). These subcentres were the very two districts chosen for comprehensive post-disaster urban redevelopment projects in February 1995.[54]

[51] For discussion of recovery concept, see, for example, (Chang, 2010; Edgington, 2010). For personal experience survey, see (Edgington, 2010, p. 210). For postdisaster population trends, see (City of Kobe, 2019).

[52] (Edgington, 2010; Tokyo Development Learning Center, 2018). Quote "which was already faltering …" is from (Edgington, 2010, p. 204). For indicator analysis of the long-term trends, see (Chang, 2010); for model-based analysis, see (duPont et al., 2015; Okuyama, 2015).

[53] (Edgington, 2010); quote "Except for a new emphasis …" is from p. 115 and "had been 'on the drawing board'…" is from p. 119.

[54] (Edgington, 2010, pp. 106–107).

Although the disaster would seem to have provided unanticipated new opportunities for urban transformation, the institutional constraints of Japan's urban planning model "shaped how quickly the city could rebuild, whether the planners could improve the city's safety, what other improvements could be carried out, and what (if anything) could be done for the most disadvantaged communities in Kobe."[55]

Despite public efforts to assist the low-income areas of the city, the spatial differentials that had been evident before the earthquake persisted in the years following it. Recovery lagged in the inner city, particularly in Nagata ward. The predisaster decline of the synthetic shoe manufacturing industry, which had been centered there, accelerated. Many younger people and families moved to new suburban housing, and "the inner-city population of Kobe – especially in Nagata ward – continued its pre-quake trend and 'hollowed out,' which led to a collapse of many communities in terms of shopping and local jobs as well as community services." The wealthier east side of the city, which had also suffered extensive damage, rebuilt and recovered more quickly. Within two years, new housing construction there already exceeded the number of lost units, in part reflecting more favorable real estate market conditions: "As the eastern part of the urban area is located suitably for those who commute to Osaka, it was expected to form a housing market for middle-income people and there has been substantial new housing construction in this area." (Indeed, housing was initially oversupplied in the east, which experienced increasing vacancy rates, while simultaneously in short supply in the western parts of the city.) Overall, the gap between the fortunes of the eastern and western sides of the city widened following the earthquake.[56]

One contributor to these dynamics was the differential availability of reconstruction financing. At the time, there were few government disaster assistance programs, and "Japan's approach after disasters had generally been to repair public infrastructure, with individuals relying on themselves for their own recovery, especially in terms of housing and income support." Moreover, only 3% of property had been insured for earthquake. In the lower-income areas in particular, many households lacked the financial means to rebuild their houses. In terms of postdisaster housing assistance policy, a "single-track approach failed to support the entire population of the disaster-stricken area."[57]

Reconstruction in the inner city also faced impediments related to safety standards, property rights, and even postdisaster reconstruction planning itself.

[55] (Edgington, 2010, p. 13).

[56] For east–west differentials, see (Edgington, 2010; Hirayama, 2000). For shoe manufacturing, see (City of Kobe, 2019; Edgington, 2010; Tokyo Development Learning Center, 2018). Quote "the inner-city population ..." is from (Edgington, 2010, p. 75); "As the eastern part ..." is from (Hirayama, 2000, p. 117).

[57] Insurance rate is from (Edgington, 2010); quote "Japan's approach ..." is from p. 56. Quote "a single-track approach ..." is from (Maly & Shiozaki, 2012, p. 56).

> Many existing houses which did not meet the requirements of the Building Standards Act [because they predated the Act] collapsed and/or were burned down … When rebuilt, however, the new houses must be adjacent to a road of four metres or more in width, and in general the building-to-site area ratio should be 60 per cent or less. It is difficult therefore to rebuild a house in a small site on a narrow road … More than half of the building lots in the inner-city area are not adjacent to a road of sufficient width.[58]

Property rights in the old neighborhoods were complex and often involved multiple parties for a single building; moreover, with the deaths of many elderly residents, ownership succession and associated conflicts further complicated matters. Reconstruction plans had designated a number of heavily damaged areas for large-scale land readjustment and redevelopment, but rebuilding in these areas actually lagged behind the rest of the city:[59] "In other words, land readjustment projects and large-scale urban redevelopment actually *stalled* recovery, in part because of the heavy-handed way in which the city took its initial steps, in part because of the complexities of inner-city property rights when land readjustment programs were being implemented, and in part because of lack of cooperation among local residents."[60]

In the meantime, the city's outlying suburban wards, which had suffered much less damage in the earthquake, recovered quickly and continued to grow after the disaster: "The rapid suburbanization of Kobe would be one of the lasting legacies of the 1995 earthquake."[61]

Building on reclaimed land continued to be a distinctive feature of urban development in the postearthquake years. Port Island Second Stage was completed after the earthquake, and further into the bay, Kobe airport was constructed on a new artificial island, despite residents' opposition and public debt implications. The city further invested in attracting new firms in rapidly growing sectors such as robotics, information technology, and medical and pharmaceutical industries. Most notably, a new Kobe Biomedical Innovation Cluster (KBIC) was developed at the center of Port Island Second Stage (on unused land where previous plans had envisioned a theme park). Although the life sciences industry in Kobe was small before the earthquake, within 20 years, KBIC had developed into the leading biomedical cluster in the country with hundreds of firms.[62]

In terms of disaster risk, after recovering from the catastrophic earthquake, the city became in many respects safer. Many of the most hazardous structures had been destroyed and replaced with buildings meeting more recent codes. Lessons from the disaster for engineering design were incorporated into revised building and bridge standards, for example, to address the problem of soft first stories in

[58] (Hirayama, 2000, pp. 125–126). [59] For property rights and conflicts, see (Hirayama, 2000).
[60] (Edgington, 2010, p. 176). [61] (Edgington, 2010, p. 75). See also (Chang, 2010; Hirayama, 2000).
[62] (Edgington, 2010). For KBIC, see (Tokyo Development Learning Center, 2018).

RC buildings. After the Kobe earthquake, earthquake engineering technologies for base isolation and passive structural control became commonly applied in the design of larger, taller buildings. To address risk in existing buildings, a seismic retrofit program was undertaken for schools, and subsidies helped to retrofit nearly 40,000 homes.[63]

Public infrastructure was also upgraded to mitigate the risk of future disasters. Reflecting lessons from the earthquake, Kobe invested in major risk reduction improvements to its water system, in particular, replacing higher priority, vulnerable distribution pipes with seismically resistant ones, developing an expanded system for storing water, and constructing a third transmission main under the densely developed urban area for emergency supply and backup. Infrastructure investments have also been made in anticipation of a future earthquake on the Nankai Trough subduction zone, where, according to the historical seismic record, great offshore earthquakes have occurred in the decades following an inland fault earthquake in the region. Tsunami mitigation measures, including raising and fortifying seawalls, were completed in 2023.[64]

Yet disaster vulnerability remains. In August 2018, Typhoon Jebi made landfall at Kobe (among other locations along its track) as a category 3 storm, causing record windspeeds and record levels of storm surge and waves around Osaka Bay. Numerous flood gates and coastal embankments had been constructed to protect urbanized areas from flooding, but development that was located on the seaward side of these protective structures (e.g., former waterfront industrial sites converted to retail uses) flooded. Coastal inundation damage was especially pronounced on artificial islands in the bay. On Rokko Island, emergency response facilities were flooded, and a vertical evacuation order (to upper building stories) was issued for all of the 20,000 residents. Cars and containers became floating debris, storm surge and waves damaged port infrastructure, and the island was briefly cut off due to access road flooding. At Port Island, a tunnel – constructed after the Kobe earthquake to provide the island with redundant access – was closed for two days due to flood risk. Kansai International Airport in Osaka, also on an artificial island, was cut off for days when a drifting ship crashed into an access bridge.[65]

Lessons learned from the earthquake have also been incorporated into national policies on disaster assistance. Restrictions on compensating private homeowners were eased, funding programs developed, and postdisaster public housing provided in ways that better support community recovery. Moreover, social issues

[63] For revised standards, see (Kawashima & Unjoh, 1997; Nakashima & Chusilp, 2003). For base isolation, see (Nakashima & Chusilp, 2003). For seismic retrofit program, see (Edgington, 2010).

[64] For water system investments, see (Sakaki et al., 2014) and Kobe City Waterworks Bureau website (https://kobe-wb.jp/seibi/). For Nankai Trough earthquake, see (UNCRD, 1995). For tsunami mitigation, see (Kobe City International Division, 2023).

[65] (Mori et al., 2019). See also (Takabatake et al., 2018).

such as the "benefit of keeping communities together through the entire resettlement process, and the special needs of elderly evacuees and others is much better understood, and these issues are increasingly considered along with the physical reconstruction."[66] The evolution of government assistance policies will also be part of the dynamics in future disasters.

5.3 Christchurch

The Canterbury Plains region where the city of Christchurch, New Zealand, is located is framed by the Southern Alps range to the west, the Waimakariri River to the north, the Pacific coast to the east, and extinct volcanoes to the south. These landscape features all relate to the region's geologic dynamism. New Zealand is located at an active tectonic junction between the Indian–Australian and Pacific crustal plates. Uplift and buckling processes have been forming the Southern Alps over the last 15 million years, and earthquakes are an inherent part of these mountain-building processes. Flowing down from the mountain range, a number of rivers – relatively short ones, in global comparison – run eastward to the Pacific coast, bringing considerable quantities of sediment from the alpine watersheds. Over geologic time, the rivers' alluvial fans have built up the coastal Canterbury Plains with gravel deposits over 500 m deep. In the sector of the plains where Christchurch is located, the agent of land formation has been the Waimakariri River, its floodplain spreading to the ocean and, in the area south of Christchurch, meeting up against the Port Hills and Banks Peninsula, where the eroded cones of a volcanic complex protrude from the sea.[67]

The Waimakariri is a 150 km long braided river whose course has shifted, according to the geologic record, many times across this landscape. Although the river's route today lies north of Christchurch, at various periods within the last several thousand years the river has met the sea in other locations – for example, to the city's east at the Avon–Heathcote Estuary as well as to the city's south around Banks Peninsula. The plain is crisscrossed with old channels of the river, many filled in with gravel, sand, and silt. Groundwater, plentiful in aquifers beneath the plain, is recharged by seepage from the Waimakariri River. The water table is high, within 1–2 m from the surface in the eastern area of Christchurch. Originally, the lands were primarily comprised of swamps.[68]

[66] (Maly & Shiozaki, 2012, p. 62).

[67] In New Zealand, it is increasingly common to refer to places by both their English and Maori names (e.g., Aotearoa New Zealand, Ōtautahi Christchurch, the Ōtākaro Avon river, the Ōpāwaho Heathcote river) and to use Maori terms for certain concepts (e.g., pākehā for New Zealanders of European descent). Here, only English names and terms are used since these would be familiar to an international readership. For geology and physical setting, see (Brown et al., 1995).

[68] (Brown et al., 1995; Hughes et al., 2015; Reinfelds & Nanson, 1993). For water table, see (Rogers et al., 2014). For swamps, see (Pawson, 2000).

Springs give rise to creeks, streams, and small rivers in this landscape: The Avon and Heathcote Rivers, in particular, flow eastward through Christchurch and into a shallow, intertidal estuary that is mostly enclosed by a 4 km long spit. Some 6,500 years ago, the coastline lay near what is today the western edge of the Christchurch CBD. Because of this geologic history of landscape formation on the floodplain and coast, the western areas of the city tend to be underlain with alluvial gravels while the eastern portions are generally comprised of coastal dunes and estuarine or tidal wetland sediments.[69]

Before European colonizers arrived, the region had been inhabited by Indigenous Maori peoples, who were hunter-gatherers. Their villages clustered around the Banks Peninsula rather than in the swamplands, and they moved seasonally to harvest waterfowl, eels, flax, and other foods and commodities from the productive ecosystems of the marshes and estuary. The area that today lies within the Christchurch city boundaries contained seasonal rather than permanent Maori settlements (located on areas of higher and drier ground) and was traversed by trails running along sandy ridges through the swamps.[70]

* * *

Urbanization began with the European settlers who arrived in the middle of the nineteenth century (Figure 5.2). Christchurch was founded, unambiguously and deliberately, as an English colonial town. As was common in New Zealand in that era, it was established by a private agency: The Canterbury Association in London "had bought the land for its settlement from the New Zealand Company and … hoped to sell 100,000 acres to cover its expenses and establish a colony of fifteen thousand people, with a bishop." It instructed its surveyor to select a site for the new town that met certain criteria: a minimum acreage of land for the town itself; ready access to a port; and access to land for farming. A location near the small harbor at Lyttelton was initially deemed preferable; however, it would have necessitated expensive reclamation to meet the acreage requirements. Instead, an alternate site on the Avon River was chosen – it was swampy and "an obvious compromise between the limits of boat navigation on the Avon, the nearest elevated dry land to the coast, and the nearest sources of timber."[71]

The town was planned from the start. Its 1850 plan delineated a rectangular town site, a regular grid pattern of streets, Cathedral Square at the center, a large

[69] For estuary, see (Findlay & Kirk, 1988). For prehistoric coastline, see (Cubrinovski & Robinson, 2016). For sediments, see (Hughes et al., 2015).

[70] For Indigenous livelihoods, see (Hobbs et al., 2022; Pawson & Holland, 2005; Wilson, 2013). For area within city boundaries, see (Rice & Sharfe, 2008; Wilson, 2013). In the early nineteenth century, the area was controlled by the Ngāi Tahu tribe.

[71] Quote "had bought the land …" is from (Rice & Sharfe, 2008, p. 15). See also (Hamer, 1995). Quote "an obvious compromise …" is from (Rice & Sharfe, 2008, p. 14). See also (Pawson, 2000; Wilson, 2013).

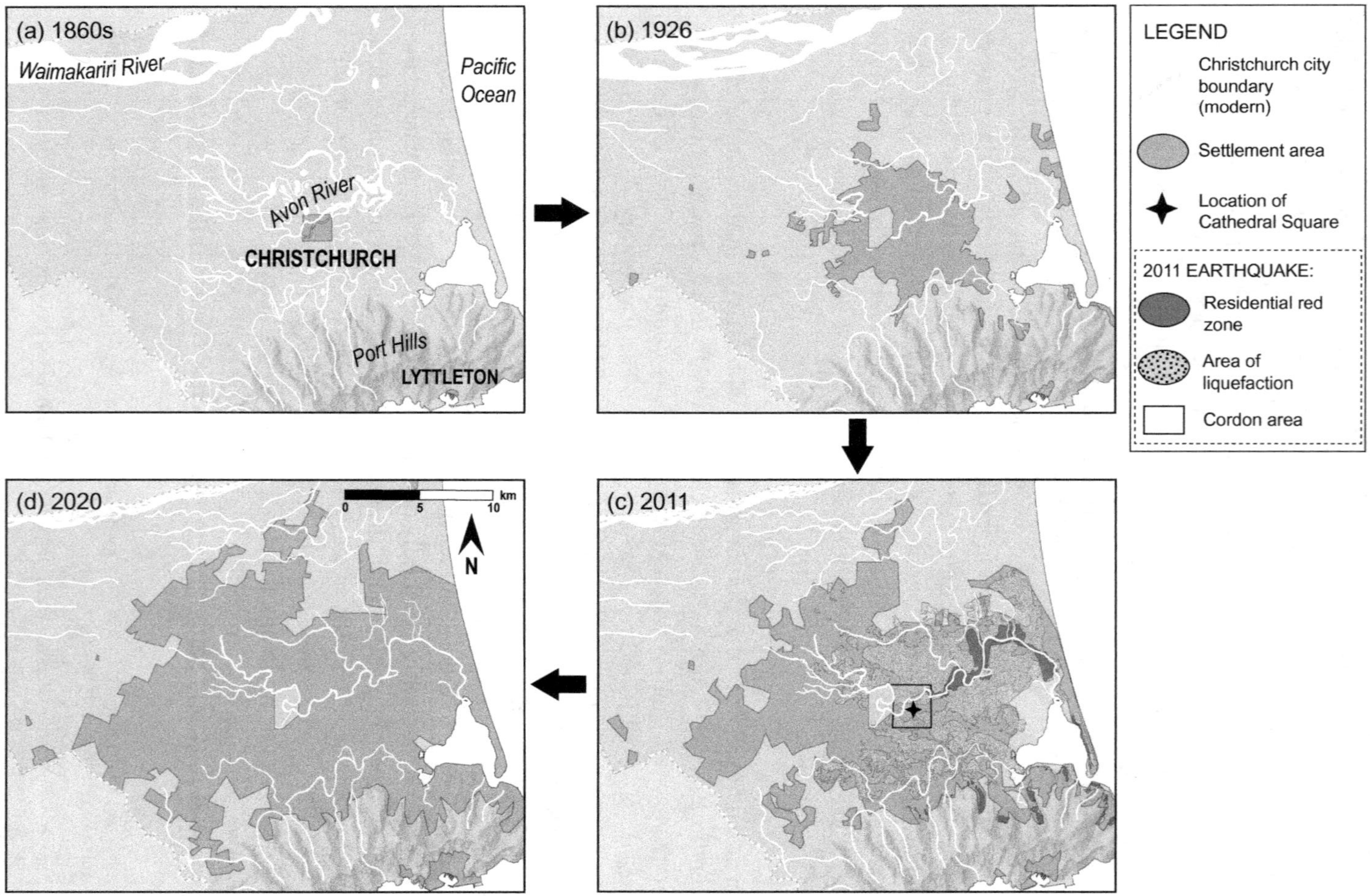

Figure 5.2 Christchurch, urban expansion 1860s–2020. (Data based on: Archives New Zealand, n.d.; Canterbury Maps and Partners, n.d.; Chang et al., 2014; Christchurch City Council, n.d.-a; Orchard, 2017; Rogers et al., 2014; Saunders & Becker, 2015; White et al., 2007. Maps by Charlotte Milne.)

park and other public spaces, and tracts of regularly sized lots for sale. These features largely remain in Christchurch today, and the original town site, bordered on all four sides by wide avenues, grew into the city's downtown. Lot sizes were large – "a significant allocation of town land was recognized as an essential form of bait to attract investors" – but this caused an "excessive dispersal of settlement" because many of the plots were owned by absentee speculators. Moreover, since the land was largely swampy and poorly drained, in the early town, "settlers chose the drier, more elevated locations, and vast areas remained in a state of nature among the irregularly scattered dwellings." The regularity of the town plan belied the inconvenient realities of the terrain.[72]

Christchurch's economy in its early days was precarious. In the initial decades of colonization, many towns were established in New Zealand, "among which for a time a highly competitive relationship existed as they jostled to acquire the assets that would give them the edge in the struggle to become the dominant town in the region." The most pressing issue for 1850s Christchurch was improving transportation access to Lyttelton harbor on the other side of the Port Hills. Road and water access to Lyttelton was hazardous, but digging a tunnel was considered too expensive for a small settlement. The economy was saved, it has been said, by sheep: Only with the rapid growth in wool exports did the government gain the revenue and confidence to make the capital investment. With the opening of Lyttelton Tunnel in 1867 and the connection of railroad service (which had reached the town in 1863), Christchurch gained a secure footing for economic growth and became commercially viable.[73]

Rail transport was critical: "It became of vital importance not just for the growth but even for the very survival of a town that it be located on a railway route. Towns that … [were] bypassed or unable to achieve such a location almost invariably languished." The new rail station was located south of Christchurch town where there was still available land, leading to subsequent clustering of industrial and warehousing activities in that area. By 1876, with the arrival of waves of European immigrants, the town had a population of 12,000.[74]

In this early phase as a frontier town, Christchurch experienced numerous hazards. Earthquakes were among the lesser problems. The most significant seismic event occurred in 1869 – a shallow earthquake centered some 3 km southwest of central Christchurch; although its magnitude is unknown, ground shaking intensity in the town has been estimated at MMI VII. The earthquake caused widespread

[72] (Hamer, 1995; Rice & Sharfe, 2008). Quote "a significant allocation of town land …" is from (Hamer, 1995, p. 16); "settlers chose the drier, more elevated locations …" is from p. 11.

[73] Quote "among which for a time a highly competitive relationship …" is from (Hamer, 1995, p. 19). For early economic conditions, see (Rice & Sharfe, 2008).

[74] Quote "It became of vital importance …" is from (Hamer, 1995, p. 27). For rail station and European immigrants, see (Rice & Sharfe, 2008).

damage to chimneys and to the contents of homes and stores. The side of a brick house collapsed and the stone spire of one church was extensively cracked, yet there were some masonry buildings that remained undamaged. A second strong earthquake occurred in 1870, but while this event was larger in magnitude, it was also deeper and centered about 30 km away. It, too, caused minor damage to chimney and building contents. Beyond these two events, no other significant near-field earthquakes shook Christchurch until the Canterbury sequence of 2010–2011; these were thus "the only historical events that provided an insight into the occurrence and effects of moderate magnitude earthquakes on faults hidden beneath the alluvial plains upon which Christchurch city is situated."[75]

Riverine flooding posed a much more present threat. As early as 1859, engineering studies determined that the then-current bed of the Waimakariri River "was the fourth it had occupied in recent times; floodwaters within the previous two or three years had 'found vent' by the north arm of the Avon." Initially, some limited flood protection works were attempted but easily overwhelmed. A storm in 1868 was particularly destructive:[76]

> Ships were wrecked in Lyttelton Harbour, and the heavy rain caused surface flooding in many places. Most serious of all, the Waimakariri River burst its banks and flowed into its ancient channels on the northwest side of Christchurch. Much of the water came down the Avon, and flowed a metre deep across the Market Place (now Victoria Square). Many shops and houses were damaged by floodwaters and silt deposits.[77]

This disaster ramped up efforts to address the flood problem: "The popular view was that the river should not be allowed to interfere with the work of building a city." A River Board was established, "money was spent on bigger and more extensive groynes," and trees were planted in efforts to confine the river. Floods nevertheless continued to occur; for example, an 1879 storm caused major flooding that disrupted railroads not just around Christchurch but throughout the South Island of New Zealand; the response was better drainage, bigger bridges, and enlarged culverts.[78]

To some extent, flood impacts reflected the newcomers' lack of familiarity with the landscape. "Settlers from Britain were unaccustomed to fast-flowing, mountain-fed watercourses that rose rapidly and without warning. New Zealand's rivers, especially the wide braided rivers of the South Island, posed such a threat to [the settlers] that drowning became nicknamed the 'New Zealand death.'" This lack of familiarity extended to railroad construction. In 1863, a rail bridge was

[75] (Downes & Yetton, 2012); quote "the only historical events …" is from p. 199. See also (Brown et al., 1995).

[76] Quote "was the fourth it had occupied …" is from (Pawson, 2000, p. 72).

[77] (Rice & Sharfe, 2008, p. 35).

[78] Quotes "the popular view …" and "money was spent …" are from (Pawson, 2000, p. 74). See also (Brown et al., 1995). For railroad system response, see (Brett, 2019).

constructed over the Heathcote River in what is today suburban Christchurch; within two years, "the river had scoured the foundations and limited the weight of trains that could cross." In 1867, a new rail bridge opened south of Christchurch, but it was underdesigned and swept away by floodwaters the next year. It was a common occurrence, and engineers soon learned from these experiences and improved their designs and interventions.[79]

> The reactive repairs of the 1860s – mending bridges, stabilizing embankments, distributing fresh ballast – led to preventative measures in the 1870s. The Railways Department incorporated longer bridges, more culverts and better drainage, and altered waterflows with stopbanks [levees], groynes and other measures … by the late 1880s the Railways Department had modified rivers such that they had fewer and less-damaging effects on most lines.[80]

The twin priorities driving these investments were securing transport operations and protecting agricultural production.[81]

Disease, too, presented a chronic hazard. Christchurch in the 1870s was not a healthy place. Epidemics occurred annually; in one outbreak, typhoid killed 152 people. "Christchurch had become notorious as New Zealand's 'fever capital,' with much higher mortality rates from diphtheria, typhoid and scarlet fever than the other main centres." The public health problems derived from poor sanitation, which were aggravated by hospital and brewery waste pollution in the Avon River, wells contaminated by nearby cesspools, and household and animal waste left on unpaved streets.[82]

* * *

Growth therefore required addressing sewerage. A Drainage Board was set up in 1875, and by the late 1880s, Christchurch became the first of New Zealand's main centers to have wastewater management infrastructure: "Rainwater would be channelled into streams and rivers, while sewage and household waste were kept separate and carried into large brick underground sewers." With the construction of these networks, many streams and creeks were converted into piped or boarded drains. In terms of public health, the drainage system also "helped indirectly, because ground water seeped into the system through the pipe joints and significantly lowered the water table, making the city a drier and healthier place than before. The elimination of cesspits largely solved the typhoid problem, and the effect on the city's death rate was dramatic." Public infrastructure for water supply, though, lagged that for drainage because Christchurch

[79] (Brett, 2019); quote "Settlers from Britain …" is from p. 5, and "the river had scoured …" is from p. 8.
[80] (Brett, 2019, p. 25). [81] (Brett, 2019).
[82] (Pawson, 2000; Rice & Sharfe, 2008). Quote "Christchurch had become notorious …" is from (Rice & Sharfe, 2008, p. 42).

had ready access to fresh water from underground aquifers. But eventually, with urbanization, aquifer levels declined, water extraction costs increased, and demand from population expansion grew. The urban water supply network was completed in 1909.[83]

As Christchurch's population grew over the next few decades, households spread out of the original town site into new suburbs that were enabled by the transportation technology of the day – trams powered by horses or, later, by steam and eventually electricity. The tramway network radiated out from the city center and stimulated residential development along its routes. Companies seeking to promote real estate invested heavily in the tram system in the 1880s and 1890s, which reached its maximum extent in 1914. In the years between World Wars I and II, "only the bicycle competed with the tram as the way most people of Christchurch moved about the city." The tram network not only promoted suburbanization but reinforced the central city's economic role: "The years that trams were a key part of the city's transport system coincided with the years the central city drew its largest numbers of people from the suburbs, to work, shop or seek entertainment."[84]

Over this period, Christchurch grew to become the largest city on the South Island and the second largest (after Auckland) in New Zealand. Population expanded from some 44,000 in 1886 to 80,000 by 1911 and 135,000 in 1939. Along the way, the city absorbed several adjoining suburban boroughs through administrative amalgamation. Economically, the city's prosperity remained tied to that of the agricultural hinterland, especially the production of wool and wheat for export. The invention of refrigeration and refrigerated shipping was key to economic growth, with the region exporting frozen meat to England and other distant lands from the 1880s onward.[85]

Christchurch's building stock evolved along with the growth in population and wealth. Early buildings, which were constructed of wood, "were regarded by those who built them as temporary expedients." In the 1870s, a number of wooden churches were replaced by stone structures.[86] Gradually, the townscape transformed: "Through much of the second half of the 19th century in central Christchurch, older, smaller wooden buildings co-existed with large, newer masonry structures. Through the prosperous years from the late 1890s to 1914

[83] Quote "Rainwater would be channelled …" is from (Rice & Sharfe, 2008, p. 51). For piping, see (Wilson, 2013). Quote "helped indirectly …" is from (Rice & Sharfe, 2008, p. 52). For water supply network, see (Pawson, 2000).

[84] (Hamer, 1995; Wilson, 2013). Quote "only the bicycle …" is from (Wilson, 2013, p. 63) and "the years that trams …" is from p. 62.

[85] (Rice & Sharfe, 2008). See also (Gibson, 1971). Population figures reflect the territorial amalgamation that occurred in 1903.

[86] Quote "were regarded by those who built them …" is from (Wilson, 2013, p. 105). For churches, see (Rice & Sharfe, 2008).

most (though not quite all) of the remaining wooden buildings were replaced by large, handsome commercial buildings in permanent materials."[87]

The inner city experienced a building boom in the early 1900s and became nearly fully built up. The Anglican cathedral (on Cathedral Square) was completed in 1904, as was the Roman Catholic cathedral. Residential uses became scarce in the central city as the early houses were replaced by commercial structures. The area within the four avenues that framed the original town site came to be largely comprised of buildings for shopping, entertainment, education, government, and financial and other businesses. By the beginning of World War I, "the central city was dominated by 'permanent' masonry commercial buildings, mostly of three to five stories, plus substantial masonry churches and public buildings." This urban landscape remained largely unchanged in the years between 1914 and 1945, a period of war and economic depression during which few new buildings were constructed.[88]

Considering the vulnerability of masonry buildings to earthquake shaking, it is fortunate that no major seismic events occurred during these decades of early urban growth. Smaller earthquakes were experienced periodically, however, and the spire of the Anglican cathedral was damaged while under construction in 1881, 1888, and again in 1901. After the latter earthquake, "it was decided to rebuild the upper section in timber sheathed in copper, to reduce the risk of future earthquake damage." No liquefaction was reported in either these events or the earlier, more damaging, 1869 earthquake, potentially due to sparse urban development and the size of the earthquakes.[89]

Disease remained more deadly, while frequent flooding continued to pose problems. The 1918 Spanish influenza epidemic killed over 500 people in Christchurch – the city's deadliest disaster. Between 1920 and 1953, Christchurch experienced 26 flood events. By the 1930s, the authorities had decided to embark on an ambitious strategy to control the Waimakariri River:[90]

> It aimed to prevent overflows and, by confining the lower course to a relatively narrow and shorter channel, to flush the build-up of gravel out to the sea. The old South Branch was closed off and Wright's Cut was excavated to bypass a sharp loop. A comprehensive stopbank [levee] and groyne system was constructed. Work on this scheme lasted into the 1950s.[91]

This strategy, to confine the river to an artificial channel along the northern edge of the floodplain, was intended to protect Christchurch and its suburbs from flooding.

87 (Wilson, 2013, p. 107).

88 (Rice & Sharfe, 2008; Wilson, 2013). Quote "the central city was dominated …" is from (Wilson, 2013, p. 111).

89 (Brown et al., 1995; Canterbury Earthquakes Royal Commission, 2012; Rice & Sharfe, 2008). Quote "it was decided to rebuild …" is from (Rice & Sharfe, 2008, p. 64). See (Rice & Sharfe, 2008) for 1901 damage and (Brown et al., 1995) for other earthquakes and comments.

90 For Spanish influenza, see (Rice & Sharfe, 2008). For floods, see (Pawson & Holland, 2005).

91 (Pawson, 2000, pp. 74–75).

By the time it was completed, land on the river's old South Branch had been largely reclaimed. Over the ensuing decades, the scheme succeeded in preventing major flood disasters, but "at the price … of ever-increasing investment in stopbanks [levees], revetments, and plantings – and with the effect of ever-greater urban expansion over the flood plain."[92]

* * *

The decades following World War II were mostly years of prosperity, and Christchurch grew substantially. Its population expanded from about 150,000 to about 373,000 just before the 2010–2011 Canterbury earthquake sequence. Territorial amalgamation and local government reform meant that by the 1990s, the Christchurch City Council was administering a "coherent urban area" administratively separate from the rural hinterland. The city's economy grew apace and diversified; in addition to the traditional agricultural processing, export-oriented manufacturing and tourism emerged as important sectors. Completion of the Lyttelton road tunnel in 1964 enabled direct road access to the port, which was transformed by containerization, with new facilities constructed on reclaimed land.[93]

In the postwar decades, people came to rely increasingly on automobiles for their mobility. The housing demand that accompanied population and economic growth was almost entirely accommodated through car-oriented suburban sprawl. New development filled in land between the old tram lines and extended beyond their terminals. Government policies "encouraged and often restricted homebuyers to purchase new housing on the urban periphery." By the end of the 1960s, "new streets and houses had taken over large areas of farmland in the north-east and north-west, while many vacant blocks across the southern suburbs were now built over. [To the east on the coast] New Brighton was now physically joined to the city by a continuous built-up area."[94]

Retailing and employment also decentralized. From the mid-1960s, suburban shopping malls drew retailers and consumers away from the inner city. New manufacturing jobs were predominantly located in suburban industrial zones. Churches in the new suburbs contributed to declining congregations in the inner city. Professional service companies decentralized to a lesser degree, however, and largely remained in the city center.[95]

[92] (Pawson, 2000); quote "at the price …" is from pp. 206–207.

[93] (Christchurch City Council, 2010; Rice & Sharfe, 2008; Thorns & Schrader, n.d.). Quote "coherent urban area" is from (Rice & Sharfe, 2008, p. 146). See also (Wilson, 2013).

[94] (Buchanan et al., 2006; Memon, 2003; Rice & Sharfe, 2008; Wilson, 2013). Quote "encouraged and often restricted homebuyers …" is from (Buchanan et al., 2006, p. 345); "new streets and houses …" is from (Rice & Sharfe, 2008, p. 131).

[95] (Memon, 2003; Rice & Sharfe, 2008; Wilson, 2013).

In the postwar era, institutions of city and regional planning were developed and exerted a new influence on urban development. Land-use regulation and zoning came into force in the 1950s, for example. In response to concerns about emerging urbanization problems – "the provision and efficient utilisation of urban infrastructure, the loss of productive agricultural land on the urban periphery, increasing cross-city travel, traffic congestion, and decline of the central business district and inner city neighbourhoods" – planning authorities sought to contain urban growth within the older built-up area while encouraging decentralized growth in a few satellite centers. From 1950 to 1990, a 4 to 5 km wide "green belt" (a zone excluding non-farm dwellings) was designated around the urban core, beyond which the plans provided for satellite towns. Motivation notwithstanding, in practice, the policy does not appear to have been particularly successful at containing urban growth: "The green belt policy did not anticipate the strong pressures for rural-residential decentralisation around Christchurch. Nor could it promote, on its own, infilling and redevelopment of the main urban area within Christchurch at higher population densities."[96]

The green belt policy was effectively dismantled by subsequent legislation. After the 1991 Resource Management Act (RMA) came into effect, the green belt was no longer enforced. The RMA shifted policy and planning "from the control and direction of land use and its socio economic consequences, to the 'sustainable management' of the biophysical effects of land use decisions." In place of government regulation to guide urban growth, the RMA sought to achieve environmental goals while relying more heavily on market mechanisms. As with preceding planning systems, this regime also did not achieve effective growth management, and the outcome was a rapid acceleration of new residential development in the peripheral parts of the metropolitan area.[97]

At the same time, from the 1990s, environmental values were becoming more prominent in urban and regional planning. For example, initiatives were undertaken to restore some areas of former wetlands "to attract birds, protect plants and provide recreational opportunity." Christchurch City Council, in considering improvements to the aging drainage infrastructure, developed a Wetlands and Waterways Strategy that recognized the importance of not only drainage but also recreation, biodiversity, culture, and other values; initiatives included retrofitting and developing new stormwater drainage using naturalized systems.[98]

[96] For land use and zoning, see (Swaffield, 2012; Wilson, 2013). Quote "the provision and efficient utilisation …" is from (Memon, 2003, p. 31) and "the green belt policy did not anticipate …" is from p. 34. For green belt, see (Memon, 2003; Swaffield, 2012).

[97] Quote "from the control and direction of land use …" is from (Swaffield, 2012, p. 408). For RMA, see (Memon, 2003). For peripheral development, see (Buchanan et al., 2006; Memon, 2003).

[98] Quote "to attract birds …" is from (Pawson, 2000, p. 84). For Wetlands and Waterways Strategy, see (Swaffield, 2012).

In the process of urban expansion, disparities within the city – in particular, between the more affluent west side of the city and the relatively disadvantaged east – became more pronounced. Broadly speaking, in Christchurch, "there is a northwest-to-southeast gradient of affluence, with neighbourhoods in the west and northwest of the city having higher than average household incomes and property values." According to New Zealand's Index of Social Deprivation, a composite metric reflecting aspects such as low income and inadequate housing, the most deprived neighborhoods prior to the 2010–2011 earthquakes were located mainly to the east and south of the city center, and the least deprived areas to the northwest. The most deprived neighborhoods also corresponded to areas with a high proportion of Maori people.[99]

Notably, however, court proceedings in the 1990s led to a major settlement between the Crown and Ngāi Tahu, the principal Maori tribe of the South Island. The Crown was found to have seriously breached its historic treaty obligations; the settlement, which included lands and city properties, made Ngāi Tahu "a significant new force in Christchurch's property and business sectors." The settlement "brought some re-dress to the Iwi [tribe], setting precedents for Treaty-led planning in Aotearoa New Zealand."[100]

Changes to Christchurch in the postwar decades entailed not only suburban expansion but also transformation of the central city. In the 1960s and 1970s, construction of high-rise commercial buildings caused "more change to the townscape in twenty years than in the previous fifty." Many older commercial buildings were torn down to build modern office blocks and hotels: "Every week, it seemed, old brick buildings in the inner city were reduced to piles of rubble and replaced with plain boxes of glass and steel." Around Cathedral Square, the spire of the cathedral became dwarfed by new high-rises. New mid-rise buildings were also constructed throughout the central city. Christchurch Hospital was "completely rebuilt … with a succession of major buildings gradually replacing the old brick wards." This construction boom reflected the city's changing economy, "driven by a commercial demand for higher quality office space (in the case of the office buildings) and the growth of the tourist industry (in the case of the hotels)." It came to an end with the stock market crash of 1987. By that time, "the ample supply of office space in the buildings erected before the crash was sufficient for demand for such space until the early 21st century," and little new commercial construction occurred downtown until the 2000s. By the time of the 2010–2011 earthquakes, the CBD

[99] For disparities, see (Rice & Sharfe, 2008). Quote "there is a northwest-to-southeast gradient …" is from (Cloke et al., 2023, ch. 3). For Index of Social Deprivation, see (White et al., 2008). For Maori people, see (Hobbs et al., 2022).

[100] Quote "a significant new force …" is from (Rice & Sharfe, 2008, p. 160); "brought some re-dress …" is from (Hobbs et al., 2022, p. 5).

was in relative decline and had substantial commercial vacancies, especially in older buildings: "Low investment returns were an element of the widespread recognition that before the earthquake sequence parts of the commercial central city were economically depressed."[101]

In the decades of substantial growth between World War II and the 2010–2011 Canterbury earthquake sequence, no major disasters struck Christchurch. But the city's risk profile was rapidly transforming – not only from urban development but also from direct efforts to manage and mitigate disaster risk. Riverine flood management for the Waimakariri continued along the previously established approach of containing the river, with further investments made to remove large quantities of accumulated gravel from the channel. New concerns arose, however, about climate change and flood hazards related to increased rainfall and rising sea levels. The Christchurch City Council developed a planning requirement for all new buildings in a designated Flood Management Area to have minimum floor elevations at a specified height (2.72 m) above mean sea level.[102]

> This plan change to address the flood hazard had been bitterly fought through the courts over many years and was due to come into effect in January 2011. Prior to the [2010–2011] earthquakes, CCC [Christchurch City Council] knew that many properties in the eastern suburbs were already too low lying and were therefore highly susceptible to both flood and tsunami inundation.[103]

The city's primary natural hazard was perceived to be flooding, aggravated in part by drainage-induced ground settlement.[104]

Meanwhile, the earthquake threat was becoming better understood. Overall, seismic hazard in Christchurch before 2010–2011 was considered "moderate, about half that of Wellington, New Zealand's capital city." Engineering design standards and building codes began to reflect earthquake considerations. The first seismic design standards were developed in New Zealand following the destructive 1931 Hawkes Bay (Napier) earthquake on the North Island, which caused 256 deaths. After that disaster, construction practices rapidly moved away from unreinforced masonry (URM), and a 1965 amendment to the design standard prohibited construction of new URM buildings altogether. The early standards "provided the basic loads and forces to be considered in design," and subsequent ones introduced important methodological improvements, especially ductility and capacity design provisions in a 1976 standard. Actual construction practices may for various reasons lead or

[101] (Rice & Sharfe, 2008); quote "more change to the townscape ..." is from p. 128, "Every week, it seemed, ..." is from p. 140, and "completely rebuilt ..." is from p. 159. Quote "driven by a commercial demand ..." is from (Wilson, 2013, p. 116) and "the ample supply of office space ..." is from p. 117. For CBD vacancies, see (Chang et al., 2014). Quote "Low investment returns ..." is from (Cloke et al., 2023, ch. 6).

[102] For flood management on the Waimakariri, see (Pawson, 2000). [103] (Rogers et al., 2014, p. 494).

[104] (Hughes et al., 2015).

lag the official engineering design standards in effect at the time; nonetheless, the standards provide useful benchmarks for assessing how buildings of different construction vintages can generally be expected to perform in an earthquake.[105]

The 1976 changes are considered to demarcate the first "modern" seismic code for RC construction, and subsequent updates further improved design standards as earthquake engineering knowledge advanced. RC buildings that predate modern codes are considered "non-ductile" structures that under sufficiently strong shaking could fail suddenly in brittle ways. At the time of the 2010–2011 earthquakes, the vast majority of multistory buildings in the Christchurch CBD were RC structures, many dating from the 1960s and 1980s. The city's policy toward seismically weak buildings was "a passive approach, whereby earthquake-prone buildings were identified but retrofits would typically only be required with a change of use or significant modifications."[106]

The potential for ground failure in earthquakes was not, however, as systematically addressed as the risk of damage to structures such as buildings and bridges.

> The requirements for structural engineering were set out in [professional design standards] … but there were no specific requirements for geotechnical investigations. The susceptibility of the land to undergo liquefaction was recognized and mapped, but not widely appreciated. A significant tsunami hazard was considered to be present for some eastern suburbs, but it was the flood hazard that was of greatest concern for natural hazard planners.[107]

Maps of liquefaction potential from the 1990s identified broad areas of the city, particularly in eastern Christchurch, where a combination of susceptible soils (silt, sand, peat) and high water table (often less than 1 m below ground level) indicated high potential for liquefaction in earthquakes.[108]

Improved knowledge about earthquake risk in the Christchurch region also spurred action on the part of infrastructure organizations. For example, the electric power distribution utility, Orion, began investing in seismic risk reduction from the mid-1990s after participating in an engineering study on natural hazards and lifeline infrastructure risk in the Christchurch region. It seismically strengthened some 260 URM substation buildings, upgraded key bridges carrying electric power assets, and planned a backup "hot-site" for its network control center. By 2010, the utility could claim that all of its district substations and major cables met seismic standards of the day. The lifelines study similarly spurred seismic risk reduction and emergency

[105] Quote "moderate, about half that of Wellington …" is from (Rogers et al., 2014, p. 494). For seismic design standards, see (Kam et al., 2011; MacRae et al., 2011). Quote "provided the basic loads …" is from (MacRae et al., 2011, p. 1–1). See also (Canterbury Earthquakes Royal Commission, 2012).

[106] For seismic codes, see (Kam et al., 2011; MacRae et al., 2011). For non-ductile structures, see (Kam et al., 2011). Quote "a passive approach …" is from (Chang et al., 2014, p. 517).

[107] (Rogers et al., 2014, p. 494).

[108] (Brown et al., 1995).

preparedness on the part of other organizations responsible for electric power transmission, gas, communications, water, port infrastructure, and bridges.[109]

In the postwar decades, insurance also emerged as a major mechanism for addressing natural hazard risk. In 1945, following numerous earthquake disasters around the country, the national government established the Earthquake and War Damage Commission – later renamed the Earthquake Commission (EQC) – "to provide affordable natural disaster insurance to help communities recover from natural disasters." The state-owned insurer provided insurance for "homes, their contents and land against damage by earthquake, volcanic eruption, natural landslip, hydrothermal activity, tsunami and fire following any of these natural disasters." The cover was offered as an automatic extension to fire insurance policies purchased from private companies. At the time of the 2010–2011 events, as many as 95% of homeowners were estimated to have held EQC insurance, which would cover up to NZ$100,000 in earthquake-related damages, with losses over this "cap" covered by the private insurer; "This dual scheme effectively means that the state takes on a portion of the risk associated with living in a seismically active country." Insurance for businesses, though outside of EQC's scope, was also commonly purchased. For both businesses and households, the available insurance was considered inexpensive. By the time of the 2010–2011 earthquakes, New Zealand was among the most highly insured countries in the world.[110]

* * *

The 2010–2011 Canterbury earthquake sequence began in September 2010 with a shallow M_w 7.1 seismic event that ruptured a previously unknown fault underneath the Canterbury Plains. This Darfield earthquake, with epicentral location some 40 km west of Christchurch, caused ground shaking at levels "close to those that would have been used for building design under the current [standards]" – broadly speaking, it was a severe earthquake comparable to a 500-year return period event. In Christchurch city, widespread damage occurred to unreinforced masonry and old stone buildings, and the eastern suburbs experienced broad areas of liquefaction "with silt oozing to the surface and lateral spreading of the land causing damage to houses and infrastructure." There were no fatalities.[111]

[109] For Orion, see (Giovinazzi et al., 2011; Kwasinski et al., 2014; Massie & Watson, 2011; Orion New Zealand Ltd., 2010). For lifelines study and other organizations, see (Fenwick, 2012; Giovinazzi et al., 2011).

[110] See (Brown et al., 2013; Public Inquiry into the Earthquake Commission, 2020). Quote "to provide affordable earthquake insurance …" is from (Toka Tū Ake EQC, n.d.); "homes, their contents and land …" is from (Brown et al., 2013, p. 4). For NZ$100,000 limit, see www.eqc.govt.nz/insurance-and-claims/canterbury-earthquake/canterbury-claims/building-claims/. Quote "This dual scheme …" is from (Cloke et al., 2023, ch. 3). For insurance considered inexpensive, see (King et al., 2014).

[111] (Berryman, 2012; Canterbury Earthquakes Royal Commission, 2012). Quote "close to those that would have been used …" is from (Canterbury Earthquakes Royal Commission, 2012, p. 33); "with silt oozing …" is from p. 32.

In the ensuing months and years, the Darfield earthquake was followed by thousands of aftershocks, several of which were notably damaging. The epicentral locations of the aftershock sequence trended, as a general pattern, toward the east. In December 2010, a M_w 4.7 aftershock occurred that was centered within the Christchurch CBD (1.8 km northwest of Christchurch Cathedral) at a depth of 4 km; while not large in magnitude, because of its location and shallow depth, the earthquake led to some damage in the central city.[112]

The most devastating event of the sequence was the February 2011 M_w 6.2 Christchurch earthquake, which caused 185 fatalities and triggered a formal declaration of a national state of emergency. The earthquake occurred with epicentral location some 10 km south of the city center in the Port Hills, rupturing a previously unknown fault at a shallow depth, up to within 1 km of the surface. Ground motions were extremely high – up to 0.8g (80% of gravity) in the CBD – and were comparable to or exceeded what could be expected in an earthquake with a 2,500-year recurrence interval. Nearly half of the city experienced liquefaction, and deadly rockfalls occurred in the Port Hills. The CBD and eastern suburbs suffered particularly severe losses. Around 75% of the city's housing stock (over 150,000 homes) were damaged to some extent, with losses exceeding NZ$100,000 for some 20% of them. Further aftershocks followed; events in June and December 2011 (M_w 6.0 and 5.9, respectively) further damaged already weakened buildings, including the cathedral at the city center, and again caused liquefaction in the eastern suburbs. In total, the city lost some 12,000 houses and 1,500 commercial buildings that were demolished. The earthquakes and subsequent reconstruction generated 40 years' worth of construction and demolition waste.[113]

Beyond the human impacts, property and economic losses in the Canterbury earthquake sequence were catastrophic. All told, the cost of repairing and rebuilding residential, commercial, and infrastructure damage was initially estimated at NZ$20 billion (US$15 billion) in 2011 dollar terms, or equivalent to 10% of the country's gross domestic product (GDP), and later revised to NZ$40 billion in 2015 dollar terms. About 80% of losses were covered by insurance, which is exceptionally high by global standards. The Canterbury earthquakes "resulted in the largest volume of insurance claims in New Zealand's history, and … the fourth largest insurance event in global history." Already by 2012, it was reported that "claims made to the government EQC net of reinsurance cover exceed $7

[112] (Canterbury Earthquakes Royal Commission, 2012).

[113] (Canterbury Earthquakes Royal Commission, 2012). Distance from (Bradley, 2012). For liquefaction and rockfalls, see (Cubrinovski & Robinson, 2016). For housing stock losses, see (Parker & Steenkamp, 2012). For further aftershocks, see (Berryman, 2012; Canterbury Earthquakes Royal Commission, 2012; Wilson, 2013). For total buildings lost, see (Brand & Nicholson, 2016). For waste, see (Potter et al., 2015).

billion, and have exhausted its funds. The additional liability of the EQC is to be met by the Crown."[114]

The intensity of ground motions and the persistence of major aftershocks surprised experts and the populace alike. But given the levels of shaking that were actually experienced, buildings in the CBD generally performed as engineers would have expected. That is not to say that they survived the shaking undamaged but rather that they were often damaged to degrees and in ways consistent with how they had been built, according to the governing building codes (if any) of the era.[115]

In the city center, nearly half of the building stock had been constructed before the introduction of modern seismic codes. In the February 2011 earthquake, URM and stone buildings dating from the 1930s and earlier experienced widespread damage and killed 39 people. Over 85% of URM buildings suffered anywhere from moderate to complete damage, but those that had been seismically retrofitted before the earthquakes did better. As for mid- and high-rise buildings in the CBD, nearly all of which were built of reinforced concrete, older construction vintages dating from the 1930s–1970s, before modern seismic building codes, were typically damaged in ways that were "well known by designers and … have already been addressed in the current standards" – for example, with columns exhibiting "X"-shaped cracks characteristic of brittle shear failure. Some 54% of these older RC buildings were tagged Red (unsafe) or Yellow (restricted use) in postearthquake safety inspections. One collapsed entirely, with 18 fatalities.[116]

More recently constructed multistory RC buildings were on the whole less damaged, although as many as 44% were tagged Yellow or Red. Considering that the buildings experienced shaking that greatly exceeded the level to which they were designed, and that seismic codes are intended to minimize life safety risks rather than prevent damage entirely, "a large majority of the RC buildings, particularly the modern (post-1976) buildings with capacity-design consideration, performed as expected of them in a severe earthquake" – at least as expected by engineers. One structure, however, the Canterbury Television (CTV) building built in the mid-1980s, pancaked catastrophically and caused 115 deaths. Forensic investigations found deficiencies in its design and construction.[117]

114 For economic losses, see (Parker & Steenkamp, 2012; Wood et al., 2016). For insured loss, see (King et al., 2014). Quote "resulted in the largest volume of insurance claims …" is from (EQC Earthquake Commission, 2013, p. 4); "claims made to the government EQC …" is from (Parker & Steenkamp, 2012, pp. 15–16).

115 For building performance compared to expectations, see (Kam et al., 2011).

116 For buildings constructed before modern seismic codes, see (Kam et al., 2011). For URMs, see (Moon et al., 2014). Quote "well known by designers …" is from (Canterbury Earthquakes Royal Commission, 2012, Vol. 2, pp. 107–108). For safety inspection tags, see (Kam et al., 2011).

117 (Kam et al., 2011); quote "a large majority of the RC buildings …" is from p. 271. For CTV building, see (Canterbury Earthquakes Royal Commission, 2012, Vol. 6).

In the aftermath of the February 2011 earthquake, for public safety reasons, civil defense authorities severely limited public access to the entire CBD. A "cordon" – a fenced and guarded perimeter – was set up around the area bounded by the four avenues, around 110 city blocks (4 km^2) with some 3,000 buildings. This had the immediate effect of displacing not only central city residents but also some 6,000 businesses and 25% of the city's jobs. Over the ensuing months, city blocks were gradually taken out of the designated area until the cordon was completely eliminated over two years later. Within the cordon, conditions were established to streamline safety inspections, construction activities, and demolitions; for example, normal permitting requirements were relaxed. The national government created a new agency, the Canterbury Earthquake Recovery Authority (CERA), to lead the recovery effort and gave it unique powers to expedite the demolition of damaged buildings. Ultimately, in the CBD, nearly all of the unretrofitted URM buildings (and even 70%–80% of the retrofitted ones) were torn down, as were some 60% of multistory RC buildings. As much as 70% of the CBD's commercial building stock for offices, retail, and hospitality may have been torn down.[118]

This unusually high rate of demolition in the downtown reflected a complex postdisaster decision-making environment. Building damage was one factor in the decision to demolish, but often not the only one. Many buildings that were not severely damaged and technically could have been repaired were not. Decision-making regarding buildings' fates was influenced by uncertainties associated with the prolonged aftershock sequence, policy changes toward earthquake-prone buildings, insurance payout conditions, and drawn-out and complex insurance claims processes – as well as the cordon itself and CERA's authorities. "The overall effect of these multiple, interacting factors and decisions has probably been an acceleration of the process of eliminating the poorer (low seismic resistance) building stock."[119]

In the eastern suburbs, liquefaction and associated ground failure caused widespread damage to homes and infrastructure. As strong shaking caused the saturated, loosely consolidated soils to liquefy, large quantities of sand, silt, and water were ejected from below ground to the surface: "Sediment build-up was sufficient to partially bury automobiles and block streets." In total, the earthquakes generated some 900,000 tons of liquefaction silt that had to be removed. The land subsided, often unevenly, causing damage to the foundations of thousands of single-family houses. Nearly 60,000 homes were impacted by liquefaction, 20,000 of them severely. In some areas, water released from the ground as well as from broken water and sewer mains flooded streets. Along the margins of rivers

[118] (Chang et al., 2014; Kam et al., 2011; Kim et al., 2017; King et al., 2014). For URMs, see (Moon et al., 2014). For CBD commercial stock, see (Cloke et al., 2023, ch. 6).

[119] (Chang et al., 2014; Kim et al., 2017). Quote "The overall effect …" is from (Chang et al., 2014, p. 527).

and streams, liquefaction was often accompanied by lateral spreading of the ground – "large permanent ground displacements towards the waterway, slumping and associated settlement." This lateral spreading was especially destructive as it "induced very large and non-uniform ground deformation causing stretching of the ground, foundations and then the building itself. The conventional slab-on-grade and concrete perimeter foundations of residential buildings could not resist such loads or deformation."[120]

Liquefaction and associated ground failure also severely damaged bridges and buried infrastructure. Lateral spreading rotated the supporting abutments of numerous road bridges spanning the Avon River. Damage to underground electric power cables caused widespread power outages, though emergency repairs largely restored power relatively quickly. The potable water system experienced exceptionally high damage rates (nearly 1 repair per kilometer of pipe). In areas with liquefaction, buried pipelines were damaged at 5–15 times the rate in nonliquefied ground. Damage to sewer pipes was similarly severe and took longer to repair. Among other effects from liquefaction, "damaged sewer and storm water drainage pipes were filled with sands, reducing or completely eliminating their ability to drain water." Liquefaction damage at the main wastewater treatment plant led to raw sewage being dumped into local rivers and estuaries. Potable water supply was disrupted to half of Christchurch city; although largely restored within a month, residents were required to boil water for many weeks due to potential sewage contamination.[121]

As disruptive as infrastructure damage was in the earthquakes, it would undoubtedly have been worse had the utilities not previously invested in seismic risk reduction. In the case of Orion, the electric distribution utility, only one of 314 upgraded URM substation buildings failed. Although its administrative buildings in the CBD were rendered unusable in the February 2011 earthquake, within hours, the company was able to reestablish its control center in a backup site, thanks to prior emergency planning. The utility's NZ$6 million seismic upgrade program may have averted NZ$30–50 million in losses, not to mention "weeks and even months of continuous power cuts across most of Christchurch." The city's gas system also presented a remarkable success story. The gas network sustained virtually no damage in the earthquakes and no gas-related fires broke

[120] Quote "sediment build-up …" is from (Davis et al., 2015, p. 7). Tonnage of liquefaction silt is from (Potter et al., 2015). Subsidence damage is from (Van Ballegooy et al., 2014). For liquefaction damage, see (Cubrinovski & Robinson, 2016). Water system damage is from (Davis et al., 2015). Quote "large permanent ground displacements …" is from (Cubrinovski & Robinson, 2016, p. 189). Quote "induced very large and non-uniform ground deformation …" is from (Cubrinovski et al., 2012, p. 268).

[121] For damage to bridge abutments, see (Cubrinovski et al., 2012). For electric power damage, see (Giovinazzi et al., 2011). For damage to potable water and sewer systems, see (O'Rourke et al., 2014). Quote "damaged sewer and storm water drainage pipes …" is from (Davis et al., 2015, p. 6). For raw sewage dumping, see (Davis et al., 2015; Giovinazzi et al., 2011). For boil water requirement, see (Giovinazzi et al., 2011).

out, an outcome that was attributable to the utility's use of highly ductile polyethylene pipes. This practice reflected "lessons learnt following the Kobe earthquake and the participation in the emergency preparedness activities organised by the Canterbury Lifelines Group."[122]

* * *

The extent of earthquake damage and demolitions meant that Christchurch would be dramatically altered – but how would it rebuild? In the CBD, initially the local government (the Christchurch City Council) was in charge of recovery planning. It solicited public input through a popular "Share an Idea" campaign and developed a Draft Central City Plan (Draft CCP). In April 2012, however, a Christchurch Central Development Unit (CCDU) was created within the national agency CERA with an "urgent mandate to deliver a reconstruction blueprint for the downtown area within 100 days." The resulting Christchurch Central Recovery Plan 2012 (CCRP) – developed through a "technocratic top-down 'masterplan'" process – superseded the Draft CCP but adopted a number of its provisions.[123]

Broadly, the reconstruction plan sought "to provide an enhanced network of green open spaces based around the Otakaro (Avon River) and Cathedral Square, to rebuild a more compact low rise commercial core, to increase the number and density of inner-city residents, and to promote mixed-use developments in areas surrounding the core." A foundational assumption was "the maintenance of the existing street and land ownership patterns" in the city center. The government would acquire 16% of the land in the central city to reduce the footprint of the CBD and locate key infrastructure projects. A frame around the downtown's east, south, and north would "reshape central Christchurch," providing new greenspace and helping to "deliver a more compact core"; the idea was "to improve the concentration of commercial uses (and in turn the intensity of urban activity) and to stimulate the growth of significant residential population able to drive demand for everyday goods and services." A series of "anchor projects" financed by national and local governments – a convention center, central library, hospital campus, stadium, and other projects – would catalyze private sector investment in the redevelopment. Building heights within the CBD would be restricted to six to seven stories:[124]

[122] (Giovinazzi et al., 2011; Kwasinski et al., 2014). Quote "weeks and even months of continuous power cuts ..." is from (Giovinazzi et al., 2011, p. 410). For gas system, see (O'Rourke et al., 2014). Quote "lessons learnt following the Kobe earthquake ..." is from (Giovinazzi et al., 2011, p. 411).

[123] (Brand & Nicholson, 2016). Quote "urgent mandate to deliver ..." is from (Chang et al., 2014, p. 526). For CCRP document, see (Canterbury Earthquake Recovery Authority, 2012).

[124] (Brand & Nicholson, 2016); quote "to provide an enhanced network ..." is from p. 166 and "the maintenance of the existing street ..." is from p. 165. Quote "to improve the concentration ..." is from (Canterbury Earthquake Recovery Authority, 2012, p. 35).

> This was initially the result of strong public resistance to the idea of returning to high rise towers … Subsequent economic assessments found that six or seven storey buildings gave the best returns on investment due to the additional cost of seismic strengthening required above this height for Christchurch ground conditions. The economic analysis also suggested that given the expected office demand in the Christchurch market, the six to seven storey model spread development more equitably across the central city, benefiting a number of landowners rather than concentrating the office floor space in a few isolated towers.[125]

In the eastern suburbs, the scale of liquefaction-related land damage in the city was enormous and led to an unusual postdisaster outcome – the government's decision to abandon a substantial area of previously developed urban land. In the worst-hit areas of the eastern suburbs, liquefaction sediments had to be cleaned up, land damage addressed, houses repaired from the foundations up, and substantial utility infrastructure restored. For many places, especially where land had been severely impacted by lateral spreading, rebuilding was deemed impractical and uneconomical. Moreover, land subsidence, lateral spreading, changes in river channel, and settling of levees had "significantly increased flood risk from the Avon river, requiring emergency levee construction and new storm water network construction." The earthquakes "caused floodplain subsidence in excess of 0.5 to 1 m along tidal stretches of the two main urban rivers, greatly enhancing the spatial extent and severity of inundation hazards posed by 100-year floods, storm surges, and sea-level rise." Furthermore, "with groundwater levels (i.e., fully saturated soils) now closer to the ground surface, there is less soil above the water table and therefore less capacity to absorb water during storm events." In the eastern suburb of Bexley, "the high tide demonstrated that some areas had become more vulnerable to flooding as a result of the earthquake-induced subsidence."[126]

After the September 2010 Darfield earthquake, governments and communities alike had wanted to "rebuild everywhere, wherever possible" with improvements for greater earthquake resilience. The February 2011 earthquake, however, was "a game-changer": "Considering the time that large-scale land improvement works would take, as well as the prolonged disruption and distress to the residents that this would entail, the Government actively looked to withdraw from some of the worst-affected or most vulnerable residential areas." Moreover, the financial case for rebuilding was poor:[127]

[125] (Brand & Nicholson, 2016, p. 173).

[126] For rebuilding deemed impractical, see (Cubrinovski et al., 2012; Van Ballegooy et al., 2014). Quote "significantly increased flood risk …" is from (Giovinazzi et al., 2011, p. 404). Quote "caused floodplain subsidence …" is from (Hughes et al., 2015, p. 4) and "with groundwater levels (i.e., fully saturated soils) …" is from pp. 7–8. Quote "the high tide demonstrated …" is from (Rogers et al., 2014, p. 502).

[127] (Rogers et al., 2014, p. 503).

Neither insurance policies nor the EQC Act (1993) provide for betterment. In many cases, the land is not suitable for the types of buildings that had been constructed on the land, so putting these properties back to the position they were in immediately before the earthquake was not going to solve the underlying problem. This would also potentially leave insurers with the same exposure, the risk appetite for which has been rapidly diminishing.[128]

After several damaging earthquakes and innumerable aftershocks, many residents also no longer wanted to rebuild in place. The sequence of events demonstrated that "new land use planning solutions were required … it was not business as usual." CERA designated a "residential red zone" within which rebuilding would not be permitted.[129]

The rationale for strategically retreating or "red zoning" land was primarily an economic one where land remediation or protection was either technically unfeasible or the cost was greater than the value of the land and buildings. The potential cost of land remediation or protection was calculated based on local area solutions. Where this cost exceeded the cost of purchasing the properties at a pre-earthquake valuation, the land decision was made to strategically retreat and the land was purchased using the exceptional powers of the CER [Canterbury Earthquake Recovery] Act.[130]

Owners of over 7,200 properties in the residential red zone were offered a buyout by the government (which would then have the task of recovering money from insurers, including EQC), and nearly all accepted. Houses in the red zone were then removed, and the land "retired."[131]

* * *

The population of Christchurch initially declined by about 6% after the earthquake, losing some 21,000 residents out of 372,600 prior to the disaster. The situation turned around as the rebuild got under way and, due in large part to an inflow of reconstruction workers, the city had regained predisaster population numbers by 2017; thereafter, it continued growing and by 2022 had reached 389,000. Many people displaced from the city relocated to more outlying areas within the Canterbury region: The surrounding Selwyn and Waimakariri districts grew from 85,500 predisaster to 99,000 in 2013, and subsequently continued to expand more rapidly than Christchurch, reaching 147,200 people by 2022.[132]

128 (Rogers et al., 2014, p. 504).
129 (Rogers et al., 2014). Quote "new land use planning solutions …" is from (Saunders & Becker, 2015, p. 77).
130 (Brand & Nicholson, 2016, p. 167).
131 (Rogers et al., 2014). This discussion pertains to the residential red zone designated in flat, liquefaction-prone areas. A separate red zone affecting over 700 properties was also established for part of the Port Hills that was at risk of rockfalls and cliff collapse; see (Saunders & Becker, 2015).
132 Statistics from (Christchurch City Council, n.d.-b, 2010, 2013, 2016). Predisaster population is the estimated figure for 2009.

The economic recovery followed roughly the same trend. Five years after the earthquakes, one assessment reported: "Construction sector activity has increased markedly over the past five years. Most other sectors appear resilient, with notable exceptions being tourism and education, where activity is down sharply." One study found that over 95% of businesses "are still operating within the region, although, on average, with reduced income, reduced employees and higher costs." The total number of jobs in Christchurch city declined from 189,000 (in 2009) to 184,000 (in 2012), then recovered to 203,000 (in 2015) and grew to 224,000 (in 2022).[133]

Within the CBD, however, reconstruction and recovery unfolded with some complexity. After seven years, the situation was considered yet "fragile," and progress after 10 years "both uneven and fitful." Despite the scale of dislocation and demolitions in the central city, "there was never any question about rebuilding the central city as a multifunctional urban space in situ, regardless of the difficulties faced"; indeed, the disaster "refocused pre-earthquake attempts to stem its decline in the face of growing suburban competition, particularly from retailing, hospitality and allied services." But commercial rebuilding in the downtown was slow to take off – delayed by issues of insurance settlement, financing, and land title amalgamations – and lagged both infrastructure repairs and housing reconstruction in the rest of the city.[134]

Rather than leading the rebuild as intended, many of the anchor projects were delayed: 10 years after the earthquakes, the convention center had just opened, for example, while the stadium and metro sports facility were "still anticipated." In 2022, the central city still had nearly 200 vacant sites, predominantly used for car parking. Early reconstruction in the CBD tended to take place on its edges, particularly to the less damaged north, west, and south. This was influenced in part by the cordon:[135]

> While the intention of the cordon was to facilitate recovery, the "early starter" private investors generally favoured sites outside the cordoned-off area. This has been particularly noticeable in the renaissance of areas such as Victoria Street and Addington which were outside the central city "red zone." There has been a significant lag between rebuilding on sites inside the cordon when compared to sites outside.[136]

Displaced businesses and government offices relocated to the edge of town, leasing spaces in formerly vacant structures "after owners rapidly converted them to

[133] Quote "construction sector activity ..." is from (Wood et al., 2016, p. 3); "are still operating ..." is from (Stevenson et al., 2011, p. 4). Statistics are from the Christchurch City Council.

[134] Quotes "fragile" and "both uneven and fitful" are from (Cloke et al., 2023, ch. 6, 5); quote "there was never any question ..." is from ch. 6. For delay in commercial rebuilding downtown, see (Wood et al., 2016, p. 3); see also (Cloke et al., 2023).

[135] Quote "still anticipated" is from (Cloke et al., 2023, ch. 4). Vacant sites are from (Christchurch City Council, 2022).

[136] (Brand & Nicholson, 2016, p. 172).

offices, retail and hospitality spaces to take advantage of the high demand and tenants' willingness to sign rental contracts for long enough periods." Generally, many businesses moved to the relatively undamaged western and southwestern parts of the city.[137]

Retail sector recovery in the CBD continued to face the predisaster challenge of competing with shopping centers in the suburbs. Before the earthquakes, there had been 499 retail businesses in the central city area, fewer than the 629 in the major suburban centers; afterward, the numbers in the city center declined to 320 (in 2012) and 288 (in 2015), while those in the suburbs grew to 683 (in 2012) and 663 (in 2015). In the central city, retail became "dominated by a range of big brand retailers, especially in fashion, which can afford the significant rents charged in expensive, post-earthquake buildings." Across all sectors, by 2022, the CBD had nearly 4,400 businesses with 42,000 employees – still lower than the 6,000 businesses and 50,000 workers predisaster.[138]

Planning for CBD recovery had also included incentivizing the construction of medium-density housing to attract more residents to the central city. This was partially successful: "By 2022 some of the housing objectives of the central city blueprint were being met, despite early failures, with houses being built and sold in moderately good numbers. On the other side of the ledger, a good deal of the new housing was expensive and not affordable to people on low and moderate incomes." As of 2022, about 8,000 people were living in the central city – about the same number of residents as before the earthquakes.[139]

Outside of the central city and especially on the urban margins, the postdisaster urban development pattern was one of urban sprawl, responding to housing pressures and continuation of predisaster trajectories. A shortage of housing in Christchurch following the earthquakes led to a sharp increase in house prices and rents, particularly in the suburbs to the west and south of the city that had experienced relatively little damage. Within the city, the eastern suburbs experienced the highest levels of long-term population loss.[140]

Previously, regional planning had been seeking to contain urban sprawl, but this strategy was modified following the earthquakes:

> The future for the urban region beyond Christchurch's central city was laid out in the Land Use Recovery Plan … This plan was produced recognising that the pre-existing Greater Christchurch Urban Development Strategy with its very strong emphasis on urban intensification and slow land release on the urban margins was not well suited to dealing with

[137] (Cloke et al., 2023); quote "after owners rapidly converted …" is from ch. 6.

[138] Statistics are from (Christchurch City Council, 2010, 2013, 2016). Quote "dominated by a range of big brand retailers …" is from (Cloke et al., 2023, ch. 9). Statistics for 2022 are from (Christchurch City Council, 2022).

[139] (Cloke et al., 2023); quote "by 2022 some of the housing objectives …" is from ch. 5.

[140] (Wood et al., 2016). For eastern suburbs, see (Cloke et al., 2023).

> the need to build a lot of new housing quickly … The land assigned for slow release in the Urban Development Strategy was to be made available quickly to provide for an anticipated 40,000 new households.[141]

The result was that "greenfield land, that had previously been zoned for later and much slower release, saw developers building what they knew best: a lot of financially low-risk, detached housing." Urban sprawl was also facilitated by the construction of a major new road system (planned before the earthquakes) that reduced travel times to the city's peripheral areas.[142] "One of the most visually spectacular outcomes of the housing recovery has been the construction of extensive detached-housing developments in the satellite townships of Waimakariri and Selwyn Districts. This is reflected in the south and westward redistribution of the region's population since the earthquakes."[143]

In the abandoned residential red zone, meanwhile, houses were torn down and over 600 ha of land transferred from the Crown to the city; "the eventual effect was to create large swathes of open greenspace."[144]

Christchurch was transformed in many ways by the Canterbury earthquake sequence and the subsequent reconstruction and recovery. From the perspective of earthquake risk, in emerging from the catastrophe, the city is physically safer in many ways. At a very basic level, people and organizations in Christchurch are now exceptionally aware of the seismic hazard and how to live better in earthquake country. Very tangibly, the city's large stock of earthquake-vulnerable buildings has largely been removed, replaced by new buildings that meet current seismic design standards. Damaged infrastructure has similarly been repaired in ways that will better withstand future earthquakes; for example, water mains have been replaced with pipes made from highly ductile materials that the February 2011 earthquake demonstrated to be capable of surviving severe liquefaction and lateral spreading. The country introduced a new national system in 2017 for managing earthquake-prone buildings, and guidance continues to evolve. Large areas of the eastern suburbs that were especially prone to both earthquake and flooding – and made more vulnerable by the 2010–2011 disaster – are no longer inhabited.[145]

The residential red zone has been incorporated into the ongoing transformation of the 11 km long Ōtākaro Avon river corridor, "one of the largest areas of managed retreat in an urban environment in the world." The Ōtākaro Avon River Regeneration Plan, approved in 2019, "sets out a continuous 345-hectare publicly

[141] (Cloke et al., 2023, ch. 5).
[142] (Cloke et al., 2023); quote "greenfield land …" is from ch. 5. See also (Swaffield, 2012).
[143] (Cloke et al., 2023, ch. 5). [144] (Cloke et al., 2023, ch. 10).
[145] For water main improvements, see (O'Rourke et al., 2014). For earthquake-prone building legislation, see www.building.govt.nz/managing-buildings/managing-earthquake-prone-buildings/#jumpto-new-system-for-managing-earthquake__002dprone-buildings.

accessible ‘green spine’ along the river from the city centre to the estuary. This will provide reafforested areas of native bush [vegetation] and wetland, the latter acting as retention basins as part of a city-wide flood management strategy.” Notably, the vision is not narrowly about safety from natural hazards; rather, it “emphasises a restored natural environment, and strengthened connection between people, the river and the land.” Flood hazard mitigation is approached through a holistic approach that also addresses improving water quality, restoring ecosystems, and engaging communities. One objective, for instance, is to “create a restored native habitat with good quality water so there is an abundant source of mahinga kai, birdlife and native species”; the plan explains that “for Ngāi Tūāhuriri and Ngāi Tahu, mahinga kai is an important concept that can be described as the places where natural resources are obtained, and the philosophies and practices that surround them.”[146]

5.4 Urbanization and Seismic Risk

Kobe and Christchurch are very different cities in many respects. Whether in terms of geographic setting, population size, key industries, density, or the built form of their CBDs, the two cities would seem quite distinct. Differences extend beyond the cities to their regional and national contexts. For example, Kobe is part of a much larger metropolitan region, whereas Christchurch is not. New Zealand has a national earthquake insurance program, while Japan does not. These factors matter when it comes to disaster impacts and recovery.

Yet from the perspective of risk creation, the urban development histories of Kobe and Christchurch, viewed side by side, provide some revealing insights. These lessons are considered here through the guiding questions of this book’s risk dynamics framework: How has urban development influenced the local hazard? How has it influenced exposure and vulnerability? And how have disaster events, in turn, influenced urban development? Kobe and Christchurch demonstrate that urban development processes – particularly the interrelationship between landscape, economics, and technology – play a crucial role in creating urban disaster risk, as much for earthquakes as for floods.

Urbanization does not affect the likelihood of earthquakes occurring. It can, however, influence local hazard – in terms of shaking intensity and associated ground phenomena such as liquefaction. Urbanization often involves modifying the land to make it more suitable for development, for example, through draining

[146] (Cloke et al., 2023); quote “one of the largest areas …” is from ch. 11 and “sets out a continuous 345-hectare …” is from ch. 12. Quote “emphasises a restored natural environment …” is from (Regenerate Christchurch, 2019, p. 3) and “create a restored native habitat …” is from p. 26.

swamps, filling in coastal margins, or even constructing new islands to expand the city's available land base. These types of modified lands tend to be susceptible to liquefaction and lateral spreading in earthquakes.

Major projects to shape the landscape for urban development require capital. While cost-prohibitive for small towns, large capital investments become more financially viable propositions when cities are more sizable. Moreover, land tends to be modified during periods of rapid growth, whether due to population expansion and associated pressures for new housing or for reasons of enhancing economic competitiveness to enable growth.

The scale of such efforts increases as the pressures for urban expansion intensify, as demonstrated in Kobe's sequence of coastal modification projects over the course of the twentieth century. It is worth noting that in Kobe's case, at least, this increasing scale (culminating in the construction of the large artificial islands) was in part linked to the evolving requirements of shipping technology, especially containerization and the competitive pressures to accommodate ever-larger vessels. Broadly, then, where and how a city finds space for physical expansion during periods of rapid growth influence the potential for ground failure hazards in earthquakes.

With regard to exposure – the people and property in harm's way – earthquakes differ from floods in several key respects. Typically, cities in seismically active areas are at risk from earthquakes originating in several fault zones. Some may lie directly beneath the urban area, while others (such as subduction zones capable of generating the largest magnitude earthquakes) may be hundreds of kilometers distant. Ground shaking intensity patterns in a given city can vary substantially between different earthquake events. For shaking, there is no equivalent to a 100-year floodplain. A major earthquake typically causes damage throughout a city, even as the most severe destruction may be spatially concentrated. By implication, then, for seismic risk, increasing urban population is tantamount to increasing exposure to seismic shaking. Expansion of the city into liquefaction-prone areas exacerbates this exposure.

The concept of "people and property in harm's way" can be viewed more broadly in the seismic context: Exposure is not just populations living in locations that could experience earthquake effects but people occupying buildings that are prone to earthquake damage. In Kobe, this included old, wood-frame houses with heavy tile roofs; in Christchurch, old masonry buildings; and in both cities, non-ductile concrete buildings built before modern seismic design codes. During earlier decades of urban development, the proportion of a city's population (if not the total number of people) living in these damage-prone building types would have been much higher than today, simply because those would have been the predominant types of construction.

In this sense, at least, it is plausible to describe the overall trajectory of a city's exposure to seismic hazard as ramping up through many decades of population growth and urban expansion until, with the advent of modern seismic codes, it slows and plateaus. If considered as a share of the city's population, rather than in terms of absolute numbers of people at risk, it is likely that subsequent to modern seismic codes, exposure actually declines.

In terms of property and economic value, however, the picture of exposure trends is different than for people. Seismic design codes are geared toward minimum standards to ensure life safety, not toward reducing economic losses. As demonstrated in Christchurch, damaged buildings that do not kill anyone can nonetheless end up being torn down. As urbanization progresses, cities become more densely built up, with taller buildings replacing smaller ones as demand for space intensifies. Economically, then, exposure increases without plateauing.

For floods, the "levee effect" occurs when the construction of protective structures allows – indeed, encourages – development in previously unprotected areas, affording safety in smaller hazard events but increasing losses in catastrophic ones when the levees fail. Something similar can be observed for earthquakes. Technological advances, reflected in earthquake engineering practice and building codes, enable cities in seismically prone areas to expand upward. When an earthquake occurs that exceeds what had been anticipated, more is at risk than would otherwise have been the case. It is worth remembering that every earthquake disaster brings surprises.

Urbanization influences vulnerability – the propensity to suffer loss if exposed to an earthquake – in complex ways. With technological advances, newer construction vintages of buildings, bridges, and other structures are generally less prone to damage, so physical vulnerability decreases over time. If a city's era of major growth took place many decades in the past, the built environment may be comprised primarily of more vulnerable stock; in contrast, a city whose growth has just recently accelerated would have a different vulnerability profile.

Most cities have vastly more older buildings than newer ones. Moreover, the oldest buildings are concentrated in the oldest neighborhoods, generally toward the city center, while more recent construction is predominant in the suburbs and outskirts. Eventually, older buildings may be replaced by newer, taller, better engineered structures when development pressures and increases in land value are sufficient. As seen in both Kobe and Christchurch, such development pressures are influenced by economic conditions, population growth, land availability constraints, and transportation technologies, among other factors.

Within an earthquake-prone city, older neighborhoods are often hotspots of not only physical vulnerability but also social vulnerability. Rents may be lower and housing more affordable, hence occupied by low-income households or elderly people with limited financial means. In the aftermath of a damaging earthquake, reconstruction may bring in more higher-value properties, leading to a loss of affordable housing, as in the Christchurch case. In Kobe's inner city wards, recovery was slow, complicated by complex property ownership arrangements, improvement efforts such as widening streets, and other issues. In both cities, postearthquake housing loss accelerated construction in outlying, greenfield locations.

Disasters influence urban development in ways both direct and indirect. Reconstruction following earthquakes, as with other types of hazards, typically continues and often accelerates predisaster trends. In both Kobe and Christchurch, for example, postearthquake recovery hastened ongoing suburbanization. Moreover, reconstruction plans incorporated urban planning ideas and projects that had been envisioned before the earthquakes; the availability of financial assistance from the national government helped with implementation. Reliance on technological solutions to the earthquake problem, too, was accelerated, for example, with the increased adoption of base isolation and passive structural control systems in new high-rise buildings after the Kobe earthquake.

Yet major disasters can shift the direction of urban development, as demonstrated by the planned abandonment, or managed retreat, from Christchurch's residential red zone. It is noteworthy that this policy, although environmentally beneficial, was also economically motivated: Rebuilding safely in the red zone would have been too costly, as earthquake damage to the land had rendered it too prone to flooding.

More broadly, disasters trigger learning and adaptation. Major earthquakes provide lessons that are translated into professional practice, for example, into improving building code provisions. The influence extends to cities well beyond the disaster area. In the case of Christchurch's natural gas system, for instance, lessons from the Kobe earthquake had been incorporated into pipeline retrofits that successfully averted damage in the Canterbury earthquake sequence. Learning from other cities is especially critical for seismic risk, since for any individual city, significant earthquakes occur much less frequently than, say, major storms and floods.

Disasters also lead societies to develop more diversified strategies for reducing risk. As the Kobe and Christchurch histories demonstrate, many institutionalized mechanisms for addressing earthquakes – building code improvements, construction practice regulations, government insurance schemes, disaster relief funds for households, and others – were instituted following major disasters.

6

Reconsidering Disaster Risk Reduction

6.1 Legacy in the Landscape

Many scholars and observers have argued that "natural disasters" are far from natural occurrences over which human society has little agency, that natural hazard events turn into disasters only because of social conditions and decisions. In this book, I have investigated this thesis at the level of cities. The six case studies demonstrate that not only are "natural disasters" far from being natural and random occurrences but they are a collateral outcome of how cities grow. It is striking how a version of a common risk narrative runs through cases as distinct as Vienna and Calgary, New Orleans and New York, Kobe and Christchurch. In many specific ways, these cities demonstrate that disaster risk today is a legacy of urban history.

Hazards are characteristic of the physical landscape on which cities develop. Many cities were founded as small settlements on the shores of navigable waterways such as rivers or coasts. Such sites provided economic and strategic advantages, particularly for transport and trade, that were important for the towns as they competed with other settlements, attracted population, and developed into cities. The benefits of such sites came with risks. Floods are natural occurrences in such terrains; indeed, they are part of the geomorphological processes that created the land itself over geologic time. In the early history of many cities, flood disasters occurred frequently – and so did other devastating events such as deadly epidemics and fires. Once a town was planted and took root, it persisted at its original location, rebuilding after every disaster.

Consequently, a modern city's risk remains influenced by the economic and technological considerations of its founding era, which guided the original town site in relation to the landscape and its associated hazards. The specifics of the logic differ across historic eras and hence provide one axis of differentiation between old and young cities. Moreover, over time, the economic logic of the site may even become obsolete – but the location of the urban core, typically near the river or coast, remains.

As a town grows into a city, it densifies at its core and expands outward to accommodate more people and economic activities. Within the local region, the initial town settlement was typically located at a site of comparable safety, such as near the river but on higher ground. Growing populations, however, create pressures for expanding into more hazardous lands. Typically, capital investments would be undertaken to create new developable land – investments such as draining swamps, stabilizing river courses, or dumping fill into a bay to extend the shoreline outward. Technology would overcome the inherent constraints of the landscape and produce expanses of new, low-lying land available for urban development. The specifics varied across the six cities, but in each case, urbanization transformed the physical landscape of land and water.

Urban development itself elevates property values and stimulates further, denser, construction to accommodate the increasing demand by populations and economic activities in the growing city. While developers profit from this, local governments are also incentivized by tax revenues to promote growth. In some cases, they may take an active role, for example, by building transportation and other infrastructure. Over time, particularly in geographically constrained settings, the efforts at landscape transformation increase in scale. Examples include Kobe's artificial islands and New York's filling in of extensive coastal wetlands.

With urban growth, the number of people and value of property at risk from natural hazards – particularly floods – rise, and so too does the pressure to safeguard them. The well-known "levee effect" or "safe development paradox" occurs frequently: Flood protection works lead to more urban development in hazard-protected areas. As a consequence, the potential losses in a catastrophic event that overwhelms the defenses are heightened. Whether in relation to flood or seismic hazards, cities become increasingly dependent on technological solutions such as flood control structures and earthquake engineering.

What is striking from the case studies is the degree to which this ratcheting up of technological dependence is a deliberate strategy of urban development, even in the aftermath of disaster events. The Great Danube Regulation and its subsequent enlargement allowed Vienna to develop new neighborhoods in the previously unstable floodplain. After Hurricane Betsy in 1965, the New Orleans levee system was substantially expanded on the business case that it would protect new land that could be urbanized. In the hazards and disasters literature, the levee effect has been raised as a critique of flood management strategies that paradoxically end up increasing risk. What has been perhaps underappreciated is how a city facing economic pressures to grow across a landscape will, with few if any exceptions, choose to rely increasingly on technology to manage the hazard-related barriers to such growth.

With this self-reinforcing dynamic of urban development and hazard protection, the situation becomes increasingly difficult to reverse. Addressing hazard risk becomes very "path dependent" as future options are constrained by past decisions. This persistence in the urban landscape entails not only the durability of physical structures such as flood protection works and buildings on the floodplain but also associated vested interests – institutions charged with the expensive task of maintaining flood protection, for instance, and residents owning homes in the floodplain.[1]

Perhaps the clearest evidence of such path dependency is the scarcity of examples of retreat from hazard lands that have already been developed into urban neighborhoods, even in the aftermath of major disasters. Following Hurricane Katrina, a proposal to shrink the city's footprint in ways that would reduce flood risk met with strong public resistance. After Hurricane Sandy, New York City's response was adamantly against coastal retreat. Only on Staten Island, in a few of the lowest-density areas facing the highest storm surges, were properties bought out and land turned to greenspace (through a State-level initiative). In Calgary, the buyout program that was instituted after the record flood was voluntary, had low uptake, and made little impact.

Among the case studies, Christchurch's residential red zone provided the most remarkable example of substantial postdisaster managed retreat. It is exceptional in vision and implementation. But it is worth noting that the buyout areas were low-density residential neighborhoods where neither land remediation nor flood protection was an economically (or technically) viable option. In this sense, the exception helps to prove the rule.

As cities grow, larger and more sophisticated engineering works render formerly common hazard events infrequent. Technologies such as flood control works serve to diminish the natural dynamics of landscape processes, thereby creating stable environmental conditions that facilitate urban development. One unintended consequence is that urban populations become more and more distanced from an awareness of these natural dynamic processes, such as riverine flooding. The occurrence of fewer damaging events reduces the collective memory of disasters, an effect that is accelerated with the inflow of newcomers who are unfamiliar with the local landscape and its hazards. Over time, there is a collective loss of hazard awareness.

What happens during eras of rapid growth, when pressures intensify for more housing and urban development, is especially consequential. It is typically during periods of rapid urban growth that there is sufficient pressure and economic justification for making expensive capital investments, whether those be for flood protection structures or bridges that connect formerly peripheral areas to the urban core. Engineering works are designed according to the technologies and practices of their day. Once constructed, buildings and infrastructure often endure for many decades.

[1] For path dependency in flood management, see, for example, (Gralepois et al., 2016).

From the perspective of disaster risk, suburbanization and sprawl can sometimes be helpful, for example, if growth extends away from the most flood-prone areas. Newer neighborhoods in more peripheral areas would tend to experience less damage in a disaster due to both location and technological improvements such as higher design standards in building codes.

The corollary to these observations, however, is that older cities – and especially older neighborhoods within older cities – are often especially vulnerable in disasters. Buildings in a neighborhood tend to be similar in vintage, having been constructed at around the same time. In many cities, older neighborhoods that have not been redeveloped or gentrified represent concentrated pockets of disaster risk. The buildings may predate modern safety standards (such as for seismic hazard), be in poorer condition and command lower rents, and be providing more affordable housing for low-income populations. Similarly, the older neighborhoods' utility and transportation infrastructure may be more vulnerable to damage and disruption. Retrofits such as seismic strengthening or elevating the building for flood resistance are likely to be financially impractical, if not technically infeasible. Kobe's inner city wards provide an example of how such physically vulnerable areas with socially vulnerable populations tend to experience the worst losses and have the greatest difficulty in recovering after a major disaster. In Hurricane Sandy, the severity of impacts in Manhattan's older Lower East Side and Brooklyn–Queens waterfront areas similarly reflect this pattern.

This is not to say, however, that the urban core is always the most vulnerable area, nor that its vulnerability relentlessly worsens with time, nor that the most socially vulnerable populations are always residing in the most at-risk locations. The city is continually changing. Older areas may be redeveloped or become gentrified (displacing vulnerable populations in the process), technologies and building standards improve, and urban planning interventions can directly or indirectly mitigate disaster risk. Along Calgary's older riverfront areas, for example, physical and social vulnerability changed over the decades. At the time of the 2013 flood, the inundated neighborhoods comprised mainly affluent residents, whereas in prior decades, those same areas had been mainly populated by low- to middle-income households. In Manhattan, newer waterfront developments such as Battery Park City experienced relatively little damage and disruption, having been designed to more recent standards on the basis of better risk information.

Destructive disasters periodically punctuate a city's urban development trajectory. In the short term, cities often do become safer after disasters, in that construction with modern standards replaces what was lost. Yet because the underlying economic drivers and institutional structures remain, reconstruction typically continues predisaster development trends in terms of where the city rebuilds and expands. Disadvantaged neighborhoods often lag in recovery, while places with favorable economic conditions rebound quickly. Cities that had been experiencing population decline, financial difficulties, and other governance challenges at the time of the disaster, such as New Orleans before Hurricane Katrina, face much greater difficulties in recovery.

Particularly destructive events tend to spur not only rebuilding but also a diversification in strategies for managing future hazards. This often entails expanding the role of the local government and involving higher levels such as state or provincial and national governments. New approaches may be tried in addition to, but not replacing, previous strategies. Examples from the case studies include the creation of national insurance policies, efforts at regional-scale risk mitigation (such as coastal restoration in Louisiana or flood protection for the larger New York–New Jersey metropolitan area), and nature-based or hybrid solutions for flood risk (such as New York's Living Breakwaters project or Christchurch's Ōtākaro Avon river corridor).

Over the course of urban history, government policy and urban planning have played increasingly important roles in addressing urban disaster risk. Across the case studies, markets – meaning the private sector forces and structures that drive urban development – appear to have had little incentive to reduce disaster risk. Markets do not deal well with long-term hazards. Government regulations such as building codes are thus crucial, as they mandate minimum safety standards that over time incorporate better scientific and engineering understanding. Moreover, they can serve as a form of vital institutional memory of local hazards. But since they typically apply only to new construction, they leave unaddressed the substantially larger and more intractable problem of existing buildings that predate modern standards.

6.2 Any City

Early in the process of writing this book, I faced a crucial question: Which cities should I choose for the case studies? I selected Vienna, Calgary, New Orleans, New York, Kobe, and Christchurch on the basis of their individual instructive value (their disaster experience, for instance, as well as the richness of the available scholarship) and for their collective diversity. Now after having delved into these cases, I suspect that the initial decision may have been less momentous than originally appeared. I suspect that even if I had chosen other cities, the empirical evidence would have led to the same broad conclusions.

This is of course a hypothesis to be confirmed by further research, and there is one important caveat: The risk narrative may differ for cities in developing countries or what is referred to as the Global South. Nonmarket economies, informal settlements, extreme intraurban wealth disparities, and weak planning institutions and governance arrangements, among other factors, influence urbanization patterns in ways that can be expected to affect how a city's disaster risk evolves over time. These factors also appeared in the early histories of some of the case studies in this book but not with the same population and spatial scale, technological era, or globalized economic context. An interesting, open question is therefore how differences in political and economic structures influence the creation and evolution of urban disaster risk.

This study raises many other questions, too, and suggests further research needs. In the interest of tractability, I have focused on the urban built environment rather than a city's inhabitants. While there are connections to the populations at risk – for example, in the processes leading to risk hotspots within a city – there remains a need to critically examine the dynamic interrelationship between physical and social vulnerability. Such an investigation would necessarily involve much greater attention than I have paid to social groups, inequities, institutional structures, and political power.

A second research need pertains to the role of individual people and decisions. Here, I have focused on the broad arc of the risk narrative and emphasized the long-term, structural dimensions of urbanization from an urban economic perspective. This approach de-emphasizes the role of influential individuals (e.g., powerful mayors and visionary urban planners) as well as effective collectives (e.g., citizens' groups). It is also insensitive to key decisions, decision-making processes, political influences, and conflicts. It can be criticized, perhaps, for lacking in imagination about what might otherwise have been. I hope, however, that it provides a useful complement to more in-depth studies of individual cities and disasters that illuminate the roles of influential individuals, critical decisions, and urban visions. Much as we would like to think that enlightened individuals and wise choices can make a substantial difference, systemic aspects do also matter: Choices are constrained, not all paths are possible, and some are more likely than others.

A third question relates to how applicable the findings are to other types of natural hazards. Floods and earthquakes are certainly very different hazards, but they both cause substantial property damage in urban environments. Other hazards – extreme heat events, for example – do not. Yet while urbanization may not influence disaster risk in the same way for other hazards as for floods and earthquakes, it is reasonable to hypothesize that urban development history does matter. In extreme heat events, many cities have concentrations of vulnerable populations such as low-income senior citizens living in older, unretrofitted apartment buildings prone to overheating. Low-income neighborhoods often have streetscapes lacking in trees that could provide vital shade and cooling – another legacy of historic urban development patterns.

* * *

The city where I live, Vancouver, Canada, is not one of the case studies in this book. Its urban history is comparatively short (similar to Calgary's) and from the perspective of natural hazards rather uneventful. It would have made a relatively bland case study for this book. Vancouver was destroyed by an urban fire in 1886, just two months after being incorporated as a city, when all but three houses were burned down. Recovery proceeded quickly and brick structures replaced wooden ones. Aside from this Great Fire in its early days, the city has not experienced a major disaster. Yet in writing the case studies, I came to recognize that, even so, Vancouver's risk story, too, resonates with those of the six cities.[2]

Vancouver is located on the delta of the Fraser, a major river that drains a watershed the size of Great Britain. The Fraser River runs from the Rocky Mountains to the Salish Sea on Canada's Pacific coast. "Before European settlement, the mighty Fraser River was untamed – it regularly overtopped its banks … Beginning in 1864, dykes were built along the Fraser River and its tributaries to protect people and property from flooding." The largest recorded flood on the Fraser occurred in 1894, when the region was sparsely settled; despite its size, therefore, the inundation caused little damage. In ensuing decades, "the lower Fraser Valley [transformed] into a highly developed agricultural area with growing suburban communities and commercial centres," so that in the great flood of 1948, numerous dike collapses led to extensive inundation over agricultural lands. Following the 1948 flood, the dike system was repaired and expanded: "By 1960, some 375 km of river and sea dykes provided protection to most of the vulnerable floodplain and reclaimed tidal lands … By 1994, the [federal and provincial] governments had spent almost $300 million on flood-control structures and programs." By 2003, over Can$13 billion worth of property had been constructed behind the diking system, and nearly 350,000 people resided on the lower Fraser River floodplain. At the time, analysts noted that the diking system had been designed to withstand an event the size of the 1894 flood of record, and "there is a one-in-three chance that a flood [as large as the 1894 event] or larger will occur in the next 60 years."[3]

In 2021, two days of intense precipitation from an atmospheric river event caused dike breaches and led to extensive flooding in the Fraser Valley upstream of Metro Vancouver. It was the costliest extreme weather disaster in the province's history, with substantial damage to farms, homes, and transportation infrastructure. Moreover, "many of those affected by the flooding … learned for the first time that their homes and farms were located on a former lakebed – Sumas Lake," which returned with the flood. The lake, which had once been at the heart of a rich

[2] For fire, see (Mackie, 2024).

[3] For Fraser River, see Fraser Basin Council: www.fraserbasin.bc.ca/about_fraser_basin.html. For flood history, see (Clague et al., 2003); quotes are from pp. 67, 72, 73.

ecosystem and was vital to Indigenous peoples of the region, had been drained in the 1920s to create agricultural land for settlers.[4]

The Vancouver metropolitan region, located downstream from the inundated area, was not flooded in the 2021 disaster. (Its main impact was being cut off from the rest of Canada because flooding and landslides disrupted all highway and rail connections through the Fraser River corridor.) But risk from flooding in the heavily urbanized area has nonetheless been rapidly building up.

Metro Vancouver, which includes the City of Vancouver and numerous other municipalities, has a population approaching 3 million (in 2023) and faces both riverine and coastal storm surge flooding. Climate change is exacerbating both.

> A 500-year flood event – i.e., a flood of a magnitude that currently is estimated to have a 0.2% chance of occurring in any given year – could, by the year 2100, be 10 times more likely to occur … due to the effects of climate change … Today, approximately 20 dikes would be overtopped by such a flood, but by 2100, that flood would cause all existing river dikes to be overtopped, unless significant dike upgrades were implemented.[5]

Analysts have estimated that a 500-year coastal flood would cause Can$19 billion in losses today (2023) but Can$25 billion if it occurred in 2100. Similarly, losses from a 500-year river flood would be Can$23 billion today but Can$33 billion in 2100 – just from inundating more of what already exists, without considering any future increases in population or urban development.[6]

Flooding would be concentrated in just a few especially low-lying communities. Within the metropolitan region, the municipality of Richmond (where Vancouver International Airport is located) would be especially hard hit. Richmond is a flat, low-lying island city built on the Fraser River delta. Average land elevation is 1 m above sea level. (Provincial guidance advises municipalities to plan for 1 m of sea-level rise by 2100.) The city is entirely ringed by 49 km of dikes, and the flood protection system also includes drainage pipes, culverts, and pump stations. Ground subsidence is exacerbating the flood risk. In a major earthquake – and there is a significant seismic hazard – most of the critical dikes across the region, including Richmond's perimeter dike, would be vulnerable to additional subsidence and damage.[7]

[4] The likelihood of extreme rainfall events like the one in 2021 has been substantially aggravated by human-caused climate change (Gillett et al., 2022). For Sumas Lake, see (Finn et al., 2024); quote is from p. 2.

[5] (Fraser Basin Council, 2023, pp. 3–4).

[6] (Fraser Basin Council, 2023). The Fraser River flood event would affect not only Metro Vancouver but also communities upstream in the Fraser Valley. The coastal flood event would primarily affect Metro Vancouver. Inflation is also not considered in the estimates.

[7] (Fraser Basin Council, 2023). More than 60 First Nations (Indigenous) communities that are located on reserves and treaty lands also face high risk, as do the municipalities of Delta in Metro Vancouver and Chilliwack in the Fraser Valley. For Richmond, see also (City of Richmond, 2019, 2022). Metro Vancouver comprises the cities of Vancouver and Richmond as well as 19 other municipalities, one unincorporated area, and one treaty First Nation (https://metrovancouver.org/about-us).

Richmond lies immediately south of the City of Vancouver, across a bridge. Historically, it developed somewhat later than other municipalities in the metro region. In 1966, for example, Richmond had a population of just 50,000 at a time when the City of Vancouver had 410,000. Eventually, however, development pressures reached into the flood-prone area. Regional planners had long been aware of the hazard:[8]

> In the 1996 Livable Region Strategic Plan (LRSP) of Metro Vancouver … one of the guiding principles was to avoid putting additional population in areas of the region subject to hazards … Richmond was known to be particularly hazardous due to its floodplain location, low elevation, liquefaction-prone soils, and the vulnerability of its saucer-shaped topography … Yet constraining growth for hazard avoidance was not palatable to the City of Richmond, and this resistance threatened the adoption of the LRSP since all municipalities had to agree to it. Subsequent negotiations led to a memorandum of understanding: Richmond would support the LRSP, and the region would accept growth in Richmond up to the population limits in the City's official community plan.[9]

By 2021, Richmond's population had reached some 210,000 people, of which 60% comprised international immigrants, the vast majority from Asia. The City's Dikes Master Plan currently involves an accelerated timeline for raising the height of the flood protection structures.[10]

Nor is Richmond the only example in Metro Vancouver of urbanization pressures on flood-prone lands. In the City of Vancouver, as the sea level rises, the coastal floodplain will be expanding into low-lying areas where the land had historically been modified in the process of urban development. This includes waterfront areas of the city's Inner Harbor, where "many competing land uses have been made possible by land reclamation through infilling of near-shore areas," and the False Creek Flats, which had once been a tidal mud flat – a coastal wetland regularly covered by and exposed with the tides – prior to urban settlement. The mud flats were filled in by the city in the early twentieth century to create land for rail yards. Later, "as industry shifted, changed, and moved out of False Creek, the area became the centre of numerous urban revitalization efforts in the 1970s that continue through to this day." False Creek currently has over 38,000 residents and $19 billion in property value. A new campus is under construction on the flats for one of the city's main hospitals, which will move there from its current downtown location outside the coastal floodplain. The City is actively engaging in coastal adaptation planning for False Creek; among other initiatives, it has run a design

[8] Population data are from BC Stats, www2.gov.bc.ca/assets/gov/data/statistics/people-population-community/population/municipal_census_pop_1921_2021.pdf.
[9] (Chang et al., 2019, pp. 153–155).
[10] Population data are from Statistics Canada, 2021 Census of Population (www12.statcan.gc.ca). For Richmond's flood protection plans, see www.richmond.ca/services/water-sewer-flood/dikes.htm.

competition and engaged in innovative solutions to "adapt to rising sea levels while accommodating urban development and fostering ecological revitalization."[11]

Like Kobe and Christchurch, the Vancouver region is at risk from not only riverine and coastal flooding but also earthquakes. As in those other cities, many of the lands at risk of flooding are also highly susceptible to liquefaction in a seismic event – areas including the city of Richmond, Vancouver International Airport, Vancouver's harbor waterfront, and the False Creek flats. Like other earthquake-prone cities around the world, exposure has been increasing due to population growth; but counterbalancing this, vulnerability has been mitigated by improvements in building codes. Seismic design provisions began to be incorporated in Vancouver building codes from the early 1970s and have been periodically amended to higher standards thereafter. One study compared a hypothetical earthquake striking in 1971 versus in 2006; it found that the net effect, in terms of expected earthquake fatalities, was that "from the perspective of the urban area as a whole, improvements in earthquake engineering … have barely kept up with the growth in the number of people living in harm's way." But, in terms of physical damage and social disruption, "the overall severity of the disaster would have been notably higher in 2006 than in 1971, even as the capacity of the urban area to deal with the disaster increased."[12]

As in other cities, older neighborhoods in Vancouver represent hotspots of seismic risk where physically vulnerable building stock is often occupied by socially vulnerable population groups. In a major earthquake, the City has warned: "Large sections of downtown, the West End and the Downtown Eastside would be heavily damaged and need to be cordoned off, leaving them inaccessible for months or even longer." The Downtown Eastside (immediately east of downtown Vancouver) is the most socially vulnerable neighborhood in the region, with 70% of the population considered to be low income. The West End (immediately west of downtown) is one of the city's most densely populated neighborhoods, largely built up subsequent to the city's relaxing of building height restrictions in the late 1950s; over 220 mid- and high-rise structures were built in the neighborhood between 1962 and 1975. The West End is currently a "generally modest income community" with 33% of residents considered low income. It includes a large LGBTQ community, has traditionally served as a "landing pad" for people moving in to the city, has a high density of children, and is predominantly comprised of renters rather

[11] For coastal floodplain map and False Creek background, see (City of Vancouver, 2021); quote "as industry shifted …" is from p. 40. Quote "many competing land uses …" is from (NHC [Northwest Hydraulic Consultants], 2014, p. 7). For the downtown hospital, see https://vancouver.ca/home-property-development/new-st-pauls.aspx. For design challenge, see https://vancouver.ca/green-vancouver/sea2city-design-challenge.aspx; quote is from the website.

[12] For liquefaction map, see (Javanbakht et al., 2023). For building codes, see (Ventura et al., 2005). Quotes are from (Chang et al., 2012, p. 997).

than homeowners. Especially significant for a city with a housing affordability crisis, the West End neighborhood currently accounts for one-third of the city's total rental housing stock, 90% of which was constructed before 1975.[13]

The hallmarks of risk in any city are simultaneously singular to that context and representative of broader generalities.

6.3 Practical Significance

What is it about urbanization that gives rise to disaster risk? With insights gained from the Urban Risk Dynamics framework and the case study cities, it is worth stepping back to reflect on the practical significance of answering this question – why it matters, especially for efforts to reduce disaster risk. I would suggest that there are at least three broad reasons: It underscores why disaster risk and risk reduction should be viewed dynamically, not statically, and provides an approach for doing so. It demonstrates why understanding and tackling urban disaster risk should start with the city, rather than with the hazard or the disaster. And it illustrates why interdisciplinary perspectives are so critical to this enterprise.

Urbanization is a systemic driver of disaster risk. Cities evolve in systematic ways that can be broadly anticipated, in patterns characterized by change along with persistence. The same dynamic forces and pressures that connect the past to the present will continue to shape today's city into its future form. Recognizing this can help analysts and policy-makers to plan better for disaster risk not just today but into the future. Rather than consider future conditions solely in scientific terms, it is critical to simultaneously and realistically consider them in social scientific terms. Urban change often outpaces climate change and, moreover, also modifies the local hazard. Anticipating urban change is complex, but concepts and methodologies from fields such as geography, urban planning, regional science, and urban economics provide tools for doing so.

Considering risk dynamically can help address policy-relevant questions such as which risk mitigation measures to invest in, at what scale, where, and when. For example, the timing of mitigation measures in the context of urban growth and change appears critical. Approaches such as managed retreat may be feasible in areas where the local hazard is high and urban density is low (e.g., Christchurch's residential red zone or New York's buyouts on Staten Island). After an area becomes intensely developed, property values and entrenched interests render such approaches much less feasible; instead, the realistic solution space may involve new approaches, likely involving greater reliance on technology, to

[13] Quote "large sections of downtown ..." is from (City of Vancouver, 2019, p. 42); for Downtown Eastside, see p. 31. For West End, see (City of Vancouver, 2017); quotes are from pp. 10, 9.

protect people and property in ways that accommodate the hazard. Similarly, anticipating urban change can help identify not only today's risk hotspots within the city but also areas that may become future concentrations of risk. It can help to identify critical challenges that may be encountered in postdisaster recovery, such as a potential loss of affordable rental housing stock in a neighborhood that under predisaster conditions is already under gentrification pressures. In other words, thinking about urban change can help planners proactively prepare for reducing risk and recovering from disaster.

Understanding urban disaster risk should start with the city, rather than the disaster. Disasters do not "happen to" a city but rather are an outcome of the city's particular conditions at the moment in its history when the hazard event occurs.

Experts and professionals in the field are accustomed to viewing the disaster risk problem through a specialist lens, that is, to focusing on the hazard or the disaster. Centering the city helps to clarify why disaster risk reduction is often so challenging to prioritize in the agendas of elected officials, private businesses, and urban residents. It can also help in identifying potential alliances with advocates for other societal objectives where actions to reduce disaster risk can simultaneously help with goals such as housing affordability, climate change mitigation, or environmental protection. Centering the city also helps to consider risk from a multihazard standpoint, for example, to identify neighborhoods that are at high risk from floods as well as earthquakes and to develop building regulations that address both hazards. (It is possible to take actions that help with one while hurting with the other; for example, houses with garages and other nonliving spaces on the ground floor for flood reasons may have structural designs that render them prone to soft-story damage in earthquakes.)

Centering the city also suggests that risk reduction examples and lessons can be effectively shared between urban areas with similar risk profiles. Port cities with industrial waterfronts facing both seismic and sea-level rise hazards may find more relevant risk reduction lessons from other similar cities than, say, from beach towns outside of seismic zones that have tourism-based economies. Historic cities with flood-prone downtown cores may learn more from other similar places than from suburban towns experimenting with nature-based solutions to reduce flood risk.[14]

More fundamentally, centering the city suggests that to truly reduce future disaster losses, government policies must address the fundamental risk-producing institutions and processes of urban growth and change – property rights, real

[14] The Resilient Coasts Canada (Resilient-C) platform that my students and I have developed provides an example of a tool for a community to identify other places with similar risk profiles and to access information on how they are addressing risk (https://resilient-c.ubc.ca). See also (Chang et al., 2015, 2018, 2020).

estate markets, risk subsidization, and even the relationship between urban society and the physical landscape – and recognize their underlying economic logics. Structural changes to urban development processes are much more challenging to effect than technological solutions. But innovative policies for flood insurance, disaster assistance, or land-use planning may be more effective in reducing risk if designed to incentivize actions (such as gradual retreat from high-risk areas) rather than simply restrict or prohibit them.

Finally, examining the role of urbanization illustrates why interdisciplinary perspectives are so critical to understanding and addressing disaster risk. The complexity of "urbanization" that shapes a city's risk profile over time does not fall neatly into the intellectual domain of any discipline or subdiscipline. For example, the case studies demonstrated that cities require expanses of flat land contiguous to existing urban development as they expand during periods of rapid population growth; that they will create such land if necessary, whether by filling in coastal waters or marshlands; and that this expansion typically increases exposure and vulnerability to floods and earthquake. This observation integrates knowledge from disciplines as distinct as geomorphology and economics, or geotechnical engineering and urban planning. Similarly, developing risk reduction approaches will require interdisciplinary connections if solutions are to be effective – technically as well as in terms of implementation, avoiding unintended consequences, and ensuring that socially marginalized groups are not further disadvantaged. Insights from fields such as sociology, law, and public policy, among others, will be critically important.

The need for interdisciplinary collaboration extends beyond those researchers, students, and professionals specializing in different disciplines related to hazards and disasters. Many who work in other fields that influence the urban environment – transportation engineers, construction managers, land-use planners, real estate developers, and many others – might consider the problems of "natural hazards" and "disasters" to be the distant domain of emergency managers. But it is the ordinary, everyday urban growth and change that, more than emergency planning efforts, will shape the legacy of disaster risk for today's children and for future generations.

References

Abboud, J. M., Ryan, M. C., & Osborn, G. D. (2018). Groundwater flooding in a river-connected alluvial aquifer. *Journal of Flood Risk Management*, *11*(4), e12334. https://doi.org/10.1111/jfr3.12334

Abramson, D., Chobany, C., Merdjanoff, A., Lynch, K., Janda, I., Choi, C., Isufi, K., Kapur, R., McCool, A., Sogluizzo, M., Zambiazzi, E., & Piltch-Loeb, R. (2022). *Ten years after Sandy: Charting a region's recovery*. NYU Center for Public Health Disaster Science.

Anderson, D. L., Mitchell, D., & Tinawi, R. (1996). Performance of concrete bridges during the Hyogo-ken Nanbu (Kobe) earthquake on January 17, 1995. *Canadian Journal of Civil Engineering*, *23*, 714–726.

Angel, S., Parent, J., & Civco, D. L. (2012). The fragmentation of urban landscapes: Global evidence of a key attribute of the spatial structure of cities, 1990–2000. *Environment and Urbanization*, *24*(1), 249–283. https://doi.org/10.1177/0956247811433536

Archives New Zealand (n.d.). Crown Grant Index Record Map: Christchurch District (c. 1905). *Crown Grant Plans*. Accessed December 10, 2024 from: https://archway.howison.co.nz/item/R22668377

Armstrong, C., Nelles, H. V., & Evenden, M. D. (2009). *The river returns: An environmental history of the Bow*. McGill-Queen's University Press.

Arnott, R. (2011). What planners need to know about the "New Urban Economics." In N. Brooks, K. Donaghy, & G.-J. Knaap (Eds.), *The Oxford handbook of urban economics and planning* (pp. 51–78). Oxford University Press. https://doi.org/10.1093/oxfordhb/9780195380620.013.0004

Babson, A. L., Bennett, R. O., Adamowicz, S., & Stevens, S. (2020). Coastal impacts, recovery, and resilience post-Hurricane Sandy in the Northeastern US. *Estuaries and Coasts*, *43*(7), 1603–1609. https://doi.org/10.1007/s12237-020-00809-x

Baics, G., & Meisterlin, L. (2016). Zoning before zoning: Land use and density in mid-nineteenth-century New York City. *Annals of the American Association of Geographers*, *106*(5), 1152–1175. https://doi.org/10.1080/24694452.2016.1177442

Bairoch, P. (1991). *Cities and economic development: From the dawn of history to the present* (C. Braider, Trans.; Paperback ed.). University of Chicago Press.

Barendrecht, M. H., Viglione, A., & Blöschl, G. (2017). A dynamic framework for flood risk. *Water Security*, *1*, 3–11. https://doi.org/10.1016/j.wasec.2017.02.001

Beasley, W. G. (1989). The foreign threat and the opening of the ports. In M. B. Jansen (Ed.), *The Cambridge history of Japan: Volume 5: The nineteenth century* (Vol. 5, pp. 259–307). Cambridge University Press. https://doi.org/10.1017/CHOL9780521223560.006

Beck, J. L., & Hall, J. F. (1986). Factors contributing to the catastrophe in Mexico City during the earthquake of September 19, 1985. *Geophysical Research Letters*, *13*(6), 593–596.

Bellafante, G. (2022, October 28). Why is New York still building on the waterfront? *The New York Times*. www.nytimes.com/2022/10/28/nyregion/waterfront-building-hurricane-sandy.html

Bernhofen, D. M., El-Sahli, Z., & Kneller, R. (2016). Estimating the effects of the container revolution on world trade. *Journal of International Economics*, *98*, 36–50. https://doi.org/10.1016/j.jinteco.2015.09.001

Berry, B. J. L. (1964). Cities as systems within systems of cities. *Papers in Regional Science*, *13*(1), 147–163. https://doi.org/10.1111/j.1435-5597.1964.tb01283.x

Berry, B. J. L. (2008). Urbanization. In Marzluff, J. M. et al. (Eds.), *Urban ecology* (pp. 25–48). Springer.

Berryman, K. (2012). Geoscience as a component of response and recovery from the Canterbury earthquake sequence of 2010–2011. *New Zealand Journal of Geology and Geophysics*, *55*(3), 313–319. https://doi.org/10.1080/00288306.2012.702674

Birkland, T. A., Burby, R. J., Conrad, D., Cortner, H., & Michener, W. K. (2003). River ecology and flood hazard mitigation. *Natural Hazards Review*, *4*(1), 46–54. https://doi.org/10.1061/(ASCE)1527-6988(2003)4:1(46)

Black, J. A. (2022). *A short history of transport in Japan from ancient times to the present*. Open Book Publishers.

Blaikie, P., Cannon, T., Davis, I., & Wisner, B. (2014). *At risk: Natural hazards, people's vulnerability and disasters*. Routledge. https://doi.org/10.4324/9780203714775

Blake, E. S., Kimberlain, T. B., Berg, R. J., Cangialosi, J. P., & Beven, J. L. II. (2013). *Tropical cyclone report: Hurricane Sandy (AL 182012) 22–29 October 2012*. National Hurricane Center.

Blake, E. S., Landsea, C. W., & Gibney, E. J. (2011). *The deadliest, costliest, and most intense United States tropical cyclones from 1851 to 2010 (and other frequently requested hurricane facts) (NOAA Technical Memorandum NWS NHC-6)*. National Weather Service.

Blakely, E. J. (2012). Recovery of the soul: Rebuilding planning in post-Katrina New Orleans. *Housing Policy Debate*, *22*(1), 117–131. https://doi.org/10.1080/10511482.2011.634428

Bloom, N. D. (2008). *Public housing that worked: New York in the twentieth century*. University of Pennsylvania Press.

Blöschl, G., Nester, T., Komma, J., Parajka, J., & Perdigão, R. A. P. (2013). The June 2013 flood in the Upper Danube Basin, and comparisons with the 2002, 1954 and 1899 floods. *Hydrology and Earth System Sciences*, *17*(12), 5197–5212. https://doi.org/10.5194/hess-17-5197-2013

Blumberg, A. F., & Bruno, M. S. (2018). *The urban ocean: The interaction of cities with water*. Cambridge University Press. https://doi.org/10.1017/9781108123839

Bosker, M. (2022). City origins. *Regional Science and Urban Economics*, *94*, 103677. https://doi.org/10.1016/j.regsciurbeco.2021.103677

Bosker, M., & Buringh, E. (2017). City seeds: Geography and the origins of the European city system. *Journal of Urban Economics*, *98*, 139–157. https://doi.org/10.1016/j.jue.2015.09.003

Bradley, B. (2012). Ground motions observed in the Darfield and Christchurch earthquakes and the importance of local site response effects. *New Zealand Journal of Geology and Geophysics*, *55*(3), 279–286. https://doi.org/10.1080/00288306.2012.674049

Brand, D., & Nicholson, H. (2016). Public space and recovery: Learning from post-earthquake Christchurch. *Journal of Urban Design*, *21*(2), 159–176. https://doi.org/10.1080/13574809.2015.1133231

Brandon, C. M., Woodruff, J. D., Orton, P. M., & Donnelly, J. P. (2016). Evidence for elevated coastal vulnerability following large-scale historical oyster bed harvesting. *Earth Surface Processes and Landforms*, *41*(8), 1136–1143. https://doi.org/10.1002/esp.3931

Brett, A. (2019). Floods and railways in nineteenth-century New Zealand. *New Zealand Journal of History*, *53*(2), 5–31.

Brooks, L., Gendron-Carrier, N., & Rua, G. (2021). The local impact of containerization. *Journal of Urban Economics*, *126*, 103388. https://doi.org/10.1016/j.jue.2021.103388

Brooks, L., & Lutz, B. (2019). Vestiges of transit: Urban persistence at a microscale. *The Review of Economics and Statistics*, *101*(3), 385–399. https://doi.org/10.1162/rest_a_00817

Brown, C., Seville, E., & Vargo, J. (2013). *The role of insurance in organisational recovery following the 2010 and 2011 Canterbury earthquakes* [Resilient Organisations Research Report 2013/04]. Resilient Organisations. www.resorgs.org.nz

Brown, L. J., Beetham, R. D., Paterson, B. R., & Weeber, J. H. (1995). Geology of Christchurch, New Zealand. *Environmental & Engineering Geoscience*, *I*(4), 427–488.

Bruneau, M., Wilson, J. C., & Tremblay, R. (1996). Performance of steel bridges during the 1995 Hyogo-ken Nanbu (Kobe, Japan) earthquake. *Canadian Journal of Civil Engineering*, *23*, 678–713.

Bryant, S. P., Davies, E. G. R., Sol, D., & Davis, S. (2022). The progression of flood risk in southern Alberta since the 2013 flood. *Journal of Flood Risk Management*, *15*(3). https://doi.org/10.1111/jfr3.12811

Buchanan, N., Barnett, R., Kingham, S., & Johnston, D. (2006). The effect of urban growth on commuting patterns in Christchurch, New Zealand. *Journal of Transport Geography*, *14*(5), 342–354. https://doi.org/10.1016/j.jtrangeo.2005.10.008

Burby, R. J. (2006). Hurricane Katrina and the paradoxes of government disaster policy: Bringing about wise governmental decisions for hazardous areas. *The Annals of the American Academy of Political and Social Science*, *604*(1), 171–191. https://doi.org/10.1177/0002716205284676

Burby, R. J., Beatley, T., Berke, P. R., Deyle, R. E., French, S. P., Godschalk, D. R., Kaiser, E. J., Kartez, J. D., May, P. J., Olshansky, R., Paterson, R. G., & Platt, R. H. (1999). Unleashing the power of planning to create disaster-resistant communities. *Journal of the American Planning Association*, *65*(3), 247–258.

Burby, R. J., Nelson, A. C., & Sanchez, T. W. (2006). The problems of containment and the promise of planning. In E. L. Birch & S. M. Wachter (Eds.), *Rebuilding urban places after disaster: Lessons from Hurricane Katrina* (pp. 47–65). University of Pennsylvania Press.

Burchfield, M., Overman, H. G., Puga, D., & Turner, M. A. (2006). Causes of sprawl: A portrait from space. *Quarterly Journal of Economics*, *121*(2), 587–633.

Bureau of Policy and Research. (2022). *Ten years after Sandy: Barriers to resilience*. Office of the New York City Comptroller Brad Lander.

Burrows, E. G., & Wallace, M. (1999). *Gotham: A history of New York City to 1898*. Oxford University Press.

Byrne, P. M., Finn, W. D. L., & Ventura, C. E. (1996). The Hyogo-ken Nanbu (Kobe) earthquake of 17 January 1995: Seismological aspects and ground motions. *Canadian Journal of Civil Engineering*, *23*, 771–777.

Calgary Emergency Management Agency. (2022). *Disaster risk report 2022*. The City of Calgary.

Calgary Public Library. (2014). *Calgary flood story*. https://floodstory.com/

Campanella, R. (2010). *Delta urbanism: New Orleans*. American Planning Association, Planners Press.

Campanella, R. (2016). Disaster and response in an experiment called New Orleans, 1700s–2000s. In *Oxford Research Encyclopedia of Natural Hazard Science*. Oxford University Press. https://doi.org/10.1093/acrefore/9780199389407.013.1

Canterbury Earthquake Recovery Authority. (2012). *Christchurch central recovery plan = Te mahere Maraka Ōtautahi*. Canterbury Earthquake Recovery Authority.

Canterbury Earthquakes Royal Commission. (2012). *Final report*. Canterbury Earthquakes Royal Commission.

Canterbury Maps and Partners. (n.d.). Original 19th century South Island survey maps (Black Maps). *Canterbury Maps*. Accessed December 10, 2024 from: www.arcgis.com/home/item.html?id=8d89b32eb335418396eb195300351c3c

Capello, R. (2014). Classical contributions: Von Thünen, Weber, Christaller, Lösch. In M. M. Fischer (Ed.), *Handbook of Regional Science* (Chap. 27). Springer-Verlag.

Castonguay, S., & Evenden, M. D. (Eds.). (2012). *Urban rivers: Remaking rivers, cities, and space in Europe and North America*. University of Pittsburgh Press.

Chang, S. E. (2000). Disasters and transport systems: Loss, recovery and competition at the Port of Kobe after the 1995 earthquake. *Journal of Transport Geography*, *8*, 53–65.

Chang, S. E. (2010). Urban disaster recovery: A measurement framework and its application to the 1995 Kobe earthquake. *Disasters*, *34*(2), 303–327.

Chang, S. E., Gregorian, M., Pathman, K., Yumagulova, L., & Tse, W. (2012). Urban growth and long-term changes in natural hazard risk. *Environment and Planning A: Economy and Space*, *44*(4), 989–1008. https://doi.org/10.1068/a43614

Chang, S. E., McDaniels, T. L., Yumagulova, L., & Stevens, M. (2019). Dynamics and governance of risk in Metro Vancouver. In P. Gurstein & T. A. Hutton (Eds.), *Planning on the edge: Vancouver and the challenges of reconciliation, social justice, and sustainable development* (pp. 155–180). UBC Press.

Chang, S. E., & Nojima, N. (2001). Measuring post-disaster transportation system performance: The 1995 Kobe earthquake in comparative perspective. *Transportation Research Part A*, *35*, 475–494.

Chang, S. E., Taylor, J. E., Elwood, K. J., Seville, E., Brunsdon, D., & Gartner, M. (2014). Urban disaster recovery in Christchurch: The central business district cordon and other critical decisions. *Earthquake Spectra*, *30*(1), 513–532. https://doi.org/10.1193/022413EQS050M

Chang, S. E., Yip, J. Z. K., Conger, T., Oulahen, G., Gray, E., & Marteleira, M. (2020). Explaining communities' adaptation strategies for coastal flood risk: Vulnerability and institutional factors. *Journal of Flood Risk Management*, *13*(4), e12646. https://doi.org/10.1111/jfr3.12646

Chang, S. E., Yip, J. Z. K., Conger, T., Oulahen, G., & Marteleira, M. (2018). Community vulnerability to coastal hazards: Developing a typology for disaster risk reduction. *Applied Geography*, *91*, 81–88. https://doi.org/10.1016/j.apgeog.2017.12.017

Chang, S. E., Yip, J. Z. K., & Tse, W. (2019). Effects of urban development on future multi-hazard risk: The case of Vancouver, Canada. *Natural Hazards*, *98*(1), 251–265. https://doi.org/10.1007/s11069-018-3510-x

Chang, S. E., Yip, J. Z. K., Van Zijll De Jong, S. L., Chaster, R., & Lowcock, A. (2015). Using vulnerability indicators to develop resilience networks: A similarity approach. *Natural Hazards*, *78*(3), 1827–1841. https://doi.org/10.1007/s11069-015-1803-x

Christchurch City Council. (n.d.-a). "Contextual historical overview: Maps." https://ccc.govt.nz/culture-and-community/heritage/heritage-in-the-city/historical-overview

Christchurch City Council. (n.d.-b). *Facts, stats and figures*. Christchurch City Council. Retrieved May 30, 2023, from https://ccc.govt.nz/culture-and-community/statistics-and-facts/facts-stats-and-figures/

Christchurch City Council. (2010). *Christchurch City fact pack 2010*. www.ccc.govt.nz/assets/Documents/Culture-Community/Stats-and-facts-on-Christchurch/fact-packs/FactPack2010-docs.pdf

Christchurch City Council. (2013). *Christchurch City fact pack 2013*. Christchurch City Council. www.ccc.govt.nz/assets/Documents/Culture-Community/Stats-and-facts-on-Christchurch/fact-packs/FactPack2013.pdf
Christchurch City Council. (2016). *Christchurch City fact pack 2016*. Christchurch City Council. www.ccc.govt.nz/assets/Documents/Culture-Community/Stats-and-facts-on-Christchurch/fact-packs/FactPack2016.pdf
Christchurch City Council. (2022). *Central city biannual update: January to June 2022*. https://ccc.govt.nz/culture-and-community/central-city-christchurch/our-progress/central-city-action-plan-reports
Church, M., Burt, T. P., Galay, V. J., & Kondolf, G. M. (2009). Rivers. In O. Slaymaker, T. Spencer, & C. Embleton-Hamann (Eds.), *Geomorphology and global environmental change* (1st ed., pp. 98–129). Cambridge University Press. https://doi.org/10.1017/CBO9780511627057.005
City of Kobe. (1998). *The Great Hanshin-Awaji Earthquake statistics and restoration progress*. City of Kobe.
City of Kobe. (2019). *Kōbe no keizai 2018 (Kobe economy 2018)*. City of Kobe.
City of Kobe Development Bureau. (1993). *Outline of the Development Bureau's projects*. City of Kobe.
City of New York. (2013). *PlaNYC: A stronger, more resilient New York*. New York City Special Initiative for Rebuilding and Resiliency. http://s-media.nyc.gov/agencies/sirr/SIRR_spreads_Hi_Res.pdf
City of New York. (2023a). *PlaNYC: Getting sustainability done*. City of New York.
City of New York. (2023b, October 18). *Laurian Farrell appointed deputy commissioner for coastal resilience at the Department of Environmental Protection*. www.nyc.gov/site/dep/news/23-041/laurian-farrell-appointed-deputy-commissioner-coastal-resilience-the-department-of
City of Richmond. (2019). *Flood protection management strategy 2019*. City of Richmond.
City of Richmond. (2022). *Flood protection at the City of Richmond*. www.letstalkrichmond.ca/floodprotection
City of Vancouver. (2017). *West End community plan*. City of Vancouver.
City of Vancouver. (2019). *Resilient Vancouver*. City of Vancouver.
City of Vancouver. (2021). *Coastal adaptation: False Creek*. City of Vancouver.
Clague, J. J., Turner, B., & Franklin, R. (2003). *Vancouver, city on the edge: Living with a dynamic geological landscape*. Tricouni Press.
Clark, C. (1951). Urban population densities. *Journal of the Royal Statistical Society. Series A (General)*, *114*(4), 490–496.
Cloke, P. J., Conradson, D., Pawson, E., & Perkins, H. C. (2023). *The post-earthquake city: Disaster and recovery in Christchurch, New Zealand*. Routledge.
Coastal Protection and Restoration Authority of Louisiana. (2023). *Louisiana's comprehensive master plan for a sustainable coast, 4th ed. (Draft)*. Coastal Protection and Restoration Authority of Louisiana.
Coch, N. K. (2015). Unique vulnerability of the New York–New Jersey metropolitan area to hurricane destruction. *Journal of Coastal Research*, *31*(1), 196. https://doi.org/10.2112/JCOASTRES-D-13-00183.1
Colten, C. E. (2002). Basin Street blues: Drainage and environmental equity in New Orleans, 1890–1930. *Journal of Historical Geography*, *28*(2), 237–257. https://doi.org/10.1006/jhge.2001.0400
Colten, C. E. (2005). *An unnatural metropolis: Wresting New Orleans from nature*. Louisiana State University Press.
Colten, C. E. (2006). Vulnerability and place: Flat land and uneven risk in New Orleans. *American Anthropologist*, *108*(4), 731–734.

Colten, C. E., & Giancarlo, A. (2011). Losing resilience on the Gulf Coast: Hurricanes and social memory. *Environment: Science and Policy for Sustainable Development*, *53*(4), 6–19. https://doi.org/10.1080/00139157.2011.588548

Colten, C. E., & Sumpter, A. R. (2009). Social memory and resilience in New Orleans. *Natural Hazards*, *48*(3), 355–364. https://doi.org/10.1007/s11069-008-9267-x

Cooley, C. H. (1894). The theory of transportation. *Publications of the American Economic Association*, *9*(3), 13–148.

Cronon, W. (1991). *Nature's metropolis: Chicago and the Great West*. W. W. Norton.

Cubrinovski, M., & Robinson, K. (2016). Lateral spreading: Evidence and interpretation from the 2010–2011 Christchurch earthquakes. *Soil Dynamics and Earthquake Engineering*, *91*, 187–201. https://doi.org/10.1016/j.soildyn.2016.09.045

Cubrinovski, M., Robinson, K., Taylor, M., Hughes, M., & Orense, R. (2012). Lateral spreading and its impacts in urban areas in the 2010–2011 Christchurch earthquakes. *New Zealand Journal of Geology and Geophysics*, *55*(3), 255–269. https://doi.org/10.1080/00288306.2012.699895

Davies, T. R. H., Korup, O., & Clague, J. J. (2021). *The geomorphic footprint of natural hazards and disasters*. Wiley-American Geophysical Union.

Davis, C. A., Giovinazzi, S., & Hart, D. E. (2015). *Liquefaction induced flooding in Christchurch, New Zealand* [Conference paper]. Proceedings of the 6th International Conference on Earthquake Geotechnical Engineering.

Davis, D. R., & Weinstein, D. E. (2002). Bones, bombs, and break points: The geography of economic activity. *American Economic Review*, *92*(5), 1269–1289.

Day, J., Hunter, R., Kemp, G., Moerschbaecher, M., & Brantley, C. (2021). The "problem" of New Orleans and diminishing sustainability of Mississippi River management – future options. *Water*, *13*(6), 813. https://doi.org/10.3390/w13060813

Day, J. W., Colten, C., & Kemp, G. P. (2019). Mississippi Delta restoration and protection: Shifting baselines, diminishing resilience, and growing nonsustainability. In E. Wolanski, J. W. Day, M. Elliott, & R. Ramachandran (Eds.), *Coasts and Estuaries* (pp. 167–186). Elsevier. https://doi.org/10.1016/B978-0-12-814003-1.00010-1

Day, J. W., & Hunter, R. G. (2022). Environmental setting of the Mississippi River Delta. In J. W. Day, R. G. Hunter, & H. C. Clark (Eds.), *Energy production in the Mississippi River Delta* (Vol. 43, pp. 7–38). Springer International Publishing. https://doi.org/10.1007/978-3-030-94526-8_2

Dewilde, B., Dumolyn, J., Lambert, B., & Vannieuwenhuyze, B. (2018). 'So one would notice the good navigability': Economic decline and the cartographic conception of urban space in late fifteenth- and sixteenth-century Bruges. *Urban History*, *45*(1), 2–25. https://doi.org/10.1017/S0963926816000742

Diaz-Fanas, G., Garini, E., Ktenidou, O.-J., Gazetas, G., Vaxevanis, T., Lan, Y. J., Heintz, J., Ma, X., Korre, E., Valles-Mattox, R., Stavridis, A., Kim, I., Hernandez-Bassal, L., Anzola, E., Berkowitz, R., Hussain, S., Jalalian, A., Carrion, H., Dominguez Maldonado, V., … Nikolaou, S. (2020). ATC M_w 7.1 Puebla–Morelos earthquake reconnaissance observations: Seismological, geotechnical, ground motions, site effects, and GIS mapping. *Earthquake Spectra*, *36*(2_suppl), 5–30. https://doi.org/10.1177/8755293020964828

Doberstein, B., Fitzgibbons, J., & Mitchell, C. (2019). Protect, accommodate, retreat or avoid (PARA): Canadian community options for flood disaster risk reduction and flood resilience. *Natural Hazards*, *98*(1), 31–50. https://doi.org/10.1007/s11069-018-3529-z

Doglioni, C. (2018). A classification of induced seismicity. *Geoscience Frontiers*, *9*(6), 1903–1909. https://doi.org/10.1016/j.gsf.2017.11.015

Douglas, I. (2013). *Cities: An environmental history*. I.B. Tauris.

Downes, G., & Yetton, M. (2012). Pre-2010 historical seismicity near Christchurch, New Zealand: The 1869 M_W 4.7–4.9 Christchurch and 1870 M_W 5.6–5.8 Lake Ellesmere earthquakes. *New Zealand Journal of Geology and Geophysics*, *55*(3), 199–205. https://doi.org/10.1080/00288306.2012.690767

Drennan, M. P. (2018). Do agglomeration economies decay over short distances? Are they stable in the face of shocks? Evidence from Manhattan. *International Journal of Urban Sciences*, *22*(1), 1–16. https://doi.org/10.1080/12265934.2017.1407253

Du, R., & Zhang, J. (2019). Walled cities and urban density in China. *Papers in Regional Science*, *98*(3), 1517–1539. https://doi.org/10.1111/pirs.12415

duPont IV, W., Noy, I., Okuyama, Y., & Sawada, Y. (2015). The long-run socio-economic consequences of a large disaster: The 1995 earthquake in Kobe. *PLOS ONE*, 10(10), e0138714. https://doi.org/10.1371/journal.pone.0138714

Duranton, G. (1999). Distance, land, and proximity: Economic analysis and the evolution of cities. *Environment and Planning A*, *31*(12), 2169–2188.

Duranton, G., & Puga, D. (2015). Urban land use. In G. Duranton, J. V. Henderson, & W. C. Strange (Eds.), *Handbook of Regional and Urban Economics* (Vol. 5A, pp. 468–559). Elsevier.

Duranton, G., & Puga, D. (2020). *The economics of urban density* [Working paper 27215]. National Bureau of Economic Research.

Economic Bureau, Kobe City Government. (1994). *Economic overview of Kobe*. Kobe City Government.

Edgington, D. W. (2010). *Reconstructing Kobe: The geography of crisis and opportunity*. UBC Press.

Edmonds, D. A., Toby, S. C., Siverd, C. G., Twilley, R., Bentley, S. J., Hagen, S., & Xu, K. (2023). Land loss due to human-altered sediment budget in the Mississippi River Delta. *Nature Sustainability*. https://doi.org/10.1038/s41893-023-01081-0

Eguchi, R. T., Goltz, J. D., Taylor, C. E., Chang, S. E., Flores, P. J., Johnson, L. A., Seligson, H. A., & Blais, N. C. (1998). Direct economic losses in the Northridge earthquake: A three-year post-event perspective. *Earthquake Spectra*, *14*(2), 245–264.

Eigner, P., & Schneider, P. (2005). Verdichtung und Expansion: Das Wachstum von Wien. In K. Brunner & P. Schneider (Eds). *Umwelt Stadt. Geschichte des Natur- und Lebensraumes Wien* (pp. 22–53). Böhlau Verlag.

Ejiagha, I. R., Ahmed, M. R., Dewan, A., Gupta, A., Rangelova, E., & Hassan, Q. K. (2022). Urban warming of the two most populated cities in the Canadian province of Alberta, and its influencing factors. *Sensors*, *22*, 2894. https://doi.org/10.3390/s22082894

Encyclopædia Britannica, Inc. (2024a). Map of Vienna (c. 1900), from the 10th edition of the Encyclopædia Britannica. *Encyclopædia Britannica*. Accessed December 10, 2024 from: www.britannica.com/place/Vienna/History#/media/1/628062/51196

Encyclopædia Britannica, Inc. (2024b). Map of New Orleans (c. 1900), from the 10th edition of the Encyclopædia Britannica. *Encyclopædia Britannica*. Accessed December 10, 2024 from: www.britannica.com/place/New-Orleans-Louisiana/The-Civil-War-and-its-aftermath#/media/1/411897/51164

Encyclopædia Britannica, Inc. (2024c). Map of New York City (c. 1900), from the 10th edition of the Encyclopædia Britannica. *Encyclopædia Britannica*. Accessed December 10, 2024 from: www.britannica.com/place/New-York-City/Growth-of-the-metropolis#/media/1/412352/51167

Ennals, P. (2014). *Opening a window to the West: The Foreign Concession at Kōbe, Japan, 1868–1899*. University of Toronto Press.

Environment and Climate Change Canada. (2013). *Canada's top 10 weather stories of 2013*. Environment and Climate Change Canada.

EQC Earthquake Commission. (2013). Annual report 2012–2013. EQC.

Fainstein, N. I., & Fainstein, S. S. (1987). Economic restructuring and the politics of land use planning in New York City. *Journal of the American Planning Association*, *53*(2), 237–248. https://doi.org/10.1080/01944368708976658

Fenwick, A. C. (2012). *The value of lifeline seismic risk mitigation in Christchurch*. New Zealand Lifelines.

Findlay, R. H., & Kirk, R. M. (1988). Post-1847 changes in the Avon-Heathcote Estuary, Christchurch: A study of the effect of urban development around a tidal estuary. *New Zealand Journal of Marine and Freshwater Research*, *22*(1), 101–127. https://doi.org/10.1080/00288330.1988.9516283

Finn, R. J. R., Ned-Kwilosintun, M., Ballantyne, L., Hamilton, I., Kwo, J., Seymour-Hourie, R., Carlson, D., Walters, K. E., Grenz, J., & Martin, T. G. (2024). Reclaiming the Xhotsa: Climate adaptation and ecosystem restoration via the return of Sumas Lake. *Frontiers in Conservation Science*, *5*, 1380083. https://doi.org/10.3389/fcosc.2024.1380083

Finn, W. D. L., Byrne, P. M., Evans, S., & Law, T. (1996). Some geotechnical aspects of the Hyogo-ken Nanbu (Kobe) earthquake of January 17, 1995. *Canadian Journal of Civil Engineering*, *23*, 778–796.

Flores-Estrella, H., Yussim, S., & Lomnitz, C. (2007). Seismic response of the Mexico City Basin: A review of twenty years of research. *Natural Hazards*, *40*(2), 357–372. https://doi.org/10.1007/s11069-006-0034-6

Foran, M. (2009). *Expansive discourses: Urban sprawl in Calgary, 1945–1978*. AU Press.

Fraser Basin Council. (2023). *Lower Mainland flood management strategy: Synthesis of technical analysis*. Fraser Basin Council. www.fraserbasin.bc.ca/water_flood.html

Fukuyama, H., & Sugano, S. (2000). Japanese seismic rehabilitation of concrete buildings after the Hyogoken-Nanbu Earthquake. *Cement and Concrete Composites*, *22*, 59–79.

Gibson, C. (1971). Urbanization in New Zealand: A comparative analysis. *Demography*, *10*(1), 71–84.

Gierlinger, S., Haidvogl, G., Gingrich, S., & Krausmann, F. (2013). Feeding and cleaning the city: The role of the urban waterscape in provision and disposal in Vienna during the industrial transformation. *Water History*, *5*(2), 219–239. https://doi.org/10.1007/s12685-013-0075-1

Gillett, N. P., Cannon, A. J., Malinina, E., Schnorbus, M., Anslow, F., Sun, Q., Kirchmeier-Young, M., Zwiers, F., Seiler, C., Zhang, X., Flato, G., Wan, H., Li, G., & Castellan, A. (2022). Human influence on the 2021 British Columbia floods. *Weather and Climate Extremes*, *36*, 100441. https://doi.org/10.1016/j.wace.2022.100441

Giovinazzi, S., Wilson, T., Davis, C., Bristow, D., Gallagher, M., Schofield, A., Villemure, M., Eidinger, J., & Tang, A. (2011). Lifelines performance and management following the 22 February 2011 Christchurch earthquake, New Zealand: Highlights of resilience. *Bulletin of the New Zealand Society for Earthquake Engineering*, *44*(4), 402–417.

Glaeser, E. L. (2005). *Urban colossus: Why is New York America's largest city? (Working paper 11398)*. National Bureau of Economic Research.

Glavovic, B. C., Dawson, R., Chow, W., Garschagen, M., Haasnoot, M., Singh, C., & Thomas, A. (2022). Cross-chapter paper 2: Cities and settlements by the sea. In H.-O. Pörtner et al. (Eds.), *Climate change 2022: Impacts, adaptation and vulnerability* (pp. 2163–2194). Cambridge University Press. https://doi.org/10.1017/9781009325844.019

Gordon, M., & Hulchanski, J. D. (1985). *The evolution of the land use planning process in Alberta 1945–1984* (Research paper no. 156). Centre for Urban and Community Studies, University of Toronto.

Gornitz, V., Couch, S., & Hartig, E. K. (2002). Impacts of sea level rise in the New York City metropolitan area. *Global and Planetary Changes*, *32*, 61–88.

Gotham, K. F., & Greenberg, M. (2014). *Crisis cities: Disaster and redevelopment in New York and New Orleans*. Oxford University Press.

Governor's Office of Storm Recovery. (2022). *Superstorm Sandy anniversary report: Ten years later: A retrospective, 2012–2022*. New York State.

Gralepois, M., Larrue, C., Wiering, M., Crabbé, A., Tapsell, S., Mees, H., Ek, K., & Szwed, M. (2016). Is flood defense changing in nature? Shifts in the flood defense strategy in six European countries. *Ecology and Society*, *21*(4), art37. https://doi.org/10.5751/ES-08907-210437

Gramling, R., Freudenburg, W. R., Laska, S., & Erikson, K. T. (2011). Obsolete and irreversible: Technology, local economic development, and the environment. *Society & Natural Resources*, *24*(6), 521–534. https://doi.org/10.1080/08941920903311417

Gray-Scholz, D., Haney, T. J., & MacQuarrie, P. (2019). Out of sight, out of mind? Geographic and social predictors of flood risk awareness. *Risk Analysis*, *39*(11), 2543–2558. https://doi.org/10.1111/risa.13357

Grübler, A. (2003). *Technology and global change*. Cambridge University Press.

Gurwitz, A. S. (2019). *Atlantic metropolis: An economic history of New York City*. Palgrave Macmillan. https://doi.org/10.1007/978-3-030-13352-8

Haer, T., Husby, T. G., Botzen, W. J. W., & Aerts, J. C. J. H. (2020). The safe development paradox: An agent-based model for flood risk under climate change in the European Union. *Global Environmental Change*, *60*, 102009. https://doi.org/10.1016/j.gloenvcha.2019.102009

Haidvogl, G. (2012). The channelization of the Danube and urban spatial development in Vienna in the nineteenth and early twentieth centuries. In S. Castonguay & M. Evenden (Eds.), *Urban rivers: Remaking rivers, cities, and space in Europe and North America* (pp. 113–129). University of Pittsburgh Press.

Haidvogl, G., Guthyne-Horvath, M., Gierlinger, S., Hohensinner, S., & Sonnlechner, C. (2013). Urban land for a growing city at the banks of a moving river: Vienna's spread into the Danube island Unterer Werd from the late 17th to the beginning of the 20th century. *Water History*, *5*(2), 195–217. https://doi.org/10.1007/s12685-013-0078-y

Haidvogl, G., Winiwarter, V., Dressel, G., Gierlinger, S., Hauer, F., Hohensinner, S., Pollack, G., Spitzbart-Glasl, C., & Raith, E. (2018). Urban waters and the development of Vienna between 1683 and 1910. *Environmental History*, *23*(4), 721–747. https://doi.org/10.1093/envhis/emy058

Hall, J., Arheimer, B., Borga, M., Brázdil, R., Claps, P., Kiss, A., Kjeldsen, T. R., Kriaučiūnienė, J., Kundzewicz, Z. W., Lang, M., Llasat, M. C., Macdonald, N., McIntyre, N., Mediero, L., Merz, B., Merz, R., Molnar, P., Montanari, A., Neuhold, C., … Blöschl, G. (2014). Understanding flood regime changes in Europe: A state-of-the-art assessment. *Hydrology and Earth System Sciences*, *18*(7), 2735–2772. https://doi.org/10.5194/hess-18-2735-2014

Hall, T. (1997). *Planning Europe's capital cities: Aspects of nineteenth-century urban development*. E & FN Spon.

Hallegatte, S., Ranger, N., Mestre, O., Dumas, P., Corfee-Morlot, J., Herweijer, C., & Wood, R. M. (2011). Assessing climate change impacts, sea level rise and storm surge risk in port cities: A case study on Copenhagen. *Climatic Change*, *104*(1), 113–137. https://doi.org/10.1007/s10584-010-9978-3

Halpin, E., & Varuso, R. (n.d.) "Case study: New Orleans Levee System (Louisiana, 2005)," *Lessons Learned from Dam Incidents and Failures*, Association of State Dam Safety Officials, accessed December 9, 2024, https://damfailures.org/case-study/new-orleans-levee-system-louisiana-2005/

Hamada, M., & Wakamatsu, K. (1996). Liquefaction, ground deformation and their caused damage to structures. In M. Hamada, T. Ohmachi, & N. Ohbo (Eds.), *The 1995 Hyogoken-Nanbu earthquake: Investigation into damage to civil engineering structures* (pp. 45–91). Committee on Earthquake Engineering, Japan Society of Civil Engineers.

Hamer, D. (1995). The making of urban New Zealand. *Journal of Urban History*, *22*(1), 6–39.

Han, A. T. (2019). The implication of regional and local growth management policies on sprawl: A case of the Calgary Metropolitan Area. *Journal of Urban Affairs*, *41*(8), 1103–1122. https://doi.org/10.1080/07352166.2019.1569467

Haney, T. J. (2022). Development, responsibility, and the creation of urban hazard risk. *City & Community*, *21*(1), 21–41. https://doi.org/10.1177/15356841211046265

Hanley, S. (1987). Urban sanitation in preindustrial Japan. *The Journal of Interdisciplinary History*, *18*(1), 1–26.

Hanlon, W. W., & Heblich, S. (2022). History and urban economics. *Regional Science and Urban Economics*, *94*, 103751. https://doi.org/10.1016/j.regsciurbeco.2021.103751

Harris, C. D., & Ullman, E. L. (1945). The nature of cities. *The Annals of the American Academy of Political and Social Science*, *242*(1), 7–17. https://doi.org/10.1177/000271624524200103

Hayashi, S., Kunitomo, M., Mikami, K., & Suzuki, K. (2022). Recent and historical background and current challenges for sediment disaster measures against climate change in Japan. *Water*, *14*(15), 2285. https://doi.org/10.3390/w14152285

Heblich, S., Trew, A., & Zylberberg, Y. (2021). East-side story: Historical pollution and persistent neighborhood sorting. *Journal of Political Economy*, *129*(5), 1508–1552.

Hein, C., & Schubert, D. (2021). Resilience, disaster, and rebuilding in modern port cities. *Journal of Urban History*, *47*(2), 235–249. https://doi.org/10.1177/0096144220925097

Herreros-Cantis, P., Olivotto, V., Grabowski, Z. J., & McPhearson, T. (2020). Shifting landscapes of coastal flood risk: Environmental (in)justice of urban change, sea level rise, and differential vulnerability in New York City. *Urban Transformations*, *2*(1), 9. https://doi.org/10.1186/s42854-020-00014-w

Hirayama, Y. (2000). Collapse and reconstruction: Housing recovery policy in Kobe after the Hanshin Great Earthquake. *Housing Studies*, *15*(1), 111–128. https://doi.org/10.1080/02673030082504

Hobbs, M., Ahuriri-Driscoll, A., Kingham, S., Wiki, J., Marek, L., Dionisio, M. R., Curl, A., Schluter, P., Banwell, K., & Mackenbach, J. D. (2022). A city profile of Ōtautahi Christchurch. *Cities*, *121*, 103481. https://doi.org/10.1016/j.cities.2021.103481

Hohenberg, P. M., & Lees, L. H. (1985). *The making of urban Europe 1000–1950*. Harvard University Press.

Hohensinner, S., Lager, B., Sonnlechner, C., Haidvogl, G., Gierlinger, S., Schmid, M., Krausmann, F., & Winiwarter, V. (2013). Changes in water and land: The reconstructed Viennese riverscape from 1500 to the present. *Water History*, *5*(2), 145–172. https://doi.org/10.1007/s12685-013-0074-2

Horowitz, A. (2020). *Katrina: A history, 1915–2015*. Harvard University Press.

Hruby, D. (2021, October 30). In Vienna, a visionary example of dealing with urban floods. *The Washington Post*.

Hughes, M. W., Quigley, M. C., van Ballegooy, S., Deam, B. L., Bradley, B. A., Hart, D. E., & Measures, R. (2015). The sinking city: Earthquakes increase flood hazard in Christchurch, New Zealand. *GSA Today*, 4–10. https://doi.org/10.1130/GSATG221A.1

Iai, S., Sugano, T., Ichii, K., Morita, T., Inagaki, H., & Inatomi, T. (1996). Performance of caisson type quay walls. In M. Hamada, T. Ohmachi, & N. Ohbo (Eds.), *The 1995 Hyogoken-Nanbu earthquake: Investigation into damage to civil engineering structures* (pp. 181–207). Committee on Earthquake Engineering, Japan Society of Civil Engineers.

IBI Group and Golder Associates. (2017). *Flood mitigation options assessment summary: A city of Calgary summary*. IBI Group and Golder Associates.

Intergovernmental Panel On Climate Change. (2023). *Climate change 2022 – Impacts, adaptation and vulnerability: Working Group II contribution to the Sixth Assessment Report of the Intergovernmental Panel on Climate Change* (1st ed.). Cambridge University Press. https://doi.org/10.1017/9781009325844

Jain, V. K., & Davidson, R. A. (2007). Application of a regional hurricane wind risk forecasting model for wood-frame houses. *Risk Analysis*, *27*(1), 45–58. https://doi.org/10.1111/j.1539-6924.2006.00858.x

Jansen, M. B. (1989). Introduction. In M. B. Jansen (Ed.), *The Cambridge history of Japan: Volume 5: The nineteenth century* (Vol. 5, pp. 1–49). Cambridge University Press. https://doi.org/10.1017/CHOL9780521223560.002

Javanbakht, A., Assaf, J., Salsabili, M., Sadrekarimi, A., Ghofrani, H., & Molnar, S. (2023). *Metro Vancouver liquefaction hazard mapping* [Conference paper]. Proceedings of the Canadian Conference – Pacific Conference on Earthquake Engineering 2023, Paper ID 275.

Jedwab, R., Johnson, N. D., & Koyama, M. (2022). Medieval cities through the lens of urban economics. *Regional Science and Urban Economics*, *94*, 103598. https://doi.org/10.1016/j.regsciurbeco.2020.103598

Jones, C. (2022). *Urban economy: Real estate economics and public policy*. Routledge, Taylor & Francis Group.

Kam, W. Y., Pampanin, S., & Elwood, K. (2011). Seismic performance of reinforced concrete buildings in the 22 February Christchurch (Lyttelton) earthquake. *Bulletin of the New Zealand Society for Earthquake Engineering*, *44*(4), 239–278.

Kanamori, H. (1995). The Kobe (Hyogo-ken Nanbu), Japan, earthquake of January 16, 1995. *Seismological Research Letters*, *66*(2), 6–10.

Kates, R. W., Colten, C. E., Laska, S., & Leatherman, S. P. (2006). Reconstruction of New Orleans after Hurricane Katrina: A research perspective. *Proceedings of the National Academy of Sciences*, *103*(40), 14653–14660. https://doi.org/10.1073/pnas.0605726103

Kawashima, K., & Unjoh, S. (1997). The damage of highway bridges in the 1995 Hyogo-ken Nanbu earthquake and its impact on Japanese seismic design. *Journal of Earthquake Engineering*, *1*(3), 505–541. https://doi.org/10.1080/13632469708962376

Kilgannon, C. (2012, November 19). A much criticized pocket of the Rockaways, built to survive a storm. *The New York Times*.

Kim, J. J., Elwood, K. J., Marquis, F., & Chang, S. E. (2017). Factors influencing post-earthquake decisions on buildings in Christchurch, New Zealand. *Earthquake Spectra*, *33*(2), 623–640. https://doi.org/10.1193/072516EQS120M

King, A., Middleton, D., Brown, C., Johnston, D., & Johal, S. (2014). Insurance: Its role in recovery from the 2010–2011 Canterbury earthquake sequence. *Earthquake Spectra*, *30*(1), 475–491. https://doi.org/10.1193/022813EQS058M

Knowles, S. G., & Kunreuther, H. C. (2014). Troubled waters: The National Flood Insurance Program in historical perspective. *Journal of Policy History*, *26*(3), 327–353. https://doi.org/10.1017/S0898030614000153

Kobe City International Division. (2023, June). Tsunami prevention for your safety & peace of mind. *Kobe*, 1–2.

Kornhauser, D. H. (1977). *Urban Japan: Its foundations and growth (2nd impr)*. Longman.

Kryžanowski, A., Brilly, M., Rusjan, S., & Schnabl, S. (2014). Structural flood-protection measures referring to several European case studies. *Natural Hazards and Earth System Sciences*, *14*(1), 135–142. https://doi.org/10.5194/nhess-14-135-2014

Kuraoka, S., & Rainer, J. H. (1996). Damage to water distribution system caused by the 1995 Hyogo-ken Nanbu earthquake. *Canadian Journal of Civil Engineering*, *23*, 665–677.

Kwasinski, A., Eidinger, J., Tang, A., & Tudo-Bornarel, C. (2014). Performance of electric power systems in the 2010–2011 Christchurch, New Zealand, earthquake sequence. *Earthquake Spectra*, *30*(1), 205–230. https://doi.org/10.1193/022813EQS056M

Lai, C. D. (1988). *Chinatowns: Towns within cities in Canada*. University of British Columbia Press.

Levinson, M. (2006a). Container shipping and the decline of New York, 1955–1975. *The Business History Review*, *80*(1), 49–80.

Levinson, M. (2006b). *The box: How the shipping container made the world smaller and the world economy bigger*. Princeton University Press.

Lewis, A. S. (2023, December 19). *After a decade of planning, New York City is raising its shoreline*. Yale Environment 360.

Lichtenberger, E. (1993). *Vienna: Bridge between cultures*. Belhaven Press; Co-published in the Americas by Halsted Press.

Lin, A., Maruyama, T., & Miyata, T. (1998). Paleoseismic events and the 1596 Keicho-Fushimi large earthquake produced by a slip on the Gosukebashi fault at the eastern Rokko Mountains, Japan. *The Island Arc*, *7*, 621–636.

Lin, J., & Rauch, F. (2022). What future for history dependence in spatial economics? *Regional Science and Urban Economics*, *94*, 103628. https://doi.org/10.1016/j.regsciurbeco.2020.103628

Mackie, J. (2024, July 12). This day in history, 1886: Vancouver rises from the ashes of the Great Fire. *Vancouver Sun*.

MacRae, G., Clifton, C., & Megget, L. (2011). *Review of NZ building codes of practice* [Report to the Royal Commission of Inquiry into the Building Failure Caused by the Christchurch Earthquakes].

Maly, E., & Shiozaki, Y. (2012). Towards a policy that supports people-centered housing recovery: Learning from housing reconstruction after the Hanshin-Awaji Earthquake in Kobe, Japan. *International Journal of Disaster Risk Science*, *3*(1), 56–65. https://doi.org/10.1007/s13753-012-0007-1

Marsh, W. M., & Kaufman, M. M. (2013). *Physical geography: Great systems and global environments*. Cambridge University Press.

Massie, A., & Watson, N. R. (2011). Impact of the Christchurch earthquakes on the electrical power system infrastructure. *Bulletin of the New Zealand Society for Earthquake Engineering*, *44*(4), 425–430.

McClearn, M., & Keller, J. (2021, December 13). How Calgary's massive, multi-million flood mitigation project aims to tame the Elbow River. *The Globe and Mail*.

McGarr, A., Simpson, D., & Seeber, L. (2002). Case histories of induced and triggered seismicity. In W. H. K. Lee, H. Kanamori, P. C. Jennings, & C. Kisslinger (Eds.), *International Handbook of Earthquake and Engineering Seismology* (Vol. 81, pp. 647–661). Elsevier. https://doi.org/10.1016/S0074-6142(02)80243-1

McGeehan, P., & Hu, W. (2017, October 29). Five years after Sandy, are we better prepared? *The New York Times*. https://nyti.ms/2iI6XZI

McGhee, D. J., Binder, S. B., & Albright, E. A. (2020). First, do no harm: Evaluating the vulnerability reduction of post-disaster home buyout programs. *Natural Hazards Review*, *21*(1), 05019002. https://doi.org/10.1061/(ASCE)NH.1527-6996.0000337

Memon, P. A. (2003). Urban growth management in Christchurch. *New Zealand Geographer*, *59*(1), 27–39.

Menoni, S. (2001). Chains of damages and failures in a metropolitan environment: Some observations on the Kobe earthquake in 1995. *Journal of Hazardous Materials*, *86*, 101–119.

Merz, B. (2017). Flood risk analysis. In *Oxford Research Encyclopedia of Natural Hazard Science*. Oxford University Press. https://doi.org/10.1093/acrefore/9780199389407.013.113

Michaels, G., & Rauch, F. (2018). Resetting the urban network: 117–2012. *The Economic Journal*, *128*(608), 378–412. https://doi.org/10.1111/ecoj.12424

Mitchell, D., DeVall, R. H., Kobayashi, K., Tinawi, R., & Tso, W. K. (1996). Damage to concrete structures due to the January 17, 1995, Hyogo-ken Nanbu (Kobe) earthquake. *Canadian Journal of Civil Engineering*, *23*, 757–770.

Mitchell, J. K. (2022). Megacity disaster risk governance. In *Oxford Research Encyclopedia of Natural Hazard Science*. Oxford University Press. https://doi.org/10.1093/acrefore/9780199389407.013.377

Moon, L., Dizhur, D., Senaldi, I., Derakhshan, H., Griffith, M., Magenes, G., & Ingham, J. (2014). The demise of the URM building stock in Christchurch during the 2010–2011 Canterbury earthquake sequence. *Earthquake Spectra*, *30*(1), 253–276. https://doi.org/10.1193/022113EQS044M

Mori, N., Yasuda, T., Arikawa, T., Kataoka, T., Nakajo, S., Suzuki, K., Yamanaka, Y., & Webb, A. (2019). 2018 Typhoon Jebi post-event survey of coastal damage in the Kansai region, Japan. *Coastal Engineering Journal*, *61*(3), 278–294. https://doi.org/10.1080/21664250.2019.1619253

Muller, P. O. (2017). Transportation and urban form: Stages in the spatial evolution of the American metropolis. In G. Giuliano & S. Hanson (Eds.), *The geography of urban transportation* (Ch.3). Guilford Publications.

Nadeau-Bonilla, C., & MacDonald, K. (2015). Calgary's 2013 Flood: Impacts, recovery and resiliency measures at Canada's largest cold weather BNR WWTP. *Proceedings of the Water Environment Federation*, *2015*(8), 3814–3827. https://doi.org/10.2175/193864715819555652

Nakashima, M., & Chusilp, P. (2003). A partial view of Japanese post-Kobe seismic design and construction practices. *Earthquake Engineering and Engineering Seismology*, *4*(1), 3–13.

National Centers for Environmental Information. (2024). *Costliest U.S. tropical cyclones*. National Oceanic and Atmospheric Administration. www.ncei.noaa.gov/access/billions/dcmi.pdf

Nelles, H. V. (2005). How did Calgary get its river parks? *Urban History Review*, *34*(1), 28–45.

NHC (Northwest Hydraulic Consultants). (2014). *City of Vancouver coastal flood risk assessment: Final report* [Report to the City of Vancouver]. NHC.

Nojima, N., & Kameda, H. (1996). Lifeline interactions in the Hanshin-Awaji earthquake disaster. In M. Hamada, T. Ohmachi, & N. Ohbo (Eds.), *The 1995 Hyogoken-Nanbu earthquake: Investigation into damage to civil engineering structures* (pp. 253–264). Committee on Earthquake Engineering, Japan Society of Civil Engineers.

NYC Department of City Planning. (n.d.). *Total and foreign-born population, New York City, 1790–2000*. City of New York. www.nyc.gov/assets/planning/download/pdf/data-maps/nyc-population/historical-population/1790-2000_nyc_total_foreign_birth.pdf

Okimura, T., Takada, S., & Koid, T. H. (1996). Outline of the Great Hanshin Earthquake, Japan 1995. *Natural Hazards*, *14*, 39–71.

Okuyama, Y. (2015). The rise and fall of the Kobe economy from the 1995 earthquake. *Journal of Disaster Research*, *10*(4), 635–640. https://doi.org/10.20965/jdr.2015.p0635

Oliveira, V. (2016). *Urban morphology: An introduction to the study of the physical form of cities*. Springer. https://doi.org/10.1007/978-3-319-32083-0

Olshansky, R. B. (2001). Land use planning for seismic safety: The Los Angeles County experience, 1971–1994. *Journal of the American Planning Association*, *67*(2), 173–185.

Olshansky, R. B., Johnson, L. A., Horne, J., & Nee, B. (2008). Planning for the rebuilding of New Orleans. *Journal of the American Planning Association*, *74*(3), 273–287. https://doi.org/10.1080/01944360802140835

O'Neil, J. M., Taillie, D., Walsh, B., Dennison, W. C., Bone, E. K., Reid, D. J., Newton, R., Strayer, D. L., Boicourt, K., Birney, L. B., Janis, S., Malinowski, P., & Fisher, M. (2016). New York Harbor: Resilience in the face of four centuries of development. *Regional Studies in Marine Science*, *8*, 274–286. https://doi.org/10.1016/j.rsma.2016.06.004

Orchard, S. (2017). Floodplain restoration principles for the Avon Ōtākaro Red Zone: Case studies and recommendations. Report prepared for the Avon Ōtākaro Network. Christchurch, New Zealand. Retrieved from https://ref.coastalrestorationtrust.org.nz/site/assets/files/9006/floodplain_restoration_principles_for_avon_otakaro_red_zone_vfinal.pdf

Orion New Zealand Ltd. (2010). *Managing our network assets*. Orion New Zealand Ltd. www.oriongroup.co.nz/corporate/corporate-publications/asset-management-plans/

O'Rourke, T. D., Jeon, S.-S., Toprak, S., Cubrinovski, M., Hughes, M., Van Ballegooy, S., & Bouziou, D. (2014). Earthquake response of underground pipeline networks in Christchurch, NZ. *Earthquake Spectra*, *30*(1), 183–204. https://doi.org/10.1193/030413EQS062M

Orton, P., Lin, N., Gornitz, V., Colle, B., Booth, J., Feng, K., Buchanan, M., Oppenheimer, M., & Patrick, L. (2019). New York City Panel on Climate Change 2019 report chapter 4: Coastal flooding. *Annals of the New York Academy of Sciences*, *1439*(1), 95–114. https://doi.org/10.1111/nyas.14011

Orton, P. M., Hall, T. M., Talke, S. A., Blumberg, A. F., Georgas, N., & Vinogradov, S. (2016). A validated tropical-extratropical flood hazard assessment for New York Harbor: Flood assessment for New York Harbor. *Journal of Geophysical Research: Oceans*. https://doi.org/10.1002/2016JC011679

Parker, M., & Steenkamp, D. (2012). The economic impact of the Canterbury earthquakes. *Reserve Bank of New Zealand Bulletin*, *75*(3), 13–25.

Pawson, E. (2000). Confronting nature. In J. Cookson & G. Dunstall (Eds.), *Southern capital, Christchurch: Towards a city biography, 1850–2000* (pp. 60–84). Canterbury University Press.

Pawson, E., & Holland, P. (2005). Lowland Canterbury landscapes in the making. *New Zealand Geographer*, *61*, 167–175.

Peabody, T. (2021). Marketing a nuisance: Sanitary landfilling as economic development at the 1939 World's Fair. In C. A. Zimring & S. H. Corey (Eds.), *Coastal metropolis: Environmental histories of modern New York City* (Ch. 8). University of Pittsburgh Press.

Pitarka, A., Irikura, K., Iwata, T., & Sekiguchi, H. (1998). Three-dimensional simulation of the near-fault ground motion for the 1995 Hyogo-ken Nanbu (Kobe), Japan, earthquake. *Bulletin of the Seismological Society of America*, *88*(2), 428–440.

Platt, R. H. (2013). *Impacts of Superstorm Sandy on New York City's new waterfront parks (Quick response report 243)*. University of Colorado Boulder.

Pomeroy, J. W., Stewart, R. E., & Whitfield, P. H. (2016). The 2013 flood event in the South Saskatchewan and Elk River basins: Causes, assessment and damages. *Canadian Water Resources Journal / Revue Canadienne Des Ressources Hydriques*, *41*(1–2), 105–117. https://doi.org/10.1080/07011784.2015.1089190

Potter, S. H., Becker, J. S., Johnston, D. M., & Rossiter, K. P. (2015). An overview of the impacts of the 2010–2011 Canterbury earthquakes. *International Journal of Disaster Risk Reduction*, *14*, 6–14. https://doi.org/10.1016/j.ijdrr.2015.01.014

Prion, H. G. L., & Filiatrault, A. (1996). Performance of timber structures during the Hyogo-ken Nanbu earthquake of 17 January 1995. *Canadian Journal of Civil Engineering*, *23*, 652–664.

Public Inquiry into the Earthquake Commission. (2020). *Report of the public inquiry into the Earthquake Commission, March 2020*. Public inquiry into the Earthquake Commission.

Quealy, K. (2020, May 15). The richest neighborhoods emptied out most as coronavirus hit New York City. *The New York Times*.

Rebuild by Design. (n.d.). *Project pages: The BIG U*. https://rebuildbydesign.org/work/funded-projects/the-big-u/

Reed, D. J., Davidson-Arnott, R., & Perillo, G. M. E. (2009). Estuaries, coastal marshes, tidal flats and coastal dunes. In O. Slaymaker, T. Spencer, & C. Embleton-Hamann (Eds.), *Geomorphology and global environmental change* (pp. 130–157). Cambridge University Press. https://doi.org/10.1017/CBO9780511627057.006

Regenerate Christchurch. (2019). *Ōtākaro Avon River corridor regeneration plan*. Regenerate Christchurch.

Reinfelds, I., & Nanson, G. (1993). Formation of braided river floodplains, Waimakariri River, New Zealand. *Sedimentology*, *40*, 1113–1127.

Reynolds, R. P., Blakely, D. E., & Ryan, S. E. (2014). *Potential reduction of social impacts during the June 2013 Alberta floods as a result of the drawdown of the Calgary Glenmore Reservoir* [Conference paper]. Proceedings of the CDA 2014 Annual Conference, Canadian Dam Association.

Rice, G., & Sharfe, J. (2008). *Christchurch changing: An illustrated history*. Canterbury University Press.

Rodrigue, J.-P. (2020). *The geography of transport systems* (5th ed.). Routledge. https://doi.org/10.4324/9780429346323

Rodrigue, J.-P., Comtois, C., & Slack, B. (2007). *The geography of transport systems (Repr)*. Routledge.

Rogers, N., Williams, K., Jacka, M., Wallace, S., & Leeves, J. (2014). Geotechnical aspects of disaster recovery planning in residential Christchurch and surrounding districts affected by liquefaction. *Earthquake Spectra*, *30*(1), 493–512. https://doi.org/10.1193/021513EQS029M

Rose, A. (2017). Benefit-cost analysis of economic resilience actions. In *Oxford Research Encyclopedia of Natural Hazard Science*. Oxford University Press. https://doi.org/10.1093/acrefore/9780199389407.013.69

Rosenzweig, C., & Solecki, W. (2014). Hurricane Sandy and adaptation pathways in New York: Lessons from a first-responder city. *Global Environmental Change*, *28*, 395–408. https://doi.org/10.1016/j.gloenvcha.2014.05.003

Rozman, G. (1986). Castle towns in transition. In G. Rozman & M. B. Jansen (Eds.), *Japan in transition: From Tokugawa to Meiji* (pp. 318–346). Princeton University Press.

Saito, T. (1997). Japanese private railway companies and their business diversification. *Japan Railway & Transport Review*, *January*, 2–9.

Sakaki, K., Matsuda, Y., Hirayama, N., & Itoh, S. (2014). Development of comprehensive evaluation procedure for anti-seismic strategies: Evaluating Kobe City's earthquake resistance improvement plan from the customer's viewpoint. *Journal of Water Supply: Research and Technology-Aqua*, *63*(2), 139–145. https://doi.org/10.2166/aqua.2013.009

Sandalack, B. A., & Nicolai, A. (2006). *The Calgary project: Urban form/urban life*. University of Calgary Press.

Sanderson, E. W. (2009). *Mannahatta: A natural history of New-York City*. Abrams.

Saunders, W. S. A., & Becker, J. S. (2015). A discussion of resilience and sustainability: Land use planning recovery from the Canterbury earthquake sequence, New Zealand. *International Journal of Disaster Risk Reduction*, *14*, 73–81. https://doi.org/10.1016/j.ijdrr.2015.01.013

Schmahmann, L., Poorthuis, A., & Chapple, K. (2022). Pandemic polycentricity? Mobility and migration patterns across New York over the course of the Covid-19 pandemic. *Cambridge Journal of Regions, Economy and Society*, *15*(3), 515–535. https://doi.org/10.1093/cjres/rsac017

Schober, B., Hauer, C., & Habersack, H. (2015). A novel assessment of the role of Danube floodplains in flood hazard reduction (FEM method). *Natural Hazards*, *75*(S1), 33–50. https://doi.org/10.1007/s11069-013-0880-y

Shiozaki, Y., & Malone, P. (1996). Tokyo, Osaka and Kobe: Island city paradise? In P. Malone (Ed.), *City, capital and water* (pp. 134–163). Routledge.

Smith, A. B. (2020). *U.S. billion-dollar weather and climate disasters, 1980–Present (NCEI Accession 0209268)* [Dataset]. NOAA National Centers for Environmental Information. https://doi.org/10.25921/STKW-7W73

Smith, P. J. (1962). Calgary: A study in urban pattern. *Economic Geography*, *38*(4), 315–329.

Soll, D. (2021). The Rockaway commute, 1950–2017: A long, strange trip. In C. A. Zimring & S. H. Corey (Eds.), *Coastal metropolis: Environmental histories of modern New York City* (Ch. 4). University of Pittsburgh Press.

Sonnlechner, C., Hohensinner, S., & Haidvogl, G. (2013). Floods, fights and a fluid river: The Viennese Danube in the sixteenth century. *Water History*, *5*(2), 173–194. https://doi.org/10.1007/s12685-013-0077-z

Sorensen, A. (2004). *The making of urban Japan: Cities and planning from Edo to the twenty-first century*. Routledge.

Squires, D. F. (1992). Quantifying anthropogenic shoreline modification of the Hudson River and Estuary from European contact to modern time. *Coastal Management*, *20*(4), 343–354. https://doi.org/10.1080/08920759209362183

Stanford, S. D., Stone, B. D., Ridge, J. C., Witte, R. W., Pardi, R. R., & Reimer, G. E. (2021). Chronology of Laurentide glaciation in New Jersey and the New York City area, United States. *Quaternary Research*, *99*, 142–167. https://doi.org/10.1017/qua.2020.71

Statistics Bureau of Japan. (2020). *Nihon chōki tōkei sōran: Historical statistics of Japan*. NetAdvance Inc. https://go.exlibris.link/MVkDg2jy

Steinberg, T. (2014). *Gotham unbound: The ecological history of greater New York*. Simon & Schuster.

Steinberg, T. (2021). Tough guys on the waterfront: Neoliberalism and the rise of resilient New York. In C. A. Zimring & S. H. Corey (Eds.), *Coastal metropolis: Environmental histories of modern New York City* (Ch. 13). University of Pittsburgh Press.

Stevenson, J., Vargo, J., Seville, E., Kachali, H., McNaughton, A., & Powell, F. (2011). *The recovery of Canterbury's organisations: A comparative analysis of the 4 September 2010, 22 February and 13 June 2011 earthquakes* (Resilient Organisations Research Report 2011/04). Resilient Organisations.

Stive, M. J. F., Cowell, P. J., & Nicholls, R. J. (2009). Beaches, cliffs and deltas. In O. Slaymaker, T. Spencer, & C. Embleton-Hamann (Eds.), *Geomorphology and global environmental change* (pp. 158–179). Cambridge University Press. https://doi.org/10.1017/CBO9780511627057.007

Stormwater Solutions. (2023, November 14). *New York requires USACE to overhaul flooding plan for NY-NJ harbor*. www.stormwater.com/stormwater-management/

flood-control/press-release/53078163/new-york-requires-usace-to-overhaul-flooding-plan-for-ny-nj-harbor

Swaffield, S. R. (2012). Reinventing spatial planning at the urban rural interface: A Christchurch, New Zealand case study. *Planning Practice and Research*, *27*(4), 405–422. https://doi.org/10.1080/02697459.2012.682472

Takabatake, T., Mäll, M., Esteban, M., Nakamura, R., Kyaw, T., Ishii, H., Valdez, J., Nishida, Y., Noya, F., & Shibayama, T. (2018). Field survey of 2018 Typhoon Jebi in Japan: Lessons for disaster risk management. *Geosciences*, *8*(11), 412. https://doi.org/10.3390/geosciences8110412

Tarr, J. A. (2021). Land use and environmental change in the Hudson-Raritan estuary region, 1700–1980, with an addendum to 2018. In C. A. Zimring & S. H. Corey (Eds.), *Coastal metropolis: Environmental histories of modern New York City* (Ch. 1). University of Pittsburgh Press.

Taylor, J., Paine, C., & FitzGibbon, J. (1995). From greenbelt to greenways: Four Canadian case studies. *Landscape and Urban Planning*, *33*, 47–64.

The City of Calgary. (2013). *Riparian strategy: Sustaining healthy rivers and communities*. The City of Calgary.

The City of Calgary. (2016). *Developed areas growth & change 2016 (draft)*. The City of Calgary.

The City of Calgary. (2018). *2018 civic census results*. The City of Calgary.

The City of Calgary. (2021). *Municipal development plan (MDP) – 2020*. The City of Calgary.

The City of Calgary. (2022a). *2021 flood mitigation and resilience annual update* [Utilities & Environmental Protection Report to Community Development Committee]. https://pub-calgary.escribemeetings.com/filestream.ashx?DocumentId=208113

The City of Calgary. (2022b). *Calgary's flood resilience plan*. The City of Calgary.

The City of Calgary, City & Community Planning Division. (1984). *Calgary river valleys plan: The plan and policies*. The City of Calgary.

The City of Calgary, Land Use By Law Sustainment Team, Development & Building Approvals, Planning Implementation. (2007). *The Calgary land use bylaw 1P2007*. The City of Calgary.

The City of Calgary, Land Use Section, Development and Land Use Division. (1980). *Land use bylaw 2P80*. The City of Calgary.

The City of Calgary, Planning, Development & Assessment. (2015). *Calgary snapshots 2015*. The City of Calgary.

The City of Calgary. (n.d.). *Calgary's river flood story*. Retrieved February 5, 2023, from https://maps.calgary.ca/RiverFlooding/

The Globe and Mail. (2013). *Calgary's flooding in detail*. www.theglobeandmail.com/report-on-business/calgarys-flooding-in-detail/article13160254/

The Globe and Mail. (2021). *How Calgary's massive, multi-million flood mitigation project aims to tame the Elbow River*. www.theglobeandmail.com/canada/article-calgarys-betting-on-a-controversial-flood-mitigation-project-to-tame/

The New York Public Library. (1776). *Plan of the city of New York in North America: Surveyed in the years 1766 & 1767*. Retrieved from https://digitalcollections.nypl.org/items/510d47df-f437-a3d9-e040-e00a18064a99

Thistlethwaite, J. (2017). The emergence of flood insurance in Canada: Navigating institutional uncertainty. *Risk Analysis*, *37*(4), 744–755. https://doi.org/10.1111/risa.12659

Thorns, D., & Schrader, B. (n.d.). City history and people: The appeal of city life. In *Te Ara: The Encyclopedia of New Zealand*. Retrieved May 31, 2023, from www.TeAra.govt.nz/en/graph/23512/population-of-the-four-main-urban-areas-1858-2006

Tierney, K. J. (2014). *The social roots of risk: Producing disasters, promoting resilience.* Stanford University Press.

Tierney, K. J. (2019). *Disasters: A sociological approach.* Polity Press.

Toka Tū Ake EQC. (n.d.). *Our history: Toka Tū Ake EQC.* Retrieved June 1, 2023, from www.eqc.govt.nz/about-eqc/our-history/

Tokyo Development Learning Center. (2018). *Kobe: Creative reconstruction.* The World Bank Group.

Townshend, I., Miller, B., & Cook, D. (2020). Neighbourhood change in Calgary: An evolving geography of income inequality and social difference. In J. L. Grant, A. Walks, & H. Ramos (Eds.), *Changing neighbourhoods: Social and spatial polarization in Canadian cities* (Ch. 9). UBC Press.

Tsu, T. Y. H. (2008). Making virtues of disaster: "Beautiful tales" from the Kobe Flood of 1938. *Asian Studies Review, 32*(2), 197–214. https://doi.org/10.1080/10357820802061100

Tsu, Y. H. (2005). The violent and the benign: How Kōbe remembers its rivers. In Y. H. Tsu, J. Van Bremen, & E. Ben-Ari (Eds.), *Perspectives on social memory in Japan* (pp. 204–227). Global Oriental Ltd.

Tsukada, T. (2012). The urban history of Osaka. *City, Culture and Society, 3*(1), 1–8. https://doi.org/10.1016/j.ccs.2012.06.002

Twilley, R. R., Bentley, S. J., Chen, Q., Edmonds, D. A., Hagen, S. C., Lam, N. S.-N., Willson, C. S., Xu, K., Braud, D., Hampton Peele, R., & McCall, A. (2016). Co-evolution of wetland landscapes, flooding, and human settlement in the Mississippi River Delta Plain. *Sustainability Science, 11*(4), 711–731. https://doi.org/10.1007/s11625-016-0374-4

United Nations Centre for Regional Development. (1995). *Comprehensive Study of the Great Hanshin Earthquake* (UNCRD Research Report Series No.12). United Nations Centre for Regional Development.

United Nations Office for Disaster Risk Reduction (Ed.). (2022). *Our world at risk: Transforming governance for a resilient future.* United Nations.

US Army Corps of Engineers. (2022). *New York-New Jersey Harbor and Tributaries (NYNJHAT) draft integrated feasibility report and Tier I environmental impact statement.* U. S. Army Corps of Engineers. www.nan.usace.army.mil/Portals/37/NYNJHATS%20Draft%20Integrated%20Feasibility%20Report%20Tier%201%20EIS_3Oct2022.pdf

Van Ballegooy, S., Malan, P., Lacrosse, V., Jacka, M. E., Cubrinovski, M., Bray, J. D., O'Rourke, T. D., Crawford, S. A., & Cowan, H. (2014). Assessment of liquefaction-induced land damage for residential Christchurch. *Earthquake Spectra, 30*(1), 31–55. https://doi.org/10.1193/031813EQS070M

van Holm, E. J., & Wyczalkowski, C. K. (2019). Gentrification in the wake of a hurricane: New Orleans after Katrina. *Urban Studies, 56*(13), 2763–2778. https://doi.org/10.1177/0042098018800445

Van Houtte, J. A. (1966). The rise and decline of the market of Bruges. *The Economic History Review, 19*(1), 29–47.

Ventura, C. E., Finn, W. D. L., Onur, T., Blanquera, A., & Rezai, M. (2005). Regional seismic risk in British Columbia: Classification of buildings and development of damage probability functions. *Canadian Journal of Civil Engineering, 32*(2), 372–387. https://doi.org/10.1139/l04-099

Vereinte Nationen (Ed.). (2015). *Making development sustainable: The future of disaster risk management.* United Nations.

Wagner, B., Hauer, C., Schoder, A., & Habersack, H. (2015). A review of hydropower in Austria: Past, present and future development. *Renewable and Sustainable Energy Reviews*, *50*, 304–314. https://doi.org/10.1016/j.rser.2015.04.169

Wagner, M., Merson, J., & Wentz, E. A. (2016). Design with nature: Key lessons from McHarg's intrinsic suitability in the wake of Hurricane Sandy. *Landscape and Urban Planning*, *155*, 33–46. https://doi.org/10.1016/j.landurbplan.2016.06.013

Wakefield, S. (2020). Making nature into infrastructure: The construction of oysters as a risk management solution in New York City. *Environment and Planning E: Nature and Space*, *3*(3), 761–785. https://doi.org/10.1177/2514848619887461

Wei, E., & Miselis, J. (2022). Geologic framework, anthropogenic impacts, and hydrodynamics contribute to variable sediment availability and shoreface morphology at the Rockaway Peninsula, NY. *Journal of Marine Science and Engineering*, *10*(7), 989. https://doi.org/10.3390/jmse10070989

White, G. F. (1945). *Human adjustment to floods: A geographical approach to the flood problem in the United States*. University of Chicago, Department of Geography.

White, P., Gunston, J., Salmond, C., Atkinson, J., & Crampton, P. (2008). *Atlas of socioeconomic deprivation in New Zealand NZDep2006*. www.health.govt.nz/system/files/documents/publications/canterbury.pdf

White, P. A., Goodrich, K., Cave, S., & Minni, G. (2007). Waterways, swamps and vegetation of Christchurch in 1856 and baseflow discharge in Christchurch city streams. Environment Canterbury, report U07/39. Retrieved from https://docs.niwa.co.nz/library/public/ECtrU07-39.pdf

Wilson, J. (2013). Contextual historical overview for Christchurch City [Report to Christchurch City Council].

Winiwarter, V., Haidvogl, G., Hohensinner, S., Hauer, F., & Bürkner, M. (2016). The long-term evolution of urban waters and their nineteenth century transformation in European cities: A comparative environmental history. *Water History*, *8*(3), 209–233. https://doi.org/10.1007/s12685-016-0172-z

Winiwarter, V., Schmid, M., & Dressel, G. (2013). Looking at half a millennium of co-existence: The Danube in Vienna as a socio-natural site. *Water History*, *5*(2), 101–119. https://doi.org/10.1007/s12685-013-0079-x

Wisner, B. (2016). Vulnerability as concept, model, metric, and tool. In *Oxford Research Encyclopedia of Natural Hazard Science*. Oxford University Press. https://doi.org/10.1093/acrefore/9780199389407.013.25

Wisner, B., Blaikie, P., Cannon, T., & Davis, I. (2004). *At risk: Natural hazards, people's vulnerability, and disasters* (2nd ed). Routledge.

Wood, A., Noy, I., & Parker, M. (2016). The Canterbury rebuild five years on from the Christchurch earthquake. *Reserve Bank of New Zealand Bulletin*, *79*(3), 3–16.

Yamasaki, T., Tanigawa, K., & Ness, G. D. (2010). Kobe and Niigata: Situation and site in the development of two Japanese port cities. In F. Broeze (Ed.), *Gateways of Asia: Port cities of Asia in the 13th–20th centuries* (pp. 233–264). Routledge.

Yaro, R., & Gutman, D. (2023, June 15). The plan to save New York from the next Sandy will ruin the waterfront. It doesn't have to. *The New York Times*.

Young, J. (2015). Infrastructure: Mass transit in 19th- and 20th-century urban America. In *Oxford Research Encyclopedia of American History*. Oxford University Press. https://doi.org/10.1093/acrefore/9780199329175.013.28

Youngman, N. (2015). The development of manufactured flood risk: New Orleans' mid-century growth machine and the hurricane of 1947. *Disasters*, *39*(s2), s166–s187. https://doi.org/10.1111/disa.12157

Zaninetti, J.-M., & Colten, C. E. (2012). Shrinking New Orleans: Post-Katrina population adjustments. *Urban Geography*, *33*(5), 675–699. https://doi.org/10.2747/0272-3638.33.5.675

Zimring, C. A. (2021). Reading Newtown Creek: Competing narratives of New York City's aquatic discardscape. In C. A. Zimring & S. H. Corey (Eds.), *Coastal metropolis: Environmental histories of modern New York City* (Ch. 12). University of Pittsburgh Press.

Zimring, C. A., & Corey, S. H. (2021). Water, infrastructure, and wastescapes. In C. A. Zimring & S. H. Corey (Eds.), *Coastal metropolis: Environmental histories of modern New York City* (Introduction). University of Pittsburgh Press.

Index

For EU product safety concerns, contact us at Calle de José Abascal, 56–1°, 28003 Madrid, Spain or eugpsr@cambridge.org.

www.ingramcontent.com/pod-product-compliance
Lightning Source LLC
LaVergne TN
LVHW080049210926
848481LV00011B/3308

* 9 7 8 1 0 0 9 6 3 3 5 4 3 *